Research Using IT

Palgrave Study Guides

A Handbook of Writing for Engineers   *Joan van Emden*
Effective Communication for Science and Technology   *Joan van Emden*
How to Write Better Essays   *Bryan Greetham*
Key Concepts in Politics   *Andrew Heywood*
Linguistic Terms and Concepts   *Geoff Finch*
Literary Terms and Criticism (second edition)   *John Peck and Martin Coyle*
The Mature Student's Guide to Writing   *Jean Rose*
The Postgraduate Research Handbook   *Gina Wisker*
Practical Criticism   *John Peck and Martin Coyle*
Research Using IT   *Hilary Coombes*
The Student's Guide to Writing   *John Peck and Martin Coyle*
The Study Skills Handbook   *Stella Cottrell*
Studying Economics   *Brian Atkinson and Susan Johns*
Studying History (second edition)   *Jeremy Black and Donald MacRaild*
Studying Mathematics and its Applications   *Peter Kahn*
Studying Psychology   *Andrew Stevenson*
Teaching Study Skills and Supporting Learning   *Stella Cottrell*

How to Begin Studying English Literature (second edition)   *Nicholas Marsh*
How to Study a Jane Austen Novel (second edition)   *Vivien Jones*
How to Study Chaucer (second edition)   *Robert Pope*
How to Study Foreign Languages   *Marilyn Lewis*
How to Study an E. M. Forster Novel   *Nigel Messenger*
How to Study a Thomas Hardy Novel   *John Peck*
How to Study James Joyce   *John Blades*
How to Study a D. H. Lawrence Novel   *Nigel Messenger*
How to Study Linguistics   *Geoff Finch*
How to Study Modern Drama   *Kenneth Pickering*
How to Study Modern Poetry   *Tony Curtis*
How to Study a Novel (second edition)   *John Peck*
How to Study a Poet (second edition)   *John Peck*
How to Study a Renaissance Play   *Chris Coles*
How to Study Romantic Poetry (second edition)   *Paul O'Flinn*
How to Study a Shakespeare Play (second edition)   *John Peck and Martin Coyle*
How to Study Television   *Keith Selby and Ron Cowdery*

www.palgravestudyguides.com

Research Using IT

Hilary Coombes

palgrave

First published 2001 by
PALGRAVE
Houndmills, Basingstoke, Hampshire RG21 6XS and
175 Fifth Avenue, New York, N.Y. 10010
Companies and representatives throughout the world

PALGRAVE is the new global academic imprint of
St. Martin's Press LLC Scholarly and Reference Division and
Palgrave Publishers Ltd (formerly Macmillan Press Ltd).

ISBN 0–333–91450–3 paperback

This book is printed on paper suitable for recycling and
made from fully managed and sustained forest sources.

A catalogue record for this book is available
from the British Library.

10 9 8 7 6 5 4 3 2 1
10 09 08 07 06 05 04 03 02 01

Printed and bound in Great Britain by
Creative Print and Design (Wales), Ebbw Vale

Contents

v

10 Finding a Voice – Sharing your Research Findings

Acknowledgements

I would like to thank Judie Jancovich, Mandy Kidd and Katy Waring for the thankless task of reading through drafts at various stages and offering helpful advice and comments. This book would not have been possible without the help and support of my publisher Suzannah Tipple and all her colleagues, so a special thank you to everyone behind the scenes at Palgrave.

I would especially like to thank my family; Victoria for all your help and particularly for editing so adeptly; Richard for keeping me bang up to date with the latest computer technology, and of course my husband Keith for running the house and putting up with my ridiculously long work hours as I toiled to complete this book as well as teach full time.

I have been motivated to write this book by students who are erroneously presumed by many to be able to pick up a wealth of computer knowledge without guidance, and who, when faced with the daunting task of wading through huge volumes of incomprehensible research books, feel like giving up before they begin. I say to them – don't give up, you *can* do it!

HILARY COOMBES

For Keith with all my love

Introduction

▶ Who is this book for?

It's for you
- if you if you want to know **how to research**
- if you want to **learn how computers can help you research** (no experience needed)
- if you want an **easy to follow step-by-step approach**
- if you want **minimum jargon**

▶ How to use this book

As you glance through this book you will see that each chapter has two parts. Part A contains everything you need to know about how to research with straightforward explanations. Part B explains the computer functions or facilities that will support what has been discussed in the earlier part of the chapter. These sections are easy to locate – look for the vertical rules running down the page. Either part can be read independently of the other and if you do use the computer to aid your research it will save you a tremendous amount of time and will virtually eliminate repetitive work.

▶ What others have said

'This is the kind of book that would have been perfect for me whilst I was studying for my degree. It provides a useful framework for planning and carrying through all levels of research. It also brings together and clearly explains a wide variety of information, which cannot be found elsewhere, on using computers and the internet for research and the presentation of results. This one book has everything you need . . . '

Katy Waring BSc Psychology graduate

'In an easy-to-understand manner, this book guides you through an exhaustive range of research methods. You learn how to analyse and present your findings in the most appropriate way aided by helpful summaries, diagrams and computer screen illustrations. I which I'd had access to such an informative aid when I was conducting my own research.'

Irene Bulmer Cert. Ed. T.Dip.WP, T.Dip.T
Lecturer in Further Education

'This book will be invaluable to university students in higher education who are increasingly expected to both conduct research and use computers in their research. It is clearly written with a refreshing lack of jargon and it is suitable for both first-time and experienced researchers.'

Judie Jancovich BA, Cert.Ed.
Widening Participation Officer, Bath Spa University College

1 Getting Started

Getting Started

PART A
▶ What is research?

Research is a tool for getting you from point A to point B. You wish to prove an idea – research it. You wish to disprove an idea – research it. You think that fact ABC is incorrect – research it, or that fact ABC is correct – then research it. Research is simply a method for investigating or collecting information.

However, don't be surprised if during the involved and rather messy process that we call research, you find that it is impossible to come to a neat, conclusive finale. You may even find yourself having to change your original stance, your investigations may turn your first preconceived arguments on their head, but if this happens it is all part and parcel of the research process and hopefully you will have learned from the experience.

If you look up the word research in a dictionary it will say something to the effect that *'research is a systematic investigation to establish facts or principles or to collect information on a subject'*. Research, in essence, is just that. But how you decide to research, what methods you choose, what style of research you adopt or even more fundamental how you identify a particular topic and area which will fulfill your needs will in the long term effect how successful your research will be.

▶ Why research

Most people research because they are forced to. At heart, unless they are saints, most human beings are lazy and we live life on a 'need to know' basis. For example, nowadays we increasingly 'need to know' how to operate a computer. We may just about be able to get by without making the effort, but look at just some of the ways in which it affects us:

- you can't apply for certain jobs as computer familiarity is stipulated
- you will have to pay someone to word process your CV or your university submissions or dissertations (more and more universities now demand word-processed work)

- you have placed yourself outside a whole area of conversation and will not understand others' enthusiasm for the digital camera or the excitement of designing a party invitation using the facilities of a desktop publishing package.

We research all sorts of things in our everyday life, for example we might read information about the various career options available to us or seek out various books about a proposed holiday destination in order to choose the resort that we feel is best suited to our needs – it is an everyday activity and can be fun. However, there are very few people who will undertake academic research just for the fun of it; it would take a very dedicated person who would embrace all the work that research entails just to prove a point. Most people start a research project because they have to, but once they are involved they find it rewarding, frustrating at times, but always the end result compensates for any frustrations along the way.

You may have to research a small project as part of your work, you may be seeking to improve your qualifications by gaining your first degree or you may even be an experienced academic undertaking a PhD thesis. Whatever your circumstances, well-organised research can be the key to your success.

▶ How to approach research (and survive)

If you are about to undertake research and feel daunted at the prospect of researching a topic and writing a paper, then look on the positive side, research can be exciting and you are about to embark on a journey of discovery which will widen your horizons and could change your whole career. Remember that most people experience some form of panic – 'I can't do this, it's not possible' is the first thing we think. But it is possible, you can research and present your findings; however, if you are going to be successful and not become totally stressed in the process, then preparation and organisation is the key to your success.

Research at its basic level usually has a pattern, as shown in Table 1.1. This process, albeit simplified, gives an indication of typical research steps. There are, of course, different ways of viewing research. For example at step 3 the researcher could have decided to test a hypothesis rather than set an objective.

TABLE 1.1

Typical pattern	Simple example
1. Original reason for research	Needed for work, college or university course, and so on
2. Decide on a specific topic/area	For example why so many young people consistently leave employment within a particular company, or fail to complete their university degree course
3. Identify objective (an objective is the goal or aim of the research)	Find out if and in what way the company or university is at fault
4. Decide and plan how the you are going to find information you need	Research the various methods available to you. Perhaps you decide in this case to issue questionnaires and conduct personal interviews with the people leaving, if they are willing. (Remember, however, that there are a lot of research methods available to you, so don't choose the first method you research.)
5. Negotiate access/ permission	Clear project with those in authority and request permission to interview leavers
6. Devise paperwork needed	Decide on the questions that need to be asked. Construct questionnaire
7. Research around the topic	Read what other people may already have written about the topic (a) in the particular company and (b) in the wider field. Finding relevant journal articles, books, and so on without computer help is very time consuming indeed. Most universities now have all indexes, abstracts and so on on a centralised network of computers which you will have to use
8. Decide timescale and/or number of staff to be involved and carry out and record questioning	Request permission from those leaving. Ask and record answers to questions
9. Analyse information obtained	Compare answers, look for similarities, what's useful, record findings. Can any conclusions be drawn?
10. Presentation of findings (the why, how, when, where and what)	Write a history of the research; decide on use of graphs, charts and so on to enhance findings
11. Finished research paper	To be submitted to employer or college/university if that is the requisite purpose or use it to seek publication or funding. Possibly decide on future study or career progression

A hypothesis – what is it?

The dictionary defines hypothesis as any 'proposition which is advanced for testing or appraisal as a generalisation about a phenomenon'. If you are new to research this explanation is not immediately straightforward. Some researchers see a hypothesis as a suggested relationship between two or more factors that can be tested against evidence. Fulcher and Scott give a very good example of this relationship:

> A model that links poverty to low pay, for example, may suggest the hypothesis that the introduction of a minimum rate of pay will reduce the level of poverty. A researcher, whose model links poverty to unemployment, however, may draw the hypothesis that a minimum rate of pay, by increasing business costs, would increase the level of unemployment and, therefore, the level of poverty. (Fulcher and Scott 1999:73–4)

You could use a hypothesis as a means of testing a 'feeling' that you have about something. In the case of why so many young people consistently leave employment within a particular company, the hypothesis could be set as any of the following (it would depend on the gut feelings of the researcher, who would endeavour to prove or disprove the idea or 'feeling'). This would give a slightly different approach to the research process.

Test whether young people leave because there are very few career prospects

Test whether young people leave because they perceive their salaries to be inadequate

Test whether young people leave because they find the work boring

By organising very carefully at the outset of research you will save yourself much time and aggravation later on. Approach research in a methodical manner and make sure that you have thought through what you want to do *before* you start.

This book will guide you step by step through the research process but, if you can set in place the tools to help you at each step of the way, you will find that not only doing the research but the writing and presentation of the finished paper will be easier. You will find using a computer to be one of the most helpful tools that you could set in place.

▶ Let the computer help you research

The research process can still (just about) be done without a computer, but you are making it very hard for yourself. Without doubt you will have to coerce or pay someone to word process the finished paper as well as the multitude of letters, questionnaires or findings that you will need typing along the way.

When you research around the topic you will definitely need to use computers in libraries when, for example, you want to find out what other people have already written in the area that you are researching. Access to the Internet, where you could gather an abundance of useful information, will also be closed to you, and you could miss much vital information that will enrich the findings of your personal research.

Compare Table 1.2 with Table 1.1. Notice just how much work a computer could do for you in your research process and imagine how much harder it will be if you rely only on old-fashioned, traditional methods.

TABLE 1.2

Typical pattern	Basic example of how a computer could help you
1. Original reason for research	Brainstorming software, such as Mind Manager
2. Decide on a specific topic/area	Use the Internet/library computers – see what's around, seek ideas, other publications, and so on
3. Identify objective	Word process lists, reviews. Forward plan using your lists – is what you plan feasible? You can copy relevant bits and replan if necessary. Keep notes saved (you will be able to automatically copy them into the research paper later – saves rewriting)
4. Decide and plan how you are going to find the information you need	Use online facilities at libraries. Keep records/notes in the required format from the outset ready for your eventual report and the bibliography of books – this alone will save you hours of work at the end. Word process the relevant quotes that you might use from the books/magazines as you proceed, save these under easy to find file names and incorporate

	later into document. Saves finding/writing out twice or using small card index systems (very time consuming). Computers will also search out 'keywords' for you, simplifying searches for specific topic information you've recorded
5. Negotiate access/ permission	Write letters using a word-processing package, mail merge and/or email facilities. Write report explaining the aims of your research to enclose with letters. Generate automatic labels for envelopes
6. Devise paperwork needed	Design questionnaires. Design grids for your use recording verbal responses to interview questions, tick boxes, checklists and forms
7. Research around the topic	Use multimedia to your advantage: online books, online encyclopedias, CD-ROM, computer videos, college and/or university campus networks links. Use scanners. Don't forget intranet and Internet facilities
8. Decide timescale and/or number of staff to be involved and carry out and record questioning	Keep totally on top of recorded information and word process a record of each day's work. Once more the advantage of having this immediately on computer is that you can copy parts of it straight into your research paper later
9. Analyse information obtained	Input information straight into database and draw out statistics needed immediately (no need for counting or maths on your part). Use spreadsheet package to draw pie or bar charts easily, or work out averages and so on
10. Presentation of findings	Using the word processor to bring all the above together into your research paper. Using a multitude of useful functions, such as the word count facility (you will no doubt be working to a maximum number of words). Using desktop publishing functions to give your paper a professional look
11. Finished research paper	Using presentation software to project pertinent points, charts, diagrams and so on on overhead projectors/screens for personal presentations. Designing eye-catching publicity using desktop publishing software. Using online facilities to advertise your research findings. Using word processors to write letters, mini-reports to publishers, magazines, external funding sources

You will see by comparing the two charts that computers could be of immense value to you in the research process.

This book has been written in such a way that if you choose not to use a computer in your research (although you will out of necessity have to use library computers for research purposes), you can read just Part A of each chapter, but I strongly advise you against taking that option. Part B of each chapter will mainly explain the computer functions or facilities that will support what has been discussed in the first part of the chapter.

PART B

▶ Why use the computer?

Quite simply, if you use a computer to conduct your research, in the long run you will save yourself an immense amount of time. You will also be able to congratulate yourself that you have come to terms with computer technology.

Fears

Learning to use new technology frightens some people, especially when they see quite young children effortlessly manipulate the keyboard and produce 'all singing, all dancing' documents. There is no need to fear a computer, it can't bite you, it won't swear at you and it won't blow up! The worst thing it can do is lose your work, but losing work is not usually the fault of the computer; but the fault of the operator who does not save their file regularly or properly.

I have been teaching information technology (IT) for more than 15 years and in that time, of the thousands of students, whose ages ranged from 16 to 75, who have been through the classroom, there was not one that didn't learn to use a computer. Granted, some students were quicker than others, especially at the initial stages, and some people do seem to have a natural affinity with computers, but there has never been one person who did not eventually manage to use a computer effectively.

Remember, providing you take things step by step and practise regularly, you can succeed. You have only yourself to blame if everything goes wrong when you decide to try some advanced techniques before you've mastered the basics such as opening files, keying in information and saving them. Aim to walk before you run then you will begin to understand what you are doing – a sure recipe for success.

Training

In an ideal world everyone would be born with the ability to manipulate computer keys and cajole a computer into doing exactly what was required, but it is not an ideal world and we still need to learn these skills. You have several choices:

1. Get hold of a computer and a textbook and try to teach yourself, which is not easy and some people find that working alone is the most difficult way of doing it. You wouldn't expect an engineer to suddenly just know how to construct bridges or a dentist to be born with the ability to treat teeth without some formal teaching.
2. You can ask a friend who is a little more experienced than you to help, but remember not everyone is good at explaining things, and just because someone can work a computer doesn't mean that they know the best way to carry out functions.
3. You can attend a training class and learn the basics. That may be all you need to give your confidence a boost and get you started. Some people blossom on their own once given the tools and ideas to develop.

It's a good idea at least to acquaint yourself with computer skills and software packages (see details later on packages, pp. 47, 182, 185) before you think about hiring or buying a computer, then you have some idea of what you want and need – which may not necessarily be the same.

Ideally the time to get acquainted with the computer is *before* you need it. Once you are involved in your research project you will find it more difficult to find the time to practise. If your research doesn't have to be started for a few months, you have the ideal period of time to develop your skills, and you could scan your local newspaper or telephone the local college to see what training courses are on offer right now.

▶ Buying a computer

The message from the ever-hungry computer industry is to buy the latest, fastest computer, but even if you have reached the point where you have decided to shell out your hard-earned money on this little box of tricks, the question of which one to choose is mind boggling. When you ask computer experts they always say buy the best you can afford, the one with the most memory, the one that comes with all the right software, and so on. To the beginner the act of buying a computer is baffling and you never know whether the helpful and friendly sales assistant is only trying to sell you a particular machine because the commission is good on that model.

The home computer is known as a PC (personal computer) and its ability to perform is often limited only by the knowledge of its user. Apart from being able to help you with your research project, it can help you to word process letters and documents; you will be able to keep a database (a list of information that you can interrogate for certain key information – explained in more detail on pp. 87–8, 183).

You will be able to use CD-ROMs on a wide variety of information, from encyclopedia facts to language-learning discs. Home accounts could be simplified and you will be able to access the Internet, go shopping or pay bills; banks are now online, so you will be able to satisfy all your banking queries and payments via your computer. Then there are the hundreds of games that are available to you – they're not just for children. The longer you delay with getting to grips with computers, the more difficult it is going to be for you in the long run.

Which computer?

If you want to buy a computer there is nothing like getting some hands-on experience before you decide (see Training pp. 7–8). Talk to your friends about their computers, are they happy with what they've bought and is there anything they would change? You can learn a lot from their mistakes.

Computer magazines can sometimes help, but, for the beginner, they can be confusing, so look at them carefully, scan the pages to see whether there are relevant pages of advice suited to first-time buyers before you decide to buy the magazine.

Buying a computer is a bit like buying a car, the model you buy depends on what you want to do with it, and how much money you have. You wouldn't buy a BMW7 instead of a Ford Fiesta if all you really needed it for was to pop into town now and then (unless image is all important to you and money no problem!). It's the same with computers, the model you buy depends on what you want to do with it, which is all the more reason to get some hands-on experience before you buy. If you decide that all you want is a bit of word processing and perhaps the ability to surf the Internet, then you won't need to pay as much as you would for a more powerful model with the latest chip and biggest memory. So you should decide in the first instance what you want from your computer and how much money you can afford. Then begin to look at advertisements in newspapers and magazines and compare prices and specifications.

Table 1.3 provides information on what the various words mean that you will encounter in advertisements for computers. However, it is only meant to be a quick guide; it is not possible within the focus of this book to cover in great detail the component parts of the computer. There are many books and articles written specifically on this topic and you would be wise to read some of them before parting with your hard-earned cash. If there are words below that you would like to know more about, consult the Glossary of terms on pp. 263–5.

Computer Support

TABLE 1.3

The CPU (central processing unit)	This is the 'brain' of your machine, think of it as akin to the human brain. It needs energy and ideally it should have at least a Pentium processor running at a minimum 133MHz to perform well
The screen (or VDU)	Available in various sizes, usually the larger the screen the more it costs. Screen size is either 14", 15"or 17" but larger screens are becoming affordable, so if you can get a good financial deal on a 17" or above, it will make everything much easier to read
The hard disk	This is where data is stored. The size of this is an indication of how much information can be stored by the computer. Aim for the largest size that you can afford so that you are not frustrated by the slowness of your machine
Memory (ROM & RAM)	ROM stands for 'read-only memory' (data that you can only look at, not alter) and RAM means 'random-access memory' (data stored here can be changed by you). All software packages inform you, usually on the outside of the box, of how many MB (megabytes) you need to install the particular software
Multimedia	Almost all new machines come with multimedia capabilities nowadays, that is, with speakers and a CD-ROM and DVD (digital versatile disc) drive. The speed of the drive tells you how fast information can be accessed
Printer	Many educational establishments will allow you to save your work on a floppy disk on your own computer and then take the disk into the college or university and print it out there. If you can do this, it will give you time to get to know the merits and disadvantages of various printers. If you decide to buy a printer at the outset and you can afford it, buy a laser printer; in the long run the replacement ink drum will be a thousand times cheaper. Often printers are bundled in as special offers when you buy a computer; if this is the case, ask what the cost of the replacement ink cartridge is for the 'free' printer. Ink cartridges do not last very long and become an expensive replacement item. A laser ink drum can last for years. You might be able to negotiate the cost of the 'free' printer off the cost of a laser printer at the outset, or off the cost of your computer
Software	Most PCs come with some basic software to get you started. If you are buying a new machine, negotiate at the outset for the latest Microsoft Office software. But whatever you do, do not rush out and buy extra software until you have had a little experience of what's on the market. Students within educational establishments can buy Microsoft software, which is the market leader, at greatly reduced rates once they are enrolled on their course, so do ask

Floppy disk	These look anything but 'floppy', as the disk itself (which is floppy) is surrounded by a hard plastic protective case. All disks nowadays are HD (high density) – the higher the density the more information the disk will hold. They come in a wide variety of prices, but the middle price range disk is usually very reliable. You will only need a couple of disks to get you started

Some educational establishments have purchasing agreements with certain computer suppliers in their area where you can obtain hardware (the computer parts themselves) and software (the disks that feed information into computer, thereby allowing it to perform certain functions) at a discount. It would be worth checking this out before you purchase anything. Also some establishments have free or inexpensive software available – if you don't ask, you don't get!

The first main consideration that you are likely to face will be between the Apple Mac and the Windows computer brand. Apple Macs traditionally have been more expensive, but are becoming more competitive; they are excellent in the field of graphic design, so if your interest might eventually be in manipulating pictures or home videos on your computer then they are well worth consideration. The Windows brand is more likely to be compatible with the equipment used in education and most office environments and Windows software has cornered the software market for the PC.

One extremely important consideration for you might be to choose a machine and software that will be compatible with the educational establishment or workplace that has led to your decision to carry out a research project. You may wish to transfer information between machines on different sites and incompatibility will cause you no end of problems if that is the case. If you plan to print your documents at university or in the workplace, choice of software could be crucial.

Buying second hand

Unless you are very sure of the reliability of the second-hand computer you are buying, then do think again. You have no way of knowing how much use it has been put to and whether component parts within the machine have been changed. The average hard disk is designed to last somewhere between two and five years; for all you know that bargain may be on its last legs. Buying a reliable second-hand machine is a matter of luck in the end. If you are buying second hand, seek the advice of the computer technician at your organisation or university if this is at all possible.

There is the added risk that older equipment may not work with modern software or replacement components, for example older monitors can't always cope with the modern video cards. In the long run, compatibility problems could lead you to wish you'd never bought the machine. At the end of the day, however, buying a computer comes down to personal choice and the size of your wallet.

2 Identifying an Area of Research

PART A

▶ The allocated research topic

You may not have a choice in what you research, it may be that you are given a particular topic area to research, or a concept to investigate. If this is the case, then if at all possible try to find some area that interests you within the given investigation. For example, let us say you are asked to research:

Why unemployment is 35% higher among unqualified people in comparison with qualified people.

Try not to fall into the trap of immediately presuming that everyone knows the answer already. If you do this, you will not only fall into a biased research outlook, but you may feel that the answer is so obvious that you are wasting your time in researching the topic. This in turn will lead you to devalue the importance of your research and you will find it extremely difficult to motivate yourself, especially if problems occur.

News reports often interpret the facts about patterns in society in a biased or provocative manner, and no doubt you will, over a long period of time, have read or listened to many news reports relating to the unemployed which will have in some way coloured your opinions.

Your research could bring a new slant on readily accepted views. Ask yourself why this statement is perceived to be true; question whether it is in fact a completely unbiased statement; what age group is being considered; are male and female being equally considered; is the issue local and what factors might be affecting the statement. It could be that, in arriving at this assertion, no consideration had been given to a large percentage of 16–18-year-olds that were attending full-time education but not yet in full-time employment. They were of employment age and could have been used in the statistical analysis.

Also an older generation of people may have been included. A whole generation of teenagers, who attended secondary modern school in the 1950s and 60s, left school aged 15 or 16, having never been given the opportunity of taking a single examination. This generation is now approaching retirement, perhaps they no longer wish to be employed, or they may be among the target redundancy age group that finds it difficult to find work. Your research could lead you to discover that the problem is not one of qualification but of age.

Questions such as these can be the start of turning an assigned topic that at first impression seems boring into one that holds immense interest. If you are going to spend a considerable amount of your time involved in research, it is important to feel motivated and interested in the topic from the outset.

▶ Choosing your own research topic

Selecting a topic to research needs careful consideration. If you have a choice, it is wise to think of several topics that might interest you and do some groundwork before settling on the final one. Don't jump straight in and adopt your first idea. Write down a list of issues that you would find interesting to explore within the remit of your research area. If your research has to be in the area of health, your initial list might include:

screening provision
preventative medicine
men and cancer
waiting list issues
the GP system in the UK
homes for the elderly and infirm

Think carefully about each proposed topic. *What* is the current state of affairs? *What* questions are raised? *What* factors are important? Asking the question *why* is also very helpful at this stage and prompts you into thinking along lines that you might otherwise have missed. For example, if we take the last topic on the list, 'homes for the elderly and infirm', your *what* questioning leads you into the area of what is the difference in options available for those who need nursing help as opposed to those who are elderly and need some help but not that of a qualified nurse. If you then ask the supplementary question *why*, you are very likely to find yourself with other areas of possible considerations, such as financial restraints, government provisions or the needs of the individual.

Questions such as these will prompt you into beginning the research process, but it is only a starting point. You need to narrow and refine your research area into a manageable size; you only have limited time to conduct this research and it is far better to produce a meaningful piece of work within a small area, than to take on more than you can manage. Narrowing and refining your goal may help you to decide the issues to be studied. You could identify a hypothesis to test, or you could write a purpose statement. Creswell makes the point that:

> the Purpose Statement establishes the direction for the research because it conveys the overall intent or purpose of a study. (Creswell 1994:56–7)

A purpose statement can be written in many ways depending on the methodology of your research. Creswell gives an example of a script for a qualitative purpose statement by asking a list of questions, the first few of these being:

> The purposes of this study is (was? will be?) to . . .
> (understand? describe? develop? discover?) the . . .
> (central concept being studied) for . . . (the unit of analysis: a person? processes? groups? site). (Creswell 1994:59)

If you applied these questions to the first research idea on your list it could look something like this:

> Screening provision – The purpose of this study is to discover the screening provision for women in Bristol

You are already beginning to narrow your research area just by adding the words women and Bristol. You could clarify it further by adding an age group (women aged between 40–60), or a region (women in the inner city area aged between 40–60).

▶ An initial literature search

Once you are fairly happy with a proposed area of research, you are ready to go on to the next important stage of investigation which you should do *before* you finally make up your mind on the exact scope of your research.

Whatever research question/s you have refined, it is very unlikely that you are the first person to have explored this area. At this stage it will be invaluable for you to discover what and how much has been written already in this province. To undertake a full-scale search of the literature is enormously time consuming. Unless you are absolutely sure that this is the area you want to research or you have been allocated a topic and have no choice in the matter, I would advise you just to skim the surface in the first instance. This chapter only covers the basic principles, so if you want to spend more time searching the literature at this early stage then read Chapter 4 of this book before you commence.

The rules governing the use of library facilities or the borrowing of books from an academic library vary from one university or college to another. Usually all members of the university may use the service without charge, and if you are studying at the establishment there will be no problem. Often reciprocal arrangements have been agreed between other libraries within a region and you will be able to use the facilities of these libraries also.

If you are not a member of the university, you need to talk to the librarian. Often, if you have enrolled on a course that has not yet started or are researching a specific topic, you will be allowed to use the facilities on the premises, but not take away any books. Some universities will charge you a small fee per academic term if you are not a university member and wish to use their facilities.

One of the starting points of a literature search is the library catalogue or library online facilities. Usually it is only the larger public libraries or the academic libraries associated with universities or larger colleges that will have the type of information you will be seeking. Your best starting point will be to consult the expert – the librarian. An experienced librarian will be invaluable to you throughout your research, so if you can coincide your visits with their quieter periods, they will be more likely to give you their undivided attention.

Nowadays most library catalogues of the books held in stock are consulted by using the library computer. You will be able to search a library catalogue to discover what books are held on your particular topic by typing in a keyword. Usually the computer will tell you how many copies of a book are in stock, at which branch or campus they are housed and whether they are on the shelves or out on loan. Lists of journals, printed extracts and indexes are also recorded on the computer in some libraries.

The books are arranged on the shelves of most libraries according to the Dewey Decimal System. There are slightly different editions of the Dewey System, but basically it is a method of book classification and arrangement with ten main subject classes, each of which is given a number. These classes are subdivided again into more specific topics, all with their own individual number. Once you have discovered the Dewey decimal number of your topic, you can easily find books in this area on the shelves because the spine of the book will show the number, and all books with that number will be placed on the shelves in one area, usually arranged alphabetically in order of author within that area.

The main Dewey subject headings are listed below.

Dewey Number	Category
000	General
100	Philosophy, Parapsychology and Occultism, Psychology
200	Religion
300	Social Sciences
400	Language
500	Natural Sciences and Mathematics
600	Technology (Applied Sciences)
700	The Arts
800	Literature and Rhetoric
900	Geography and History

These main headings are broken down further into subheadings and a more detailed list of some of the topic areas that might be of interest to the researcher is given in Table 2.1 below.

It is best to have pen and paper with you as you use the computer and write down a list of the books that might be related to your topic together with their Dewey decimal number; you can then go to the shelves and look at the books. If you are lucky, you can bookmark books, that is, highlight an interesting sounding book on the computer screen and then press a given key on the computer keyboard which then saves the book information into a list for you. You can print a list of those bookmarked publications when you've finished on the computer.

There are other computer-based facilities available in your library and these are covered in more detail in Part B of this chapter.

TABLE 2.1 DEWEY DECIMAL CLASSIFICATION

Dewey No.	Topic area	Dewey No.	Topic area
GENERAL		020	Library Science
000	General Knowledge and Computers	030	Encyclopedias
		050	General Serial Publications and Periodicals
003	Systems		
004	Computer Science	060	Organisations and Museums
005	Computer Programming, Programs and Data	070	Journalism, Educational, News Media, Documentary, Publishing
006	Special Computer Methods		
010	Bibliography	080	General Collections

Dewey No.	Topic area	Dewey No.	Topic area
090	Manuscripts, rare books, Prohibited works and other rare printed materials	320	Political Science (Politics and Governments
		330	Economics
		340	Law
PHILOSOPHY		350	Public Administration and Military Science
100	Philosophy		
110	Metaphysics	360	Social Problems and Services. Welfare.
120	Epistemology		
130	Paranormal Phenomena	370	Education. Education and the State
140	Specific Philosophies		
150	Psychology	380	Commerce, Communications, Transport
160	Logic		
170	Ethics	390	Customs, Etiquette, Folklore
180	Ancient Philosophy		
190	Modern Philosophy	**LANGUAGE**	
		407	Education, Research, Related Topics
RELIGION			
200.1	Theory of Religion. Philosophy	409	Language – Geographical
200.2	Religion: Miscellany	410	Linguistics
204	Christian Mythology	420	English and Old English
210	Natural Theology	430	German: Germanic (Teutonic) Language
220	Bible		
230	Christian Theology	440	French
240	Christian Moral and Devotional Theology	450	Italian, Romanian
		460	Spanish, Portuguese
250	Local Christian Church and Christian Religious Orders	470	Latin
		480	Hellenic Languages: Classical Greek
260	Christian Social and Ecclesiastical Theology		
		490	Other Languages
270	Christian Church History		
280	Christian Denominations and Sects	**NATURAL SCIENCES AND MATHS**	
		500	Science
290	Comparative Religion and Non-Christian Religions	507	Education, Research, Related Topics of Natural Sciences and Mathematics
SOCIAL SCIENCES		510	Mathematics
300.2	Social Sciences: Miscellaneous	520	Astronomy
300.7	Social Sciences: Education, Research, Related Topics	530	Physics
		540	Chemistry, Crystallography, Mineralogy
301	Sociology and Anthropology		
302	Social Interaction	550	Earth Sciences
303	Social Processes	560	Paleontology
304	Factors Affecting Social Behaviour. Demography	570	Life Sciences
		580	Botanical Sciences
305	Social Groups/Structures	590	Zoology
306	Culture and Institutions		
307	Communities	**TECHNOLOGY**	
310	General Statistics	600	Technology

Dewey No.	Topic area	Dewey No.	Topic area
602	Technology: Applied Sciences	**LITERATURE**	
604	Technical Drawing, Hazardous Materials Technology	800	Literature
607	Technology: Education, Research, Related Topics	801	Philosophy and Theory of Literature and Rhetoric
608	Inventions and Patents	807	Literature and Rhetoric: Education, Research, Related Topics
610	Medicine and Medical Sciences		
620	Engineering and Allied Operations	809	History, Description, Critical Appraisal of more than one Literature
630	Agriculture		
640	Home Economics and Daily Living	810	American and Canadian Literature in English
650	Management and Auxiliary Services	820	English and Old English Literature
660	Chemical Engineering	830	German Literature
670	Manufacturing	840	French Literature
680	Manufacture of Products for Specific Uses. Specific Industries	850	Italian, Romanian and Rhaeto-Romanic Languages
		860	Spanish and Portuguese Literatures
690	Buildings	870	Latin and Italian Literature
THE ARTS		880	Classical Greek and Hellenic Literature
700	Arts and Entertainment		
700.1	Philosophy and Theory of the Arts	**GEOGRAPHY AND HISTORY**	
700.9	The Arts: Historical, Geographical, Persons	900	Geography and History
		901	Philosophy and the Theory of History
701	Philosophy and Theory of Fine and Decorative Arts	907	Education, Research, Related Topics of History
710	Civic and Landscape Art		
720	Architecture	910	Geography and Travel
730	Plastic Arts, Sculpture	920	Biography, Genealogy, Insignia
740	Drawing, Decorative Arts	930	Ancient World History
750	Painting and Paintings	940	European History
760	Graphic Arts, Printmaking	950	History of Asia
770	Photography and Photographs	960	History of Africa
780	Music	970	History of North America
790	Performing and Recreational Arts	980	History of South America
		990	General History of Other Areas and the Internet

These subdivisions are broken down yet again and there is almost certainly bound to be something written in your topic area. Your librarian will point you in the right direction and will be able to open a whole new avenue of leads to search for information in your sphere.

▶ How to use the books initially

Let's say that you have found six books relating to your proposed topic. What should your next step be? The very existence of six books proves to you at once that there will be material available to you in this research area, and that is a good sign. Once you eventually consult other resources (abstracts which give short summaries of articles or books, bibliographies, encyclopedias, pamphlets, newspapers, reports, and so on), you have a considerable chance of finding other relevant information.

Start by skimming through each book for key information. Look at the chapter headings, the index, the illustrations or charts. If, for example, your research topic was 'stress within the classroom', you would look not only for headings directly associated with the topic, but also for other ideas and avenues to pursue: there may be chapters on managing conflict, coping with anger, developing relationship skills and so on. Your original idea might have been from the viewpoint of the teacher, but you could possibly find information coming from the perception of the student, which would give your research a totally different view. This is why it is important to undertake a quick literature search at this stage, as being presented with a wider picture early on will give you the opportunity to decide with certainty exactly the topic to research.

You need to keep a record of the relevant books or resources that have been useful, and make brief notes of the topics covered. It is much easier to do this on the computer rather than writing everything by hand. How to do this is explained in detail in Keeping a record and a bibliography on pp. 52–3.

▶ The framework of your topic

You may find it helpful at this early stage to draw up an outline of your findings so far. If your proposed topic was 'Teaching adults – should there be a different approach?', it may be that your ideas, added to those you have found in the books that you have skimmed, are something like Table 2.2 below. If this was the case, you would barely have started the research process but already you will be armed with many ideas to pursue.

TABLE 2.2 TEACHING ADULTS – SHOULD THERE BE A DIFFERENT APPROACH?

Basic considerations	Other considerations
1. Teach them in a different way? If so, why, how?	1. Confidence matters
	2. Career counselling
2. Their teaching needs	3. Life experiences
3. Their practical, social needs (for example children to be picked up from school and so on)	4. What do they expect?
	5. Skills needed by the teacher
	6. Understand group dynamics
4. Their personal needs	7. Dealing with difficulties

▶ Talking with others

Now that you have your own research framework, it is time to consult others before making the final decision. Bell sees this as an essential part of any research:

> Talking through problems and possible topics with colleagues is an essential stage of any plan. Their views may differ from or even conflict with your own and may suggest alternate lines of inquiry. They may be aware of sensitive aspects of certain topics which could cause difficulties at some stage or know of recent publications which are not listed in the library catalogue. (Bell 1999:11)

Most people are flattered to be asked their opinion on a given topic and are only too pleased to help. Plan your approach carefully, taking into account the workload and feelings of the person you are approaching. There would be no point in hoping for an unbiased opinion on whether you should investigate a company's treatment of their employees from a member of the staff who has just been sacked, or expecting support and ideas from someone who is working flat out to achieve a work deadline.

Consulting people requires not only time but also needs good relationship skills. You need to be prepared to receive advice with good grace. The research project that you've chosen may already have become very dear to your heart, and you may not like to hear someone pull it apart, however well intentioned. Remember that everyone is entitled to their opinion and, if you constructively use any criticism you receive, you will, in the long term, enrich your research paper by viewing things from an angle other than your own.

Most people undertaking research will have someone who is directing their project – either the manager or supervisor who first requested the research or the college or university lecturer – who will need to be regularly consulted and kept up to date throughout the research process. This could be an informal passing on of information from time to time, or a formalised timetable of meetings with deadlines. It is this person who will be in a position to agree a final research framework with you.

► Keeping a record and a bibliography

Once you have chosen your research area, you need to list everything you read around the area whether or not you quote part of it within your final research paper. If you keep a manual handwritten record of this information as you proceed, you will make your life easier in the long run. If you save this information straight to computer, you will eventually be in the envious position of putting together in a few hours what normally takes a week or more by the laborious handwritten method (see Writing the record on pp. 53–4).

► Setting a timetable

If you are undertaking research towards a degree, the timetable of when certain parts of the research process must be completed are probably set down. You will no doubt be given at the outset the date when your completed research submission must be handed in, and throughout the period you are likely to be meeting with your tutor who will check that you are on target.

If you do not have the above support and restrictions on your time, you could fall into the trap of taking forever to complete each stage. The initial literature search, for example, could become very wide and you may feel it necessary to make just one more visit to the library, request just one more book, glance through just one more journal and so on, all of which will hinder your progress without any great reward at that particular stage.

Set yourself targets and agree a tentative date when you will hand over your finished research. Your outline target for a small research project might look something like Table 2.3. All the relevant dates you would have written in **big, bold letters** in your diary.

TABLE 2.3 TIMETABLE – OUTLINE WORKING TARGET

Select a topic. Brief literature review. Consult colleagues and tutor/supervisor	4 weeks. Decide by 31 October
Decide method of research. Read relevant methodology literature. Start to read relevant subject literature, keep records and notes. Consult tutor/supervisor	8 weeks. To be finished by mid-December
Negotiate permission where necessary to carry out research. Devise questionnaires, checklists and so on. Decide how analysis will take place. Keep detailed records. Ongoing reading of subject literature. Consult tutor/supervisor	5 weeks. To be finished by 22 January
Do 'on the ground' research – plan and carry out interviews, administer questionnaires, diaries, observation study, etc. Ongoing reading of subject literature. Keep detailed records. Consult tutor/supervisor	5 weeks. To be finished by 19 February
Analyse material gathered. Comparison with checklists from literature. Bar charts, line graphs. Ongoing reading of subject literature. Keep detailed records. Consult tutor/supervisor	4 weeks. To be finished by 19 March
Writing the report, first draft. Probably consultation with tutor/supervisor	8 weeks. To be finished by 20 May
Consult tutor/supervisor. Rewriting the report	3 weeks. To be finished by 10 June
Consult tutor/supervisor. Last-minute amendments	2 weeks. To be finished by 24 June
Hand in research paper	28th June

You may need to be ruthless and force yourself to finish working on one stage and move to the next, even though you think you could do more. In some areas of the outline above, it is not necessary to work in too much detail, especially at the earlier stages. Sometimes life does not run smoothly, and your best made plans will be go awry. If this happens to you, let your tutor or supervisor know at once. Don't plod on hoping that you will catch up eventually – you may not. Keep them informed of what is happening in your life, seek their help and if necessary renegotiate the timetable.

PART B

▶ Using computerised library catalogues

The computer will prove to be an enormous time-saver when you want to find out more about a possible topic area of research, because it will enable you to search through databases of information for keywords.

Different educational establishments and public libraries use a different word to describe their catalogue of books, for example BIDS, UNICORN and LIBERTAS. Don't be put off by acronyms (names made up of initial letters) or grand sounding titles, they all do the same thing. They search through the computerised databases and produce on screen a list of the information you have requested. Sometimes you can also print out the information on screen. Most libraries offer a short instruction lesson in using the library computer catalogue and you might find it useful to join one of these sessions before you start your research.

To use some catalogues you will need to have a password in order to get in, with others you don't unless you wish to reserve a book. Manoeuvring a mouse (see Glossary of Terms, pp. 263–5) on the desk operates most catalogues; you simply point and click at the icons or words on the screen that you want. There is always an icon (or key on the computer keyboard) that allows you to go back one screen at a time if you have made an error, or to stop the search and start a new one.

You can search on several criteria. The options usually are:

- *The author with a title keyword:* you would use this search if you know the author's name and have some idea of the title or part of the title of the work, for example, author, Shakespeare: title, Midsummer.
- *A journal title:* key in the name of the journal and the computer will list all the editions of that journal that are kept in the library. Unfortunately it rarely lists the contents of each journal. You can also search the computer for a list of all the journals stocked, sometimes the information obtained will also describe briefly the kind of information contained in the journal or magazine.
- *A word or phrase:* this is a very useful computer tool because it can be used to search for almost anything on a given topic. If you keyed in *education* and *UK* the computer would produce a list of all publications held in that area. Depending on the search, you might end up with hundreds of titles, so the more specific that you can be in your choice of words, the better the results will match your requirements.
- *Browse mode:* you can browse through the complete alphabetical lists of

authors, subjects, videos or journal titles if you choose this option. It can be helpful if you have a vague idea of an author's name but no idea whether his or her books are suitable for your needs. It is also helpful to look at subject headings because this sometimes sparks off ideas that could enrich your research in areas that you hadn't considered before.

- A *personal or advanced search:* this search allows you to find publications by any combination of all the options listed so far. Once you have mastered the other methods, try this, as it can be useful and is not difficult to use. Different library catalogues will offer various advanced options, but almost all of them will offer a version of the following in some form:

  (a) *Booleon logic:* this enables you to use the special command OR when searching. For example if you keyed in male or female the computer would find all references that contain the words male or female.

  (b) *Wild cards:* if you want to search for part of a word, you may use an * as a wild card. For example, if you wanted to search for all the items that have the description 'age' (this would include ageing, ageism, ageless and so on), type age*.

For more hints on searching for information see Table 4.4, Internet search tips, p. 77.

▶ CD-ROMs

All large libraries now house CD-ROM facilities. The abbreviation CD-ROM stands for compact disc, read-only memory. In most computing circles the word 'disk' is usually spelt with a 'k', the CD-ROM spelling is different. Each disc will contain a colossal amount of information on a specific subject area that could be invaluable to you in your research process.

In most libraries you will not handle the actual disc because all the information will be loaded into a central computer, which will be networked (a system of connecting one computer or another) to all the other computers, often on all the various campus sites. Usually you access the CD-ROM that you think might be useful by using the mouse to point and click on an icon (small image) depicted on screen. Images and/or words will then appear on screen and you will be guided step by step as to what to do.

Once you have the hang of manipulating one CD-ROM, using the others will be easy because they all have a somewhat similar set-up. Most CD-ROMs initially give you a menu (list) of features to choose from, often presented in icon and written form. You will be able to display a complete alphabetical list of information contained on the CD-ROM and choose from that, or type in a keyword and request the computer to search for articles on that subject.

The CD-ROMs stocked by a library are often listed in the computer catalogue or some libraries will give you a handout containing the relevant information. Recommending a particular CD-ROM as being useful is impossible, because it will depend on your chosen research topic. However, to give you some idea of the enormous scope available to you in this format, see Table 2.4 below which indicates the types of CD-ROM that you might find at your library. This list is only a fraction of what is available at my local university (see also Library CD-ROMs, pp. 92–3).

TABLE 2.4 EXTRACT FROM A TYPICAL LIBRARY CD-ROM COLLECTION

Austen, Jane	World War II Global Conflict
Bronte Sisters	British Sign Language
Chambers Dictionary	Census 1991
DK Eyewitness Encyclopedia of Science	Changing Times
	Economist (various years)
Encarta Encyclopedia (various years)	Encarta Research Organiser
Encyclopedia of Science	Europe A-Z
Europe in the Round	FT McCarthy (various years)
Crolier Multimedia Encyclopedia	Guardian Newspaper (various years)
Illustrated Shakespeare	Iolis (law CD-ROM)
Laser Library – World Atlas	Keenan's Europe
Marketing Mix	Microsoft Art Gallery
NERLIS	Romeo and Juliet
Social Trends (various years)	TES Bookfind
The Times & Sunday Times (various years)	Ultimate Human Body
	Window on Korea
Using the World Wide Web	World Guide (various years)
Women in Business	World War II Sources and Analysis

▶ **Computerised diaries**

Setting up a proposed timetable for the research process is essential if you are to avoid last-minute panics and work through the procedure smoothly. You can do this in a normal paper diary but also on your home computer. There are quite cheap programs available that enable you to run a computer diary, although, for the researcher, they have one big advantage and one big disadvantage. The advantage is that you could request your computer to remind you, say, seven days before a deadline is due, and then six days, five days, four days and so on. Every time you turned on your computer in this period you would get a warning on screen that such-and-such should be handed in by whatever date. You couldn't possibly forget to get on with it then!

The big disadvantage is that, if you keep your diary on computer and not in a handwritten one, noting down pertinent dates is problematic. If in class your tutor gives you a tutorial appointment, you have to note it down on a piece of paper and transfer it to your computer later; pieces of paper can get lost or forgotten, so this is not an ideal situation. It is possible to send this information direct to your own computer via the Internet, or perhaps you will opt for a laptop computer that you can carry around with you, if so you will be able to record it straightaway. However, if you are a beginner using a computer, you will probably not want to be involved in this kind of computer technology at this stage.

Mobile phones

Mobile phones are able to record this kind of information; they also enable you to send a text reminder message to your home computer immediately you are given information if you wish.

WAP phones also give you limited Internet access. They have their own computer language and hook up to other computer devices on the World Wide Web. The online pages are small enough to fit onto phone screens, and you can use the phone pad to input instructions in a similar way to using the computer keyboard.

However, if technology is new to you at this moment in time and you feel a little anxious at becoming too involved so quickly, perhaps you would feel more comfortable and confident carrying a paper diary for the present, but use a computer diary program on your home computer for reminding you of the important dates. An added advantage would be that this would be the cheapest option.

▶ Keyboard skills

This is where you inwardly groan! You will soon find using the computer keyboard with two fingers frustrating and slow. Learning to touch-type properly is one of the most rewarding skills you will ever learn if you are involved with computers. The length of time taken to do anything on a computer will depend on how quickly you can key in your instructions or text, and if you are a two-fingered typist, you will, by default, be slow. You are bound to have friends who tell you that they can key in fast while using incorrect fingers for the various keys; they will even give you a demonstration. However, after 20 years' experience of working with keyboarders of all levels, I can assure you that their 'fast' is nowhere near the speed of a touch-typist who will also have the advantage of almost perfect accuracy without even a glance at the keyboard.

Once you have taught yourself the incorrect fingering, it is almost impossible to undo the habits you have developed, so why not at least make an effort at the outset to develop some of the correct habits used by a touch-typist. I am not advocating that you spend hours learning to become a touch-typist, only that you take on board good keyboarding skills while you are still a beginner.

You can do this in two ways. First, you could buy yourself a CD-ROM that teaches you to type, they are not expensive and there are lots of them on the market so there is bound to be one that suits your pocket and your home computer. The disadvantage with all of these discs is that you have to look at the screen all of the time in order to learn. This is not always what happens in the real world when you want to use a computer, often you are copying information from paper or books placed on the desk beside the computer. Providing you remember this, they will at least give you a basic grounding in using some of the correct fingers to cover the keyboard in the quickest possible manner.

Second, you could use a textbook to teach yourself keyboarding. This has the advantage that you will be taught to look away from the screen and the keyboard as you learn to manipulate the keyboard with the correct fingers. There are many of these books on the market and, once more, they are not expensive, in fact they are often cheaper than a CD-ROM. If you master some of the keyboard it will be a step that you will never regret.

3 Methods of Research

PART A

Many valuable investigations are carried out without a detailed knowledge of methods of research. However, you will enrich your research experience and have a better understanding of the whole field of research if you take some time to study the various methods that researchers use to obtain their information. In fact, if you are carrying out your research as part of an educational course, it is probably mandatory for you to do this.

There are many methods of researching a topic and it is impossible to do justice to any particular research method within the confines of this book. However, the main research methods are explained and from these you should gain ideas as to their suitability for your purpose. Once you have settled on several possible research methods, you should then pursue further reading in that area. The Bibliography at the end of this book will point you in the right direction, or your tutor/supervisor and librarian should be able to advise you.

It is not written in stone that you may only use one method of research. It may be far better to combine several research methods in order to achieve a well-balanced and meaningful conclusion.

When you begin to read about particular research methods in depth, you may find that the language used is difficult to understand; because all professions adopt their own jargon to ease communication between experts within that field. Academic researchers are no different to the medical or legal professions. Your best way of overcoming the problem is to keep updating your list of new vocabulary and meanings (see Glossary of new terms, pp. 31–2) and refer to it whenever necessary.

▶ Qualitative versus quantitative research

Most research uses either qualitative or quantitative research. If you look at the dictionary definition for these two words, you will see that for qualitative it says *relating to distinctions based on quality* and for quantitative *involving or relating to considerations of amount or size*. Taking these words a step further back to their roots (see Table 3.1), may help you to understand the broad differences.

TABLE 3.1

Some definitions of quantity	Some definitions of quality
A specified or definite amount	Character or nature of something
The aspect of anything that can be measured	Distinguishing characteristic or attribute
A large or considerable amount	Degree or standard of excellence

The majority of research methods can accommodate a qualitative or quantitative approach, sometimes both, depending on the topic and research process adopted.

Bouma and Atkinson summarise the difference between these two research procedures succinctly:

> The difference might be summarised by saying that quantitative research is structured, logical, measured, and wide. Qualitative research is more intuitive, subjective, and deep. This implies that some subjects are best investigated using quantitative whilst in others, qualitative approaches will give better results. In some cases both methods can be used. (Bouma and Atkinson 1995:208)

▶ Qualitative research

Qualitative research often lends itself to small-scale research where the researcher is engaging in unstructured interviews, life histories and observations. If the researcher is involved closely with an individual or a small group of individuals in the research process, one-to-one personal qualitative research helps to cultivate a better understanding of the experiences that have taken place.

For example, if the area of research is within the classroom, and the researcher has decided to investigate whether infant school children with summer birthdays are disadvantaged because of their age, regular qualitative interview research, maybe alongside other methods, would enable the researcher to gently build up a rapport with the children and coax relevant information that would otherwise be missed with a quantitative approach.

In the qualitative research process the researcher tries to interact with those they study, a relationship is fostered and personal interaction takes place. The language of a particular study is likely to be first person and personal. The researcher may lay their own values and biases on the information gathered. Therefore if this procedure is used, the researcher needs to be aware of their own value judgements and strive to view the gathered data from other angles and adopt an objective approach to the research.

▶ Quantitative research

The quantitative approach is entirely different. It holds that the researcher should remain independent and distant from the research process; the use of surveys, questionnaires and so on lends itself to this type of research. The quantitative researcher might approach the investigation into the disadvantages of a summer birthday in infant school children from an entirely different angle. Perhaps a standard questionnaire would be used with a large number of children in infant schools, measurable school achievement could also form part of the research. The study would probably develop generalisations in patterns that might enable the researcher to better explain or predict some phenomenon. The results from such a quantitative research paper might lead to research of the same question being undertaken from a qualitative viewpoint.

At a practical level, one-to-one-type research is very time consuming and can be costly, especially if much travel is involved. Questionnaires, especially if they are computer administered, can be easier, but these questions are covered in Chapter 6.

▶ Glossary of new terms

When you have reached the stage in your research of knowing exactly what you are going to research, you have also reached the moment of choosing the best method of doing so.

As you begin to read around methodological issues, you will no doubt be confronted with a whole new dictionary of words, which may at first confuse you. Table 3.2 is a list of some of the more commonly used words with brief descriptions of their meanings, although it is not meant to be a complete list of every single word that you are likely to come across, but it is a starting point. If you find other words unknown to you, you would be well advised to start your own list of new vocabulary in which you clarify meanings.

TABLE 3.2 NEW VOCABULARY LIST

Word	Definition
Covert	Invisible (researcher involved in a setting unknown to other people, for example making a mental note of something said)
Deduction	To arrive at
Grounded theory	An attempt to derive a theory. Built up gradually from careful naturalist observation, sometimes by constant comparison of data with emerging categories
Methodology*	Analysis and evaluation of investigative techniques; it is also concerned with the nature of knowledge – how do we know? How is knowledge constructed?
Methods of research*	The techniques applied to manipulate data and apply knowledge. Used in this narrow sense, the investigator does not question the validity of the appropriateness of undertaking research
Overt	Visible (much ethnographic work is overt, for example interviewing, clearly observing event/person)
Positivism	The same principles of investigation as used in the natural sciences (holding that experimental investigation and observation are the only sources of substantial knowledge)

* There is a tendency to use these concepts interchangeably. In particular methodology is used in literature when method would be the more appropriate word.

▶ Validity and reliability

Perhaps the two key issues to be considered before adopting any method of research is whether your research is likely to be reliable and valid. If you are unsure whether your interviewee/s would constitute a reliable research, ask yourself whether someone else conducting a similar study using identical questions would find similar findings. Careful examination of the research questions when you pilot (trial) them with a small number of people before use will also give you some measure of the reliability of your research technique. Pilot studies are covered in more detail in Chapters 5, pp. 114–15, and 6, p. 136.

In order for data to have meaning it needs to be reliable. Imagine if the examination papers for a national exam were marked using different criteria by the various examiners. It could well be that candidate A might pass the exam, while candidate B, who had similar answers to the questions, failed miserably. The marking would quite rightly be criticised on the grounds that it was not reliable.

Reliability refers to the consistency of the measuring instrument. A test that has used mathematical calculations using, for example, a clock or a measuring stick or device can usually be repeated by a different researcher with a different respondent and the data obtained will be reliable, for example office desks measured to check conformity with the allocated space per person under the Health and Safety Act. The measurement of the desk should be the same no matter who does the measuring.

Psychological tests cannot usually achieve such a high level of reliability. You may have collected data concerning social benefits within the UK and at the same time have gathered the answers to interview questions. One of the people interviewed may have just had their application for housing benefit turned down or another just fallen short of being able to claim income support. This is very likely to have had some influence on the answers you were given.

The researcher needs to strive for the reliability and validity of data, especially data that could have been influenced by the mental or emotional state or the personal circumstances of the respondents, otherwise the research findings may be meaningless.

Because the reliability of the data is strong it does not necessarily follow that the validity is also accurate. Validity tells us whether the measuring instrument is measuring what it is supposed to. A test that counts the number of untreated teeth (no fillings and so on) in the mouths of a class of 12-year-olds would produce reliable number data about sound teeth. But if that same test were used as an indication that regular tooth cleaning equalled sound teeth, its validity would be doubtful. Most people would be aware of many other factors that might affect the state of teeth – a sugar-filled diet or vitamin deficiency for example.

Validity confirms the truth of the matter and should measure accurately what it sets out to measure. There is no point in being very precise about nothing, after all what use is it to tell someone the time by a watch that is always 30 minutes slow. The watch could be described as being reliable but not valid.

It is very important that reliability and validity are carefully considered early in the research process, otherwise the eventual analyse of data could well be meaningless. You can check further some of the methods you could eventually use in testing the reliability and validity of data in Methods of testing reliability and validity (pp. 175–7).

▶ Sampling

With whom will you carry out your research? You will initially need to formulate an idea of what sort of people would be relevant to your research topic. Sampling is the process of selecting individuals from a larger population with the purpose of investigating features of that population in greater detail.

In research that I recently undertook, I investigated whether the needs of hearing impaired people had been met within the state education system. As part of this research I needed the views of the hearing impaired who had already experienced the normal state education system but were no longer involved within it. To do this I listed a sampling frame. A sampling frame is a list of people concerned. Because I did not have the time or resources to interview every person who came within that remit, I further defined the sample by choosing a small-scale representation within it. The respondents who eventually took part in the research were chosen to fit in with a range of age categories. The deaf or partially deaf people interviewed were ordinary people of average ability whose education had not been privileged or privately paid for. They were a cross section of people who had experienced some kind of state education in the UK during the past 25 years.

There are various methods of sampling that aim to control bias occurring in the sample itself. Mainly these methods fall into one of two areas – chance or random. The most common methods are listed below.

Stratified sampling

This occurs when certain features are specified in the sampling frame. In the research mentioned above, one of these features would have been someone who had been, but was no longer, involved within state education. I also needed the views of hearing impaired people so that was another specified feature.

Random sampling

Simple random sampling involves choosing random number tables or computer-produced random numbers to indicate which name to choose; people are chosen by number rather than name. Systematic random sampling involves every person (or item) involved in the sampling frame having an equal chance of being chosen, for example every tenth person on an employee list, sports club membership list or college student list and so on.

Volunteer sampling

Respondents are reached by requesting volunteers by means of using leaflets, radio or TV broadcasts, newspaper, magazine articles or advertisements. Volunteers are self-selecting, which may bias the sample in a particular direction, so careful consideration must be given to the fact that the information gained may not be representative of the population as a whole.

Multistage or cluster sampling

This involves sampling representative areas with similar areas elsewhere. This could involve, for example, sampling within 6th forms in the inner-city areas of Manchester, Bristol and Liverpool. The size of this type of research may be well outside the resources of smaller research, but the same idea could be applied to sampling that takes place in, for example, the use made of church hall premises in two or three different parts of a town or city.

Quota sampling

Market researchers often use this method but it is not necessarily as accurate or reliable as some other sampling frames. It is used when interviewers are instructed to seek a particular number of various types of possible respondent, perhaps canvassing the views of women over 60 years of age, black women, or women with small children for example.

Snowball sampling /

This sample almost describes itself; it is when one respondent recommends another who might be willing to be interviewed. Beware of only using this method because it is likely to produce a sample that is far from random.

▶ Life history research (including interviews)

Researching into the life history of one or more people can uncover remarkable revelations to the researcher, but there are technical problems, as well as the enormous amount of time needed to carry out this type of research properly.

I used this method as part of wider research when investigating deaf students' ability to integrate into mainstream education. Interviewing deaf people and learning at first hand their experiences, which related to their life and education in or out of the mainstream system, was enlightening and informative. However, before embarking on this method of research, several factors should be borne in mind.

1. First, careful consideration of the intended interviewee is needed. Not everyone makes a good informant and you need to choose prudently. Ask

yourself if the person is articulate. Do they have an axe to grind (you are not seeking a one-sided view)? The relationship between the two people needs to be broadly sympathetic in order to gain mutual respect. If you have strong views that differ from those of your interviewee, you will have to learn to suppress them if your research is to be successful.

2. It is helpful if your informant lives within easy distance, and usually busy people are unlikely to make good informants, as they will probably have little time to spare.

3. Consideration is needed as to what the interviewee hopes to gain from recounting their life history; it may be painful for them. You need only to think of the life history research that has been done with holocaust victims to understand this.

4. The ethical or moral issues involved in asking sensitive questions need careful consideration. The interviewee may reveal information that they later regret sharing with you, or they may not wish to divulge certain information that the researcher sees as crucial to the research progressing successfully. At all times the researcher has responsibilities towards the interviewee, the aims, objectives and methods of the research need to be clearly explained and the subsequent use of confidential information should be built into the safeguards of the research at the outset. The interviewee must be given sight of any information before publication is considered, and they must have the power of veto or amendment before publication goes ahead.

5. Some people will demand anonymity if they are to tell you quite personal information about their lives. Simply changing the real name in any document that you write is not enough in many cases, as it will still be possible to guess the person from the information given. If you have to disguise too many facts, you need to ask yourself whether it will compromise your research.

A key debate when designing life history research is whether your questions are to be focused and selective or whether you are going to adopt a more open style. If you are too narrow in your questioning and do not allow your respondent some free expression of thoughts, you are likely to limit the eventual findings of your research. If you allow your respondent to talk freely about a wide range of issues, you will find that you have gathered a large mass of data which might be difficult to analyse eventually. Interactionism in the main favours the latter approach but you may find yourself with masses of ramblings that are difficult to interpret meaningfully.

Life history method – summary	
Advantages	*Disadvantages*
• It can serve as a basis for confirming or questioning other versions or accounts • It can highlight important areas not previously considered by the researcher • When the respondent and researcher enjoy a sympathetic relationship, much information will be gained that would be difficult to gain by any other method • If questionnaires are used rather than one-to-one interviews, respondents are more likely to be truthful	• People's memory recounts may not be reliable, or they may reflect biased views and opinions • Researchers must not be tempted to 'lead' respondents • Questioning needs to be carefully handled – neither too narrow nor too open • Sensitive questioning needs careful thought and handling • Very time consuming

▶ Survey research

There are many different kinds of survey research and different reasons for conducting them. Probably the one that most people will be familiar with is the 'clip-board' researcher who stands on the street corner grabbing passers-by and asking them all manner of questions relating to their purchase of washing powder, tea or a multitude of other consumer products. Their results are fodder for the marketing and sales departments of large companies.

Some survey studies begin with a hypothesis, which is tested by the research. The hypothesis being tested by the washing powder manufacturer might be that consumers buy washing powder on image rather than performance, or on price rather than image and so on. Several hypotheses could be being tested in the one research process.

Often this type of method tends to be used for large-scale research projects, but it can lend itself quite well to a smaller qualitative study where a hypothesis is not necessarily needed. Careful clarification of what the researcher hopes to find out can be drawn up by writing objectives (the object of one's endeavours) at the outset and agreeing these with your tutor or supervisor.

Teenagers at school will often use this method of research when studying geography. They might be required to find out why a cross section of the population uses a certain supermarket, and, after agreeing the questionnaire with their teacher, they will stand outside the chosen supermarket asking customers to complete their questionnaires.

When constructing any questionnaire for survey use, attention should be given to the eventual analysis of the data gathered. Yes or no replies are often easier to collate, especially if you are not going to use a computer to analyse the answers; however, you may limit your research findings if you do not give the respondents an opportunity to express an opinion. Chapter 6 is devoted to everything you need to know about questionnaires and you can learn much more about their formation and analysis there.

Trend studies are a design survey advocated by some researchers, these permit the gathering of data over a period of time. Babbie sees trend studies as being a very useful tool for large research:

> A given general population may be sampled and studied at different points in time. Though different persons are studied in each survey, each sample represents the same population. The Gallup Polls conducted over the course of a political campaign are a good example of a trend study. At several times during the course of the campaign, samples of voters are selected and asked for whom they will vote. By comparing the results of these several polls, researchers might determine shifts in voting intentions. (Babbie 1990:51)

A trend study does not necessarily have to be carried out with large numbers of people and there is no reason why you could not adapt trend studies to suit your particular area of research. If, for example, you were asked to research

Survey research – summary	
Advantages	*Disadvantages*
• Can be carried out by more than one researcher • The 'sampling unit' (that is, target population to be surveyed such as housewives, dentists, teenagers and so on) can be fairly easy to define • Because information is often given anonymously people are more likely to be truthful • Can be a quick and inexpensive method of obtaining information • Well-designed coded questionnaires are easier to analyse compared with interviews, however interviews are more flexible	• The design of the survey, especially if used with large numbers, needs careful consideration in order that data analysis is efficient and meaningful • Social surveys involve systematic collection of the same type of data – blanket questions do not necessary suit all respondents, and much valuable information may be lost • Surveys are often unable to explain the behaviour they describe • There is a danger of biased interpretation • The data produced can only be generalised to the population involved

the effect of change within a company and whether the new systems were successful, you could ask employees relevant questions before and after the change, providing there is enough time to do so within the remit of your research.

▶ Action research

To undertake action research, the researcher is usually actively involved in the topic being researched and may be seeking to bring about change. Hitchcock and Hughes describe action research as being:

> an enquiry conducted into a particular issue of current concern, usually undertaken by those directly involved, with the aim of implementing a change in a specific situation. (Hitchcock and Hughes 1992:7)

This research method lends itself to research in areas such as health, race issues, women's rights, inequality and education. The researcher becomes involved with changing society and takes on the role of activist.

Often action research comes about because in the early stages of the research procedure the researcher identifies a problem or dilemma. They consider that it is worthwhile investigating further with a view to improving practice. At this point a hypothesis can be formulated on what would lead to an improvement in the situation.

Action research, just as all other research, needs planning. The methods by which the information is to be obtained need to be considered and implemented, but one of the main differences is that the researcher seeks to bring about change in some way and may no longer be viewed as being 'detached' from the process.

Action research method – summary	
Advantages	*Disadvantages*
• Can be used to bring about change	• The researcher can become very involved in the process
• Can highlight new courses of action and research	• Possibility of bias
• Both researchers and respondents may experience a raising of consciousness	• Can be demanding of the researcher in time and energy
• New insights may be gained	

▶ Observation

Observation is *not* one of the easiest methods of research for a number of reasons. Whether the researcher is known or not to those observed, the very act of just 'being there' can change behaviour. Think of the way that crowds react at a football game when they know that the television camera is turned on them. Would they wave and shout so enthusiastically, repeat chants so loudly or poke their tongue out at the camera if they thought that no one was watching?

Participant or non-participant
Research using observation falls mainly into one of two types – participant or non-participant and neither is without its problems. The non-participant observer takes no part in what is happening but records it; the participant observer actually takes part in some of the activities as well as observing what is taking place around them.

If you are considering non-participant observation you need to ask yourself several questions at the outset:

1. Will it be possible to be accepted into the group in order to observe what is happening?
2. Will you be able to remain impartial once you know the group well?
3. Will the group behave naturally knowing that you are observing them?
4. Will the information gained be representative?
5. How will you record what is said?
6. Will you tell the group what you are looking for at the outset?

Participant observers who know the group they are studying well are often unable to see all the points of view objectively because of this very familiarity with the personalities involved. Some of the questions posed above apply equally well to participant observers, for example even after entering the group the participant observer can find it difficult to be accepted.

Field work for a young female observer can sometimes have added difficulties whether the observation is participant or non-participant. Some younger female researchers may experience problems of being taken seriously especially in male-dominated settings. Sometimes, however, it can work in the opposite direction and a young female researcher, especially if perceived as pretty or attractive, may find it easier to gain access, compared to male or more mature female researchers.

Recording what is taking place

Recording objectively what you see can be problematic. If you are observing a group of people and watching their interactions over a long period, you may become involved with them and find it difficult to be impartial in your recordings. If you know the participants beforehand, you will be forearmed with inside knowledge of the personalities involved, which could lead you to a bias in your recordings and to overlook the obvious.

Assumptions are made about human behaviour, and researchers, who adhere to the positivist notion that experimental investigation and observation are the only sources of substantial knowledge, would use observation as a method to test assumptions. For example, it is generally believed that little girls play with dolls more than little boys. Setting aside the reasons why this might be, it would be possible to test this assumption by observing small children in a classroom situation when they are free to play with whatever toys are available. A tick list could be drawn up, whereby the researcher would record, over a given period, every time a child of either gender played with a doll. It would also be useful to know the length of play and how the doll was played with (some children might cuddle it, while others bang it on the head or use it as a football). This would enable the researcher to break down their findings into subcategories, such as whether the doll was used in a different manner dependent on the gender of the child.

Similar research could be carried out in the health profession, monitoring, for example, whether certain patients demanded more attention than others, which could be considered on age, gender or even the position of the hospital bed in the ward.

Observation in the office could offer information on whether smokers work less hours per week than non-smokers because of the frequent nicotine fixes needed during working hours. Or whether the telephone-selling manner of women compared to that of men encourages more telephone sales, observations on why this should be (for example tone of voice, non-confrontational approach and so on) might help employers to put into place a more effective training programme. Recording the actions and interactions observed is not easy and preparation is the key to a successful outcome. Some people use grids and tick off when certain things take place. Others invent elaborate charts where they record their findings. Perhaps if a researcher was looking at communication within meetings, with a view to improving the effectiveness and reducing the overall time given to the discussions, they might start by drawing up a seating plan showing where people sat with some form of identifying the people involved. The letter 'A' might be the chairman, 'B' might be the committee secretary and so on, then every time the chairman spoke to the secretary the researcher might scribble an 'A' by the secretary's name on the seating plan, indicating who had spoken to her. This is not easy, as the researcher needs to have contingencies ready for the unexpected – what happens when more than one person starts to speak or they all speak at the same time, or the refreshments arrive?

Recording the 'hidden agenda' or the non-verbal actions that are taking place can be outside the scope of observational research. The researcher from outside has no idea of the hidden working relationship between people when observing a situation, it is not possible to know the rivalries, tensions and friendships that, while not displayed openly, will change the interpretation of what takes place.

If it is possible to video or tape-record the observation, the researcher has a better chance of picking up on cues that would, because of the demands of the actual recording, be otherwise missed. But not everyone likes to be filmed or recorded on tape and may not give their permission. The researcher must also consider that the presence of the equipment will have an effect on the behaviour of those taking part and could change what takes place.

Observational research may arguably be best used alongside a secondary method of research when small-scale qualitative investigations are taking place. Observing children in the classroom and then carrying out individual interviews at a later date might enhance the research process and produce far more in-depth information for the researcher.

Observation methods – summary	
Advantages	*Disadvantages*
• Offers the researcher an 'insider's view' – a chance to see what people actually do and say	• The researcher's presence may change those being observed
• A participant observer is able to discover the priorities and concerns of the group studied	• Sample sizes of observation are usually small – one person can't be observing everything at once
• In some instances, observation may be the only way of gathering information, for example those who are suspicious of, or hostile to, the wider society	• Observation raises ethical questions, particularly when covert
	• Time consuming
	• Recording the findings at the time can be difficult
• Can produce in-depth information	• Lack of control over what is being observed
• More natural behaviour can be observed	• Observation is often descriptive rather than explanatory
• Able to gain overall view of social environment	• Possible observer bias
	• Possible ethical problems involved

▶ Case studies

There seems to be some confusion over the term 'case study' because this format of research has been used in many disciplines and consequently has come to mean different things to different people. Generally speaking, a case study uses documentation for a wider purpose, the documents may not be particularly interesting in themselves, but when related to a wider context they could throw valuable light on an investigation. A 'case history' has something in depth to say about a social phenomenon; this could be the outcome of research into a disaster such as a train crash. By comparing the documentation and findings of one crash against another, important social indications may be highlighted and plans implemented to improve safety. Research of this depth is outside the scope of the small-scale research project.

Within the umbrella term of 'case study', a combination of various types of research methods may be used; the use of documentation may be linked with an interview or action research approach; however, most case studies develop around a detailed and thorough study of an individual incident or case.

Blaxter et al. see the case study as ideally suited to the needs and resources of the small-scale researcher.

> It allows, indeed endorses, a focus on just one example or perhaps just two or three. This might be the researcher's place of work, of another institution or organisation with which they have a connection: a company, a voluntary organisation, a school, a ship or a prison ... Or the focus might be on one individual, or a small number of individuals, as in life history studies or analyses of how top managers have reached their positions. (Blaxter et al. 1996:6)

If you were asked to study why social workers within a particular geographical area received an unfavourable press, you might decide to adopt a case study approach to the research. You could perhaps look into the particular circumstances affecting that area or particular problems individual to the social services in that area. Past newspaper articles and reports from the social services (if they will allow you access) would be a good place to build this background material. You could then widen your documentation sources by reading relevant government papers and community agency reports. Often you will find that the knowledge gained from one article leads you on to another documentation source, rather like a detective moving from clue to clue in his quest to solve a case.

You might decide to adopt an interview technique alongside the case study approach by seeking the viewpoints of the various parties involved. Your analysis and evaluation of the situation might focus on the particular individuals involved and you might conclude that their perception of and dealings with the press were the weak link rather than the guidelines of the social services. Or it might be that, in the light of your own experience and relevant background reading, your concerns will focus on what you perceive to be an incompetent link in the accounting or reporting procedures laid down within the social services department.

Case study method – summary

Advantages	Disadvantages
• A case study can disprove or qualify a general statement • It often highlights new insights or ideas • Used as a pilot study it can sometimes generate ideas and focus research • Can shed in-depth information • Often provide light on things that are unethical or impractical to study in other ways • When used clinically over long periods researchers are enabled to explore variables and relationships • Case studies are often based on qualitative and descriptive data, therefore more likely to focus on rich, detailed, individual analysis	• Can be limited in scope • Cannot be replicated, therefore not usually suitable as a basis for generalisation • Case studies can lack control over important variables • The 'history' studied may not be representative or typical • Can be prone to bias • Cases may not be representative and so findings cannot be generalised • It is sometimes difficult for researcher to be objective since a close relationship with respondent may develop

▶ Experimental methods

There are times when in your research role you might have an idea or hunch about a possible connection between a set of events, which might enable you to put forward a hypothesis.

This is a much easier method to administer if your hypothesis has a scientific or measurable capability; in fact for many people the very word 'experiment' conjures up a picture of white-coated scientists in a laboratory using scientific equipment to prove something or show it to be false. When the variables can be controlled, such as in the laboratory, the experimental method is an ideal way of research. For example, a researcher might measure metal fatigue by subjecting it to a range of different measurable stresses. Many people have grave doubts, however, that this method can be successful when applied to humans. Taylor et al. highlight this problem succinctly:

This is partly because people act in terms of their definitions of situations. They are likely to define laboratories as artificial situations and act accordingly. As a result, their actions may be very different from their behaviour in the 'real' world. (Taylor et al. 1999:609)

Causality

For example, a researcher might wish to test whether mind over matter plays a part in relieving the symptoms of a minor ailment. This would be a measurable research process and research already exists in this field. We all know of the research work that has gone into preventing the common cold when paid volunteers are isolated and purposely given the cold virus. They are subsequently dosed with various remedies or perhaps with a harmless placebo that could not possibly have any effect on their symptoms.

This method, however, is not without its problems, and can be more haphazard than this model would seem to suggest. The variations in human behaviour, the pain barrier of individuals, the ambiguities and varying abilities of individuals to complete questionnaires and so on would all play a part in the ensuing research results.

The causal links (because someone has been given a cold virus they may 'feel' symptoms they would normally ignore because they are looking for them) within the research may be overlooked. Or causality may be outside the remit of the research being carried out, so it maybe difficult to draw definite conclusions unless the research is sound and well administered.

Smoking is another well-documented area of research, but perhaps you have a hunch that most of the staff making use of the gym facilities at your workplace are non-smokers, given that they are actively aware of their health already. It may be that you wish to encourage the management to offer help to the smokers with a package of health awareness training combined with practical support in giving up smoking, together with encouragement to use the gym to promote long-term physical and mental fitness. You may see this as a method of not only helping smokers to overcome their addiction, but it would also encourage a fitter working staff team who need less time-consuming cigarette breaks.

It would be fairly easy for you to measure numbers of people using the gym and divide them into smokers and non-smokers. It would also be fairly easy to find out whether smokers would be interested in using gym facilities and giving up smoking. However, the causal effects of why employees smoke and whether the working environment causes or exacerbates the problem, or whether existing users of the gym would welcome an influx of new members which might restrict the time availability of machines, or infringe on the perceived existing comfortable atmosphere within the gym, would be a much larger research undertaking.

The field experiment
A field experiment is when the study is carried out in the natural environment rather than in a controlled laboratory. For example, perhaps an actor will pretend to be lost and ask for directions in one experiment dressed as a tramp, and in a second repeat the same questions while dressed as a smartly suited young man. The reactions of the public can be recorded and because the experiment is taking place in natural surroundings they are more likely to be relevant to real life behaviour. Field studies are therefore described as having a degree of 'ecological validity'.

Experimental research works well in controlled large-scale situations, which may be expensive and time consuming to administer. However, there is no reason why the small-scale researcher could not adopt some of its processes providing that great care is taken in considering that all possible causes have been highlighted if not actually researched in depth.

Experimental methods – summary	
Advantages	*Disadvantages*
• Useful when variables can be controlled in a laboratory situation • The laboratory enables the experimenter to measure behaviour with greater precision • Laboratory research is easier to replicate • Field experiments enable the experiment to create contrived situations	• Ethical considerations – is it right to 'fool' human beings (for example placebo used in cold virus research)? • If people are involved the results will be inexact • Artificial and contrived behaviour likely when people involved • Experimental methods often involve volunteers who may react differently to non-volunteers

▶ Which research method to choose?

Deciding which method of research to use can be a difficult decision, especially if you have never been involved in research before. This chapter has given an indication of what is involved in the main research methods available to you, you are advised now to read in depth the method/s that interest you. Guidance for further reading is given in the Bibliography at the end of this book, and your tutor or an academic librarian will also be able to help you. Remember that you do not have to use just one method of research; your findings can be enriched and enlightened by combining the use of several methods.

Choosing one method does not mean that you have to keep to your first choice throughout the research. If you find that it's not suitable when you get down to the practicalities of the research, do not continue using it. The knowledge you will have gained in its application is not wasted; you will find that it will improve your research and give you fuel to enrich your new research method.

PART B

▶ Using word processing

Early in your research process, when you are still considering which methods of research to use, would be an ideal time to master the basics of word processing. The ability to produce your own notes, keep bibliographical references, write your own letters and begin to formulate the basis of your eventual research paper will be invaluable to you.

The underpinning skill needed to record this information in the most effective manner is (next to using the keyboard efficiently – see Keyboard skills, pp. 27–8) to be proficient at using a word processor. The majority of universities use Microsoft Office software, so it is likely that you will be using a version of 'Microsoft Word' software at your university campus. The practicalities of using the identical software at home are enormous:

- You will only need to learn one word-processing software.
- The work you produce on your home computer will be compatible with the university equipment. This will enable you to work at home or on campus with no problems of accessing previously saved documents, no matter whether they were saved at home or university.
- One word of warning here – *beware of viruses*. If you insert a computer disk in different computers it is possible to transfer any virus from one computer to another (see below).
- At university you will easily be able to print work previously saved at home (essential if you do not own your own printer).

Computer Support

Computer Support

Virus checkers

A virus can do a wide variety of things to your computer, from causing mayhem within a program, for example changing a certain letter to a different one, perhaps the 'a' to '3', every time you type it – which would be 3nnoying to s3y the le3st', to wiping out a programme entirely.

You can buy specialist virus checking software to load onto your home computer that checks for known viruses and eliminates them, and many educational establishments have a virus checking service, whereby you can have your disk checked out and cleaned of any virus present before you leave the computer section. Some universities insist that your disk is checked before you enter the computer section in order that you do not unwittingly transfer a virus onto their computers.

▶ Word-processing functions particularly relevant to research

It may be that you already have a computer using different word-processing software. It is not impossible to use two different software packages to produce your research document, but it will be more problematic for you. Probably you will end up mainly using your home computer.

It is not possible within the remit of this book to give detailed instructions on how to operate the functions of your word-processing software because it will vary from one package to another. However, I would advise you to consult the instruction book that came with your software or any online help facilities that you might have. Alternatively search your local bookshop for a relevant instruction book.

The facilities listed below are especially relevant to producing research work, and you would be well advised to learn them. If you are using Microsoft Word, detailed instructions for most of these functions can be found in this book. See the index on p. 274.

- Open a document file
- Amend text
- Save a document file
- Retrieve a document file that has been already saved
- Resave the retrieved file with a new name (thereby keeping the original work intact)
- Change font appearance and size
- Enhance the appearance of your work (embolden, underline, italics)
- Automatically number pages

- Use spellchecker and grammar checker (although you shouldn't totally rely on computer accuracy in this area)
- Word count facilities (you are usually told to write a set number of words)
- Cut a portion of text and move or copy it elsewhere (cut and paste)
- Move a portion of text to another area of the document on screen
- Move a portion of text to different document
- Use different justification techniques (align left or right, centre or justify)
- Add automatic paragraph numbering
- Change line spacing, especially learn double and single line spacing uses
- Change margins
- Use indentation techniques
- Print the whole document
- Print just one page of a multi-page document
- Sort lists of text into strict alphabetical order
- Making folders and sub-folders (sometimes referred to as directories). This is not strictly a word-processing function – see the following section.

Providing you get to grips with whatever word-processing software you intend to use, you will be in a good position to produce your research documents in the easiest manner, and the earlier you start this learning process the better.

▶ Folders (or directories)

Imagine an ordinary filing cabinet into which various paper documents are going to be placed. If paperwork is just thrown into any drawer in no particular order, it is going to be difficult to find any specific item. It is better if each filing cabinet drawer contains suspended insert folders or document pouches that are labelled accordingly, then whenever something is filed it can be inserted into the correct file. Subsequent retrieval of this information is then effortless.

It is the same with your computer. If you keep saving documents with no real thought as to arranging them in a logical order, you are making things more difficult for yourself in the long term. People in the computer world call this 'housekeeping' and in a way it is similar to keeping a house in some sort of order.

If, at the outset of your research, you set up a folder for each specific area of your work and then always save relevant work into that folder, you will, in the long term, save yourself an immense amount of time. For example, in the process of researching social work practise the following directories might have been made:

- Access – letters and problems
- Analysis
- Bibliography details
- Case management
- Contents page
- Email items
- Families (working with)
- Groups (working with)
- Index
- Information presentation
- Internet items
- Interviews
- Miscellaneous
- Questionnaires
- Record keeping (plus literature reviews)
- The research area
- The research report
- Theory vs practise

If these folders were made at the start of the research or project, then each time a relevant document is written it could be saved into the logical folder. For example, letters requesting that access be allowed into a building could be saved immediately under 'Access'; or relevant information downloaded from the Internet could initially be saved under 'Internet items'. When you are eventually offline (that is, not paying the telephone line charge to be connected to the Internet) and have more time, you could then read the documents in closer detail and transfer them to a more relevant directory. You can always add extra directories or delete useless ones at any stage, no matter which software you are using, so your initial ideas for titles are not 'set in stone'.

How to make folders on the computer
Let us say that your research was about social work practise and you had carried out several one-to-one interviews, attended a network meeting with the permission of the local social services, and looked at group working. You also had gathered 50 completed questionnaires. Your computer directory might look something like Figure 3.1 below.

In order to use folders or directories you need to get to grips with your computer's system. If you are using Microsoft, the most popular package, one of the ways you can do all this is in Windows Explorer → File → New → Folder.

Computer Support

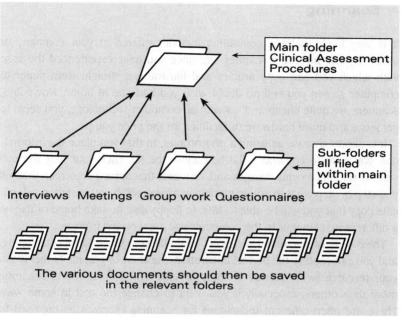

Figure 3.1

Once you have set up the folders, you need to practise saving to and retrieving from them.

To save to a folder with Microsoft:
1. File →
2. Save (or Save As if saving, updating the file and wishing to keep original intact) →
3. Save in (choose relevant computer drive, for example C) →
4. Choose the relevant folder by double clicking on it →
5. Key in appropriate file name →
6. Click on Save

To retrieve work already saved from a folder:
1. Open →
2. Look in (choose relevant computer drive, for example C) →
3. Choose the relevant folder by double clicking on it →
4. Double click on appropriate file name

The earlier in the research process that you master using folders, the easier your research process and eventual analysis will be.

▶ Scanning

It is very likely that the computing facilities offered at your company or university will include a scanner and once you have experienced the ease with which you can copy articles and illustrations straight from paper to computer screen you will no doubt wish you had one at home. Nowadays, scanners are quite cheap and, as with all computer technology, you seem to get more and more hardware or facilities for the price you pay.

It is almost as easy as using a photocopier, in that you place the information you wish to copy on a flat bed, close the lid, click your way through various screen prompts (images and/or words that appear on screen that tell you step by step what to do). In no time at all you will have on screen a duplicate copy that you will be able to save to floppy disk (to take home or use on a different machine) or to the computer you are working from.

The benefit of scanning articles is that it will save you a lot of copy typing, and you can capture the perfect illustration, pie chart or graphic to include in your research work. However, some articles lend themselves to scanning more than others, especially if you want to change the text in some way. There are often different techniques for scanning graphics as opposed to scanning text and if you experience problems with your scanned work it is as well to talk to a computer technician, just in case it is you who is doing something wrong.

You will need to cite a reference for any work that is not your own, so take details of the book or article while you have it to hand. It will save you an immense amount of frustrating time later. See the following section and Citing references and writing the bibliography, pp. 59–65, for more in-depth information.

▶ Keeping a record and a bibliography

As part of the research process, you will need to list or summarise everything you read whether or not you quote part of it within your final research paper. If you keep a record of this information as you proceed, you will save yourself a time-consuming job later.

As you read about the various styles of research, you may find information that is relevant to your proposed research. You might also wish to quote part of this information and, if this is the case, you will need to keep a detailed record. In the past researchers often kept their records on individual index cards and, although this works, it is a very old-fashioned, time-consuming way of listing information. If you keep your records on computer, you will be able to compile your bibliography (list of books or other material on the subject) at the same time as you record your book details.

If you have read a book containing information that you would like to be reminded about when you eventually write your own research document, or if you wish to quote from a book, or just record that you have read it (which gives the person assessing your research work some idea of the breadth of your reading), one of the simplest ways of recording this information is to save it in a word-processing file. There are other computing methods for doing this, but the aim of this book is to make it as easy as possible for someone new to computing.

Start by making a folder, giving it a name such as Books and articles, which will remind you that from now on this is the folder you are going to save to whenever you wish to keep book or possible future information. You might like to make sub-folders within the main Books and articles directory, with topic areas akin to your research area. For this book these would be something like:

Books on existing research
Books on methodology
Books on questionnaires
Internet articles
Magazine articles and so on

At the same time, make another folder and call it Bibliography. You will then be in a position to start a draft bibliography document which you can update as you proceed.

▷ Writing the record

Let's assume that you have read a sociology book and have been alerted and interested by a chapter that discusses parents as educators which you think might be useful in your own research. The chapter, which covers ten pages, gives the impression that parents must be able to understand and 'play up' to the school's view of good parents, interpret the teaching agenda and implement it at home in order for their children to be successfully educated. You do not agree with this theory and feel that this focus is flawed.

The information you need to record and save in your Books on education sociology directory would be as follows:

Computer Support

Topic	Parents as educators
Author (name and initials)	Bloggs, J.A.
Year of publication	2001
Title	*Education Sociology*
Edition	1st
Publisher and location	Palgrave: Basingstoke
Where book found	University Library
Dewey decimal no.	370.002

My comments
Chapter 3 (page 47 onwards) says that, in order to be a good educator, a parent must be knowledgeable about the way their child's school works, and be aware of current government initiatives. Parents can be excellent educators by caring, encouraging and helping their child, reading to them and so on. They do not need to know about the way the school works or government thinking to do this. Find research evidence to support this belief!

Possible quote to use later
'Without keeping tabs on the way in which education is proceeding, then the parent is not best placed to direct their offspring in the right direction.' (p. 49)

You may even wish to scan in part of the chapter at this point so that, when you eventually begin assembling all your researched information, you will be reminded in more detail.

Armed with the above information, you will have all the details you need to borrow the book again and reread the chapter nearer the time of writing your research paper if necessary. Or, if you believe your comments are still true after you have carried out more reading and when you are nearer to writing up your findings, you can immediately weave details into your writing at the appropriate point without being involved in any more work.

4 Collecting the Data

You will collect two kinds of data during your research. First, the historical data collected from background reading, access to written records, audio disks, video and computer sources, letters, drawings and so on. Second, the first-hand data that you generate during the research process, interview information, questionnaire returns and so on. This chapter is mainly concerned with the historical data that you will gather before you start to produce your own first-hand data.

▶ Sources of data (primary and secondary)

Because something is written does not mean that it is necessarily true, and unfortunately not all sources of data are equally valuable or reliable. If the sources are flawed or inaccurate, equally the research based on them will have little value and you will have wasted an awful lot of your personal time.

All data is either from a primary or a secondary source. Primary data is 'straight from the horse's mouth', such as original, personal letters, eye-witness accounts, official correspondence, minutes of meetings, in fact anything that is written or recorded at the time an event takes place. Secondary data is, in the main, produced after the event, and could be written or spoken.

If a friend tells you that they have to go into hospital for a minor knee operation, that is a primary source of information – you have been given this information first hand. If a second friend later reports to you that your mutual friend is going into hospital for a major hip and knee replacement operation, that is a secondary source or information – and you can see how time and gossip has made the secondary information unreliable.

The value of your research sometimes depends on how close you can get to obtaining primary data. The nearer you are to the primary source, the stronger its value as evidence, however, *you can never be sure that primary or secondary source information is accurate*. It is best to gather information from as many different sources as possible, and then you will have obtained the best possible background evidence. If during your research you come across works that are based on earlier evidence, try to see the earlier evidence also. It may be that the secondary work is valid and accurate; perhaps the latter had access to additional important information that was not available when the original was written. However, it would be wise to check, and these additional checks can all be written into your research paper to validate your own findings.

Is the data of any use?

Never accept documentary sources uncritically. It may be that the author of the work has an axe to grind, there may be political, religious or personal reasons why it is written in a certain way. You need to search for both sides of the story if possible.

Newspaper reports are at times inaccurate or biased, in an effort to persuade the reader that this or that event is oppressive or unjust, or it may persuade to foster the opposite view and show the event in the best possible light. Don't just read one newspaper's view, check against other newspapers and also see what the foreign press has to say. This will give you a balance from outside the country.

Finally look to your own prejudices. Are you searching for evidence to support your own views and dismissing out of hand information that initially seems to disagree with what you feel? You need to present a balanced case, even if you then seek to persuade the reader to agree with your views, otherwise your own research work will be unreliable and of little use.

Narrowing your search

If you are lucky, you will have been given a set reading list and this will be your starting point. If you chose your own research topic, you will have to search the library for relevant material. See the box below for hints on searching and look again at the information on An initial literature search (pp. 15–19) and Using computerised library catalogues (pp. 24–5). Make a skeleton plan of what you are looking for. Limiting the information offered to you initially will help you to focus on what is important.

If you are well prepared before you sit at the library catalogue, you will save yourself an immense amount of fruitless searching time later.

Working with and recording publications

There are two very important points to bear in mind once you have the books or journals in your hand:

1. Don't get bogged down with too much information.
2. Keep a detailed record of what you have read (see Writing the record, pp. 53–4).

Hints on searching for relevant literature

- Decide whether you only want to consult material published in the UK in the first instance. You might wish to widen your research later if UK material proves insufficient. However, you don't want to get too much material, there are only a limited number of hours in the day when you will have time to read it.
- Make a list of the possible search terms that you could use *before* you use the library catalogue. It may be that your research topic is workplace stress. 'Stress' would be your key search word, but think of other equivalent terms that would mean the same. I used a thesaurus (a book that contains lists of related words) to look up other meanings of the word 'stress' and it suggested seven other words. I could have taken this further by looking at some or all of these seven, as well as the various noun and verb meanings of stress. Book titles containing any of these seven words also might be of interest. Also, think laterally. An article about costs within the welfare state might be classified under government finance or spending.
- Decide whether you want to see only up-to-date work published in the last three or four years, or perhaps work published many years ago would also be of interest to you. You can't read everything and narrowing your initial reading material will help. You can always expand the area later.
- Another useful place to locate books and articles on your chosen topic area is the bibliographies in the back of relevant books that you have already found. If you look at the bibliography in the back of this book you will see the authors and titles of books that relate to the topics introduced in this book.

You are not reading for amusement and cannot afford to be sidetracked too often into reading non-essential material. If you want to survive research without too much anxiety at this stage, discipline yourself to looking up keywords in the publication's index and reading only the appropriate chapter/s.

If you find something interesting, *don't rely on your memory* but type the essential gist of what you have read onto your Record information or photocopy the information and highlight the pertinent areas to reread later when writing up your research document.

Other sources for obtaining information

Table 4.1 lists the publications that may be a possible starting point for consideration. This does *not* include valuable online sources, these are covered in Part B of this chapter. Not all universities or large public libraries will be able to offer all these publications, but most will be able to offer some of them and specialist librarians may well be able to point you to an alternative source of information.

TABLE 4.1

Source	Where to find
Encyclopedias	Some libraries list the encyclopedias they stock, which might give you an idea for further reading. However, many paper-based encyclopedias are now beginning to look rather dated as their CD-ROM versions become available.
HMSO publications (Her Majesty's Stationery Office)	HMSO publications are of an official or factual nature and many of them are kept in libraries. If not available at your library, consult the telephone directory for the nearest HMSO shop that can be found in most large cities.
Newspapers (current and back copies)	Most libraries stock current editions and reference libraries keep back issues. The British Humanities Index contains useful articles from various newspapers and journals, well worth consulting if available.
Official reports and policy	Many reports have become known by the name of the chairperson who presided over the committee investigating matters. For example, in 1978 Mary Warnock chaired a report that looked into special education needs, now widely known as the Warnock Report. The Library Association published a series of volumes on a selective basis and this contains indexes to these reports. Ask your librarian to view the Ford Breviates, the Select List and the Ford Lists. Also HMSO issue Monthly and Annual Catalogues that include this type of information. Details of two of the Ford publications can be found in the Bibliography but your librarian can give you a full list of the Ford publications and the years they cover.
Official statistics	General publications on statistics include the *Monthly Digest of Statistics, Financial Statistics, The Annual Abstract of Statistics, Social Trends* and *Economic Trends*. However, using the Internet is a far more rewarding way of obtaining the latest statistical information.
Parliamentary papers and their indexes	Bills of Parliament, House of Commons Papers and so on may be held by libraries (especially academic libraries) or HMSO can obtain them. The 19th-century *Subject Catalogue of the House of Commons Parliamentary Papers* (Cockton 1988) is a definitive work. Some libraries hold this on micro-fiche. The *Weekly Information Bulletin* produced by the Public Information Office of the House of Commons library provides details of the previous week's parliamentary business. It also lists forthcoming business and recent parliamentary publications.

Hansard is the official verbatim (word for word) report of the proceedings of the British Parliament.

Policy statements from large public corporations and government departments	These publications are often obtainable through HMSO or the Public Records Office although not necessarily published by them. Ask your librarian for the *Catalogue of British Official Publications* (COBOP). It is updated frequently and there is a printed index as well as a keyword index, which will help you search for information within your specific area.
Topic specific publications	There are many publications that are invaluable if you are researching within a certain area. *Social Services Abstracts* produced by the DSS or the *British Education Index* (and its American equivalent, *Education Index*) for example. Do ask your librarian for details of any publications that might be relevant to your research topic.

Video, tape, artistic data

Non-paper data is likely to be obtained in two ways. First, the first-hand data that you generate personally during the research process – audio and/or video tapes obtained while involved in interview or observation research. Second, the historic data collected as part of your background investigations that may well include video evidence, audio, commercial art or illustrations.

If it is possible to video or tape-record the observation, the researcher has a better chance of picking up on cues that would, because of the demands of the actual recording, be otherwise missed. But not everyone likes to be filmed or recorded and may not give their permission. The researcher must also consider that the presence of the equipment will have an effect on the behaviour of those taking part and could change what takes place.

▶ Citing references and writing the bibliography

As soon as you have completed a record of a book (see Keeping a record and a bibliography, pp. 52–3) you should then open your Bibliography file and enter details of the book. Remember a bibliography is simply a list of books or other material on a given subject.

The Harvard and the Vancouver System

There are two commonly used systems of referencing, one known as the *Harvard* system and the other the *Vancouver* system. The main difference between the two systems is the sequence and presentation of the reference and the fact that the Vancouver system uses footnotes on each page where you have made a book reference. The footnotes give further details of the book in question. Harvard tends to be the system that most educational establishments prefer.

There are, however, a number of other perfectly acceptable styles and you would be wise to ask the 'house style' of bibliography presentation required when you start to develop your bibliography and research paper. That way you will have all the information needed and in the correct sequence at the outset, which will save you checking back for missing information on a particular book or moving the order around at a later point. Consistency in presentation is the key; it is incorrect to mix styles.

Comparing Harvard and Vancouver book referencing

Referencing a book Harvard style	Referencing a book Vancouver style
If you are referencing a book in **Harvard style** in your bibliography, you will need to record information in this order:	If you are referencing a book in **Vancouver style** in your bibliography you will need to record information in this order:
1. The name or names of the author/s, surname first 2. The year in which the book was published (in brackets) 3. The book title (sometimes in italics or quotation marks) 4. The place of publication 5. The publisher's name	1. The name or names of the author/s, initials or first name first 2. The book title (sometimes in italics or quotations marks) 3. The place of publication 4. The publisher's name 5. The year in which the book was published (in brackets)

Harvard style example:

Brown, David (1999) *A Guide to Action Research*. Milton Keynes, Open University Press.

Vancouver style example:

David Brown. *A Guide to Action Research*. Milton Keynes, Open University Press (1999).

Referencing a chapter within a book

Books are sometimes written by several authors, and the book usually will have a theme and different people will contribute towards it by writing one chapter in the area in which they are expert. The editor/s of the book will have brought together the various contributors. If you wish to refer to one chapter only, you will need to record the information in the following order.

Harvard style	Vancouver style
1. The name or names of the chapter author/s, surname first	1. The name or names of the chapter author/s, initials or first name first
2. The year in which the book was published (in brackets)	2. The title of the article (often in quotation marks)
3. The title of the article (often in quotation marks)	3. The name of the editor(s)
4. The name of the editor(s)	4. The book title (often in italics)
5. The book title (often in italics)	5. The place of publication
6. The place of publication	6. The publisher's name
7. The publisher's name	7. The year in which the book was published (in brackets)

Harvard style example of referencing a single chapter:
Brock, David (1996) '20th Century Fox' in Judy Mail and Ron Nelson (eds) *Cinema Today*. London. BBC.

Vancouver style example of referencing a single chapter:
David Brock. '20th Century Fox' in Judy Mail and Ron Nelson (eds) *Cinema Today*. London. BBC (1996).

Your finished bibliography must be presented in alphabetical order of author surnames, so if you are given a free choice, the Harvard style would enable you to highlight all your bibliography entries when completed and sort them by computer into alphabetical order of author surname. This is another essential job that is quite time consuming when carried out manually.

Whether you put the book title in italics, quote marks or underline it, or whether you use full stops or extra spaces within the information is usually your personal choice, unless the establishment for whom you are preparing the research has definite ideas on the subject of display. Whatever style you adopt, aim for consistency in presentation as it is the key to effectively displayed and professional looking bibliographies.

Referencing an article in a magazine or journal
Usually the information needed when you are referencing an article in a journal or magazine is as follows.

Harvard style	Vancouver style
1. The author/s (surname first)	1. The author/s (first name first)
2. The date of publication (in brackets)	2. The title of the article (often in quotation marks)
3. The title of the article (often in quotation marks)	3. The title of the journal (often in italics), including the volume and number of the journal if applicable, plus the page numbers of the article
4. The title of the journal (often in italics), including the volume and number of the journal if applicable, plus the page numbers of the article	4. The date of publication (in brackets)

Harvard style example of referencing an article:

Huchison, Steven (1999) 'Software in Action'. *Microsoft Advantage.* **1**(10): 15–20.

Vancouver style example of referencing an article:

Steven Huchison 'Software in Action'. *Microsoft Advantage.* **1**(10): 15–20 (1999).

Some people also add pp. before the page numbers but it is not necessary to do so unless you wish or are specifically instructed to do so.

Referencing an author with more than one publication

If you wish to reference two books by the same author, list the books in chronological (date) order of publication. If the author happens to have published two books within the same year, add the suffixes 'a' or 'b', for example Brown (2000a) and Brown (2000b). The appropriate suffix must also be used within the text pages of your research paper.

Referencing within your text

As well as quoting books and articles in a bibliography which is presented at the end of your work, you will *also be required to acknowledge within your writing any words, statistics, summaries or quotes that are not your own, together with summaries you make using someone else's ideas, theories, data and so on.*

Brief references to another author's work (Harvard style)

If you are using the Harvard method, the author's surname and year of publication should be included. For example, if you were writing about parents as educators and you *briefly* refer to the author's work, your acknowledgement might look something like:

Bloggs (2001) says that parents cannot be good educators unless they are aware of governmental issues. Personally I do not agree with this statement, and believe that Smith (2000) is nearer the truth because . . .

In the above example, the text normally would form part of a continuous sentence, and no quotation marks or indentation of the text is necessary.

In-depth references to another author's work (Harvard style)

If you are using another author's ideas or quoting directly from their publication, then you must also add the page number to the author's name and year of publication. The directly quoted passage could be indented.

Bloggs (2001) gives alternative views of a good parent from the point of view of educational ability. He believes that middle-class parents are more likely to have the necessary skills to persuade school teachers into allowing them to play a supportive role in educating their children successfully at home, along the lines of the school curriculum and teaching methods. Pleasing the teachers plus the parents may not be in the best interest of the pupils however and he cites the following point:

'school pupils are to some extent victims of the school and their parents because it is difficult for them to please both. The pressures placed on children who find themselves in this situation sometimes forces them into a no-win position and this can force them to give-up the battle.' (Bloggs 2001 : 49)

Notice the use of the single quotation (sometimes double quotations are preferred), plus the reference to the exact page on which the quotation can be found.

If you have not directly quoted the author's words but have used their ideas, you might display the text with no indentation as follows: notice that no quotations marked are used because these are your own words.

Bloggs (2001 : 49) gives alternative views of a good parent from the point of view of educational ability. He believes that middle-class parents are more likely to have the necessary skills to persuade school teachers into allowing them to play a supportive role in educating their children successfully at home based along the lines of the school curriculum and teaching methods. He further believes that it is not in the best interest of children when they are forced into the position of having to please teachers and parents. The children may find themselves in a position where they cannot win and this can cause them to give-up trying.

Vancouver style of referencing within text

If you are using the Vancouver system of referencing within the body of your text, information about the author has to be provided by means of footnotes. The footnote is placed at the end of the passage in which the quotation or summary is made. Sometimes endnotes are used and these are placed at the end of the chapter in which the references are made.

This is quite easy to do if you are using a word processor and brief details of how to do this in Microsoft Word software can be found in Part B of this chapter, pp. 85–6. If you are using different software, look up footnotes and endnotes in the online help or your manual. Footnotes can, however, be disturbing to the eye in their display and some people find it distracting to view full book details among the text, especially if there are several books shown at the foot of each page.

Giving details of publications using the endnotes layout can be useful if each chapter of a book is written by a different author, who then gives bibliographical details at the end of their contribution to the book.

If the Vancouver style of referencing using footnotes was applied to our fictitious sociology book, it would look something like the following:

> Bloggs gives alternative views of a good parent from the point of view of educational ability. He believes that middle-class parents are more likely to have the necessary skills to persuade school teachers into allowing them to play a supportive role in educating their children successfully at home, along the lines of the school curriculum and teaching methods. Pleasing the teachers plus the parents may not be in the best interest of the pupils however and the children may find themselves in a position where they cannot win; this can cause the child to give-up trying.[1]

Notice the use of superscript numbering at the end of the quote. This matches with the appropriate book reference at the foot of the page (for example 1. John A Bloggs. *Education Sociology*. Palgrave: Basingstoke (2001) p. 49). It is possible to have several books listed in the footnote each with a different number or symbol.

Using Harvard or Vancouver style?

You may not have any choice in the system of presentation style to use for your research. The educational establishment or your employer will have fixed ideas on how they wish you to present your research, but it is likely to be based in some way on either of these systems.

If you are lucky enough to have the choice, you must be consistent, do not mix the two styles. The incidental details such as single or double quotes, use of full stops within references and so on are usually up to you and providing you are consistent in their use it will be accepted. However, some establishments have set ideas so do check before you begin.

Referencing non-print material

References to non-print material, for example audio cassette recordings or video tapes, follow a similar format to print-based publications. The specific medium used (such as film, tape and so on) are specified within the reference. For example:

Coppola, Francis Ford (Director) (1997) *The Godfather Part II.* (Film) Paramount Pictures.

Consistency in referencing

If you are going to write your manuscript by hand, then you will eventually need to hand it on to someone who can produce a word-processed version for you. You will want your finished word-processed version of your research paper to look professional and one of the ways of achieving this is to be consistent in your referencing and design layout. If you can remember to adopt a consistent style as you write, it will help your typist in the long run and they will be able to produce your manuscript in a much shorter time (see Consistency in referencing, pp. 86–7).

PART B

▶ Internet versus books

Students who rely on information that they can find on the Internet and neglect to consult books or other forms of publication are becoming an increasing worry to university and college lecturers, but that is not to say that searching the Internet for relevant information is all bad. There just has to be a balance.

Library catalogues are much more comprehensive than Web sites and it is a misconception to presume that you can find everything online, but you can find quite a lot of information and it should be *one* of the places that you look for information, especially up-to-date information. The key is to *contemplate, analyse and be critical of* the information that you find, whether it is from a printed or online source.

▶ Plagiarism

Is it your work? All your own work? Or, hand on heart, would you have to admit that, well, you did copy that bit, and that chart was downloaded from the Internet, and . . . oh dear! If you put your name on a piece of work to say that you have written it, and in actual fact parts of it were 'lifted' from elsewhere, it is known as plagiarism, which is theft. Also you will be taking praise under false pretences and, perhaps better deserved, you will also be taking criticism. Plagiarism is unjust. How would you like it if someone copied your work and didn't give you the credit? Miffed at the very least?

Stealing another person's ideas is just as bad. Turner highlights the problems that aspiring writers have when they submit their original ideas to publishers and television broadcasting companies. He quotes the writer Frederic Raphael reporting on his brush with a friendly television director who flattered him over an expensive 'brainstorming' lunch, which was supposedly organised to discuss the development of a new television programme Frederic was to have written.

> I had been swindled into spending time and energy, without fee, on a project to which no one was committed at all. My ideas were now on file; my garrulous suggestions were lodged in the minds of those who might later, without acknowledgement, make use of them. I was not wholly shattered to be told eventually, on the telephone, by the senior producer (who said that he had 'learned' a lot from 'our' experience), that the Department Head had decided to put the whole thing on ice.
> (Turner 1994:417)

Legal proceedings have been brought against such prominent bodies as the BBC, and they have been made to pay damages and costs to those who have proved that their ideas or suggestions have been used or developed without their permission. Writers have a moral right to be given credit for their work or ideas, and those of us who use them should give them credit.

It is very easy indeed to find some relevant information on the Internet and download it for your own use, but you must give credit to its author. Referencing online work is covered in detail in Part B of this Chapter (pp. 82–3) which describes how to cite any information you download from the computer. Do make sure that you follow it, and don't fall into the miserly trap of claiming other people's work as your own.

▶ Copyright

One of the basic principles of copyright is that the copyright owner holds the right to decide how someone else can use their work. It is up to you to find out whether the copyright owner has given permission for their work to be copied (see the Copyright and the HMSO paragraph, p. 70).

Copying from the World Wide Web

The World Wide Web is subject to copyright. A single Web page could be subject to several different copyrights, for example there could be a copyright for the graphics, another for the sounds used and yet another for the text. Permission from each copyright holder would be required if you wanted to copy the whole of that page.

If you want to copy and paste any part of a Web page into your own work, you should request the permission of the copyright owner. This is quite easy to do and I have found that most copyright owners are pleased to grant permission especially when the page forms part of a promotional corporate company's site. Permission is usually granted when it is explained that the copying forms part of a research programme.

If you want to ask permission to copy a Web page, all you do is send an e-mail to the Webmaster (or the owner) of the page concerned – there is usually a contact address on most Web pages – but before you do check that permission has not been granted automatically. Some Web pages already contain information and permission to print all or part of the text without requesting permission (look at the small print at the foot of the Web page). For details of how to copy see Saving or printing work from useful Internet sites, pp. 80–1.

If permission to copy cannot be found, there is sometimes a legal notice or legal information placed on the Web site. This type of information is usually located at the foot of the Web page. An example of a legal notice placed on a Web page can be seen in Figure 4.1, which was downloaded from the home page of the Web site http://www.macmillan-africa.com/

You can see at the bottom left of the page the copyright symbol © followed by the name of owner of the Web site (Macmillan Publishers Limited). Below this you can see the words 'Legal Notice'; when you move the mouse to point the arrow on screen to these words, a small hand appears indicating that there is more information that you can read on this topic. By clicking the left mouse button (while the hand is still pointing) another Web page appears

(Figure 4.2). When you read this Web page you can see that the copyright of the site belongs to Macmillan. You can now either write to Macmillan or click on the 'Contact Us' icon to request permission to copy this Web page.

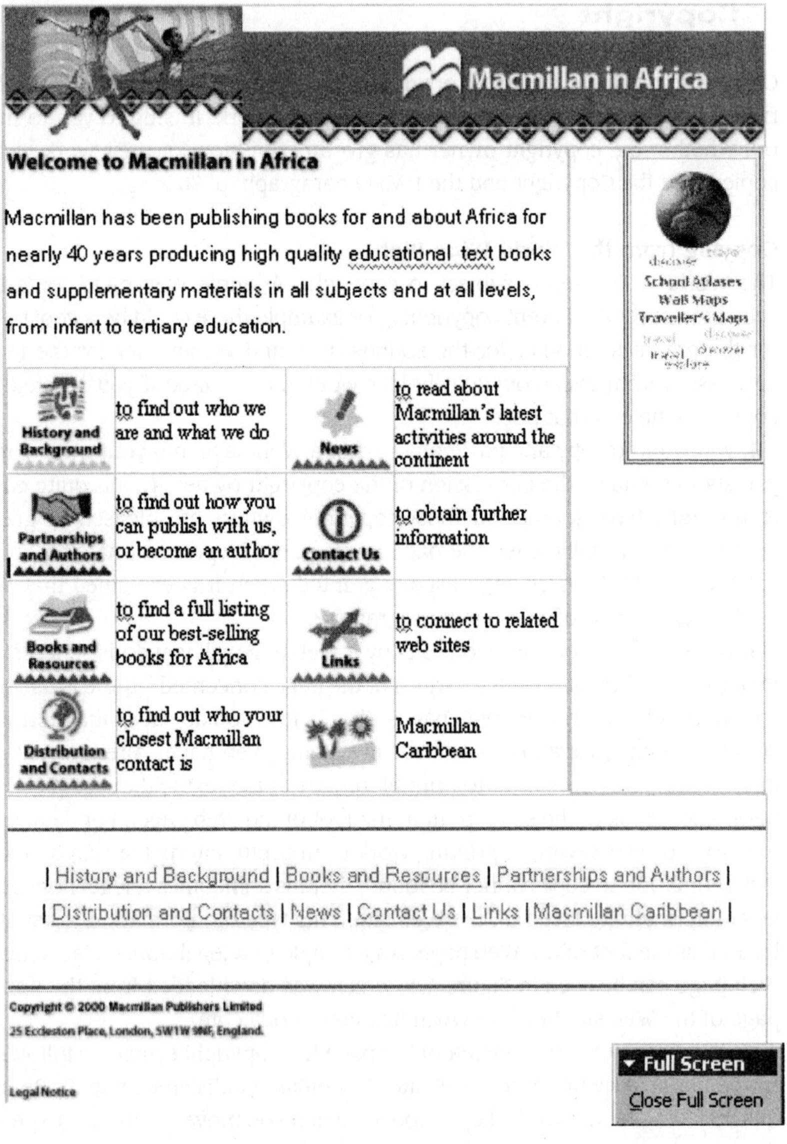
Macmillan in Africa
Welcome to Macmillan in Africa
Macmillan has been publishing books for and about Africa for nearly 40 years producing high quality educational text books and supplementary materials in all subjects and at all levels, from infant to tertiary education.
School Atlases
Wall Maps
Traveller's Maps
History and Background
to find out who we are and what we do
News
to read about Macmillan's latest activities around the continent
Partnerships and Authors
to find out how you can publish with us, or become an author
Contact Us
to obtain further information
Books and Resources
to find a full listing of our best-selling books for Africa
Links
to connect to related web sites
Distribution and Contacts
to find out who your closest Macmillan contact is
Macmillan Caribbean
| History and Background | Books and Resources | Partnerships and Authors |
| Distribution and Contacts | News | Contact Us | Links | Macmillan Caribbean |
Copyright © 2000 Macmillan Publishers Limited
25 Eccleston Place, London, SW1W 9NF, England.
Legal Notice
Full Screen
Close Full Screen

Figure 4.1 Home page of the Web site http://www.macmillan-africa.com/ produced with the kind permission of Macmillan Publishers Limited

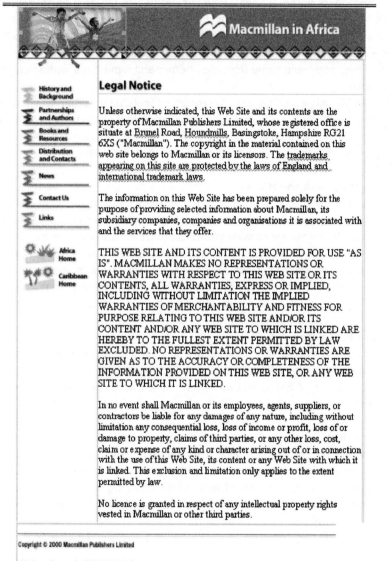

Figure 4.2 Hyper-linked legal notice page of the site http://www.macmillan-africa.com/copyright/

Fair dealing/fair use – what is it?

The UK copyright law is set out in the Copyright, Designs and Patents Act 1988. This Act makes provisions to permit some copying for the purposes of research or private study.

Section 29 of the Act deals with fair dealing for research or private study but the Act does not define fair dealing clearly and leaves that for the law courts to decide. However, it does give guidance to what is not fair dealing, for example multiple copying of a piece of work even for research purposes. So never copy something from the Internet and hand it out with your questionnaire.

Fair use allows for the use of copyrighted material in certain teaching and research situations, for example information from the Internet, providing it is used in the classroom is covered under the fair use provisions. If you want to know more visit http://www.cla.co.uk/www/internet.htm

Copyright and the HMSO

In March 1999 it was announced that HMSO would allow unrestricted copying and reproduction on certain categories of Crown copyright material in order to encourage its widespread use for reference and onward dissemination to interested bodies. Much of the information issued by the HMSO is in the form of public records, legislation, literacy, statistics and government press notices. These are areas that can be very useful in the research process. For more information search on http://www.hmso.gov.uk

Data Protection Act

The Data Protection Act 1988 relates to data stored on computers and is meant as a safeguard for individuals. The Act is wide and encompasses a huge number of issues and areas, one of which is data used for research purposes, for example it sets out information on the use of personal data processed only for research purposes.

The rights of individual data subjects is set out in detail in Part II section 7 of the Act, but section 33 deals with data used for research purposes and here some exemptions are made to the provisions under section 7. See the following box for a brief summary of some of the more important issues involved, but you really ought to have a look at the provisions of the Act for yourself and your legal requirements under it.

For more information search on http://www/hmso.gov.uk/acts/act1998/800029—e.htm

▶ Internet – understanding information

There is no limitation to what information is available online. Companies describe a wide range of things including their products, ethics and policies. Educational establishments describe their facilities and put information of

---

**Data Protection Act 1988 – data dealing with research,
history and statistics**

Summary of some of the provisions in Section 33

1. 'Research purposes' includes historical or statistical purposes.
2. The 'relevant conditions' in relation to any processing of personal data means:
   (a) that the data are not processed to support measures or decisions with respect to particular individuals, and
   (b) that the data are not processed in such a way that substantial damage or substantial distress is, or is likely to be, caused to any data subject.
3. For the purposes of the second data protection principle, the further processing of personal data only for research purposes in compliance with the relevant conditions is not to be regarded as incompatible with the purposes for which they were obtained.
4. Personal data which are processed only for research purposes in compliance with the relevant conditions may (notwithstanding the fifth data protection principle), be kept indefinitely.
5. Personal data which are processed only for research purposes are exempt from section 7 if:
   (a) they are processed in compliance with the relevant conditions, and
   (b) the results of the research or any resulting statistics are not made available in a form which identifies data subjects.

---

their courses, some put online mini lessons that can be very good. Individuals make Web pages on anything that interests them. All this information added to the numerous chat lines and advertisements that appear everywhere can make the Internet seem very confusing.

Some people criticise the Internet as being full of online trivia, but this is not the whole truth. Yes, there is a lot of enjoyable rubbish online and a lot of sites that would have no interest for you – but they might to someone else. Among all the nonsense and confusion there are sites of enormous interest, packed full of information that will be immensely valuable to a researcher.

Finding your way successfully around the Internet takes a little practise and patience, and it helps if you understand a little of Web addressing. Web addresses usually start with **http://** (known as the hypertext transfer protocol specification). However modern browsers don't require you to key in this text.

This is usually followed by **www** (World Wide Web), and then the specific address you are trying to reach (perhaps a company name). The company name will be followed by 'domain' details, which always includes a classification and country code.

Sites are sometimes classified into subject areas, for example an academic site in the United Kingdom will have the classification **ac** in the Web site address. Table 4.2 sets out some of the classification sites that are useful to know.

TABLE 4.2

Classification	Code
Academic	edu
Academic (UK only)	ac
Commerical/corporate	co
Commerical/corporate (usually a large/ international company)	com
Government sites	gov
International organisations	int
Networks (and organisations in charge of them)	net
Non-profit making organisations	org
School	sch

This classification list is growing rapidly and once you have finished reading this chapter and started to use the Internet look for new domain names by searching on http://news.bbc.co.uk/hi/english/sci/tech/ newsid1027000/1027321.stm

Table 4.3 sets out the country codes for five of the more popular countries.

TABLE 4.3

Country	Code
Australia	Au
France	fr
Germany	de
Ireland	ie
United Kingdom	uk

By deduction then, if you had a site with the Web address http://www.presentations.com you would know without opening it that it was a large commercial or corporate site, and http://www.hmso.gov.uk was a United Kingdom government site.

If you know the exact reference of the site you require, you simply key it correctly into the address area of your browser page (search engine) and press the return key. There are many browsers on the market – two that are popular in UK academic departments are Microsoft Internet Explorer and Netscape Navigator. This popularity is mirrored all over the world and is measured by the number of people who use various browsers. Always be very careful when typing in references, there should never be any spacing and full stops should be displayed exactly as the original.

► Internet – searching for information

To find information on the Internet, a computer uses search engines. There are a great many of these available, but popular ones that you may have heard of include Yahoo!, Lycos, AltaVista and Galaxy. A search engine is a Web page, not extra software that you need to buy and load onto your computer. Any computer with a modem can access search engines, and all modern computers come with the ability to surf the Internet nowadays. Most search engines work by travelling the Net, matching Web pages with pre-requested search criterion.

Loading a different search engine

Your computer will without doubt have a default search engine, if it does not suit your needs, or if you would like to try a different one, open your existing browser page (you will probably have been shown how to do this when you bought the computer) – very probably you will need to click on an icon on the desktop screen. If you are using Microsoft Internet Explorer, the icon includes a large blue e

Once you have clicked on the icon your page will look something like Figure 4.3. Click in the rectangle against the word Address, and key in the address of the search engine as illustrated in Figure 4.3. Press the return key. You will be presented with the Yahoo! opening page, as shown in Figure 4.4.

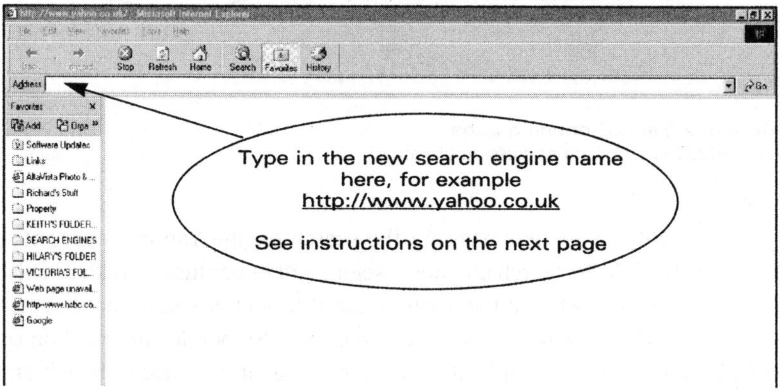

Type in the new search engine name here, for example
http://www.yahoo.co.uk

See instructions on the next page

Figure 4.3

Computer Support

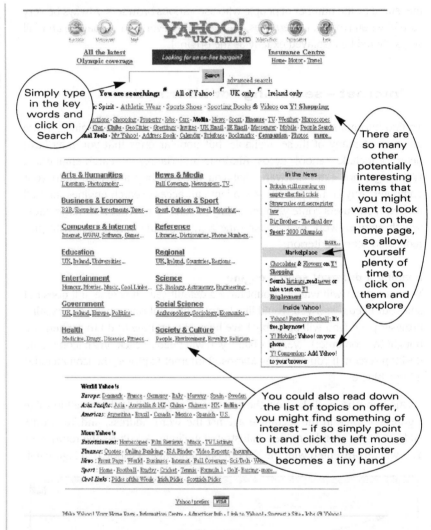

Figure 4.4 Yahoo! opening page
Reproduced with the kind permission of Yahoo!

At first sight the opening page for the search engine Yahoo! is very busy and if you are new to search engines it seems rather confusing. With practise you soon learn to focus on the areas relevant to you. If you do not have an exact Web address, you can use a search engine to look for information on specific subjects. For example, if your interest was in the field of health and you wanted to find out more about the body skeleton, simply key in 'body

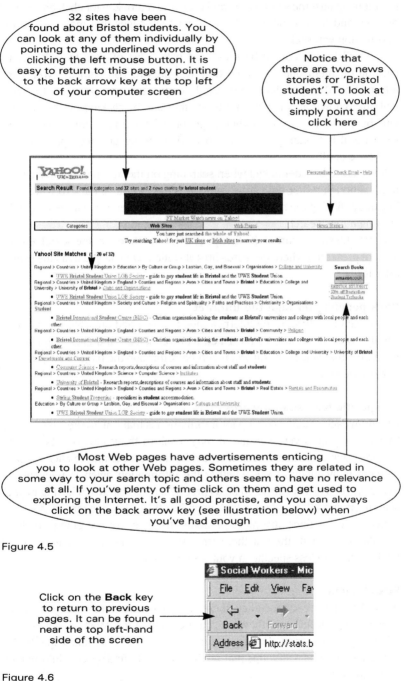

Figure 4.5

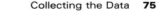

Click on the **Back** key
to return to previous
pages. It can be found
near the top left-hand
side of the screen

Figure 4.6

skeleton' against the search area and press the return key (or click on 'search' or 'go'), and the computer will search for Web pages that may contain the information you seek.

You will in due course be presented with a list of sites to visit and by clicking on them one at a time they will present you with the Web page information that you have requested. Very often one page on the Web will link (known as a hyper-link) to another and by clicking on the link you will be presented with another page of information. Sometimes this is very useful but often you will discover that the hyper-linked page has no relevance at all.

It is easy to be sidetracked when searching on the Internet, but this can be fun – although rather time consuming. It is easy to travel back to where you began by clicking the mouse on a 'Back' icon on screen (see Figure 4.6), or by starting a new search.

Figure 4.5 shows part of the first page of information that the search engine Yahoo! presented when the words bristol student were keyed in as the search criteria.

Back peddling through the Internet
If you want to return to the Internet page that you had on screen previously, simply point the mouse to the **Back** icon on screen and click (Figure 4.6). Each time that you click you will revert back through the pages that you have already viewed.

Be specific with search words
One drawback when searching for information is that unless the search word that you key in is very specific, it may result in thousands of hits (that is, possible Web page addresses). It would be time consuming to click on each of them individually to see whether the information given is relevant. To overcome this always strive to be as precise as possible when keying in your search criteria. If you know that your health skeleton query is going to concentrate on bone disorders or bone structure, try searching on these specific words first, then, if there isn't any information, it is easy to work back, becoming less specific in your search words.

Search hints
As well as striving for accuracy, there are one or two things that you can do to help yourself find exactly what you are looking for. Most search engines will recognise lower case keyed in queries with or without initial capitals. See Table 4.4 for some useful tips that might help you to find specific information more quickly.

TABLE 4.4 INTERNET SEARCH TIPS

+religion+new–Americas	Placing a + sign before a word is an instruction that the word must be included in the search, whereas a – key indicates that it should be excluded. In the example given the computer will find files that include the words religion and new but will exclude any that also contain the word Americas.
women children poverty	When keying in a 'string' of words as shown, the files found could include all three words, a combination of any two or just any one of them.
+women+children+poverty	Using the + instructs the computer to find files that contains all three words.
"Ministry of Defence"	Insert the double inverted comma (") before and after contiguous (adjoining) words. The computer will then look for these words as a complete phrase.
interview*	The asterisk* can be used as a wild card, meaning that the computer will find variable word endings of the root word, for example interviewed, interviewing, interviews.

Some search engines are a little different, for example Google doesn't recognise 'AND' and 'NOT' (+ and –), but uses a 'find more like this' system once the search is done. You will soon discover the idiosyncrasies of your favourite search engine.

Inaccurate Internet pages
Another problem encountered is the quality of the articles – anyone can put an article on the Web, so you will have to discard some unsuitable or rubbish articles along the way. This is no different to the problems encountered with written material, as anyone can write a pamphlet or print information that is inaccurate.

If you remember the classification codes (see again Tables 4.2 and 4.3) and only click on those presented with an exhaustive list of sites in the first instance, you won't waste time pursuing unhelpful information.

Other search engines to try
There are many search engines available online, and most of them have main subject areas that are further divided and subdivided. Most search engines give you the option to search UK only sites which is some cases might be a good starting point, you can 'look at the world' later. Some of the general search engines that are available are listed below:

Computer Support

- http://www.google.com
- http://www.altavista.com
- http://www.hotbot.com
- http://galaxy.com
- http://www.excite.com
- http://www.infoseek.com
- http://www.lycos.com

▶ Bookmarking useful Internet sites

When you find information that is useful and you think it will be worthwhile revisiting the site over a period of time, you can bookmark the site by adding it to your Favorites, then its online address will be saved and you can quickly revisit it whenever you wish.

Detailed instructions are given below on how to do this if you are using Microsoft Explorer, but the pattern is similar when using other packages, for example if you are using Netscape software then the word to look for is bookmark, not favorite (click on 'bookmark' and then 'add bookmark').

If you are using Microsoft Explorer and you have a Web site on screen that you wish to add to Favorites, first of all click on the word **Add** on the left of your screen. The **Add Favorite** (American spelling) dialog box will then appear (see Figure 4.7).

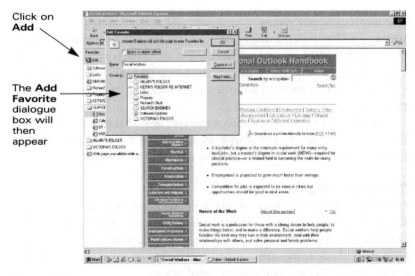

Click on **Add**

The **Add Favorite** dialogue box will then appear

Figure 4.7

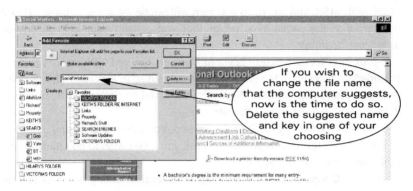

Figure 4.8

A list of existing favorite folders will appear if they have already been created. If this is the case and you can see the name of a folder you wish the Web page to be saved in then click on it (it will highlight usually in blue) and then click on OK (Figure 4.8).

You can now go on searching the Internet knowing that the Web site has been saved in the appropriate folder under Favorites.

Creating a new folder for bookmarking

If you wish to create a new folder, first of all you need to reach the screen shown in Figure 4.7 above and then click on **New Folder**. The following dialog box will appear (Figure 4.9) on top of the **Add Favorite** box. Click in the rectangle beside Folder name and key in the new folder name. Once you have done this, click OK.

Retrieving bookmarked (favorite) sites

If your Internet connections is via a cable modem, ADSL, LAN connection,

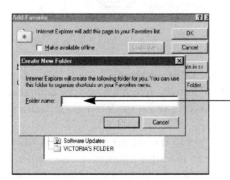

Click in rectangular box and type the name of the new folder that you would like to create

Figure 4.9

ISDN, AOL, MSN, and so on, your screen will not be the same as those printed on the following pages. It is better that you consult your help facility or instruction manual.

If your Internet connection is via modem or standard ISP (Internet Service Provider) and you want to revisit sites already saved in Favorites, simply open the appropriate folder where the work was saved by clicking on it, and then double click on the name of the site.

If you are not already on the Internet and *providing you are using a modem or standard ISP* the screen prompt will ask you if you wish to go online at this point (see Figure 4.10 below).

Click on **Connect** and the **Dial-up Connection** dialog box will appear (Figure 4.11).

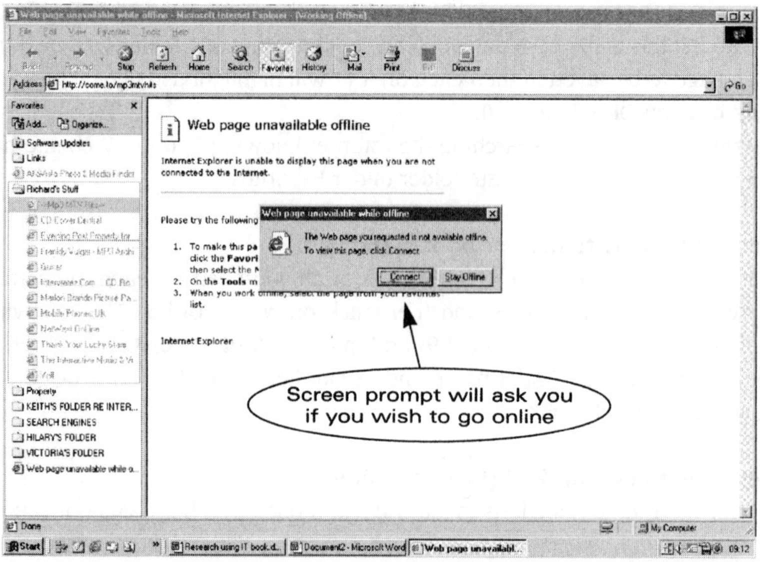

Figure 4.10

Saving or printing work from Internet sites

Alternatively you can save the information to a file on your computer's hard drive. Click on **File** and then **SaveAs** when the information you want is on screen (Figure 4.12).

The screen will then prompt you to choose the directory you wish to save your file into. In this way you can read this information later when you are offline. Even if you are not paying for the Internet connection by the minute, you may find it beneficial to gather all the related information together and

Click on
Connect in
the usual
way

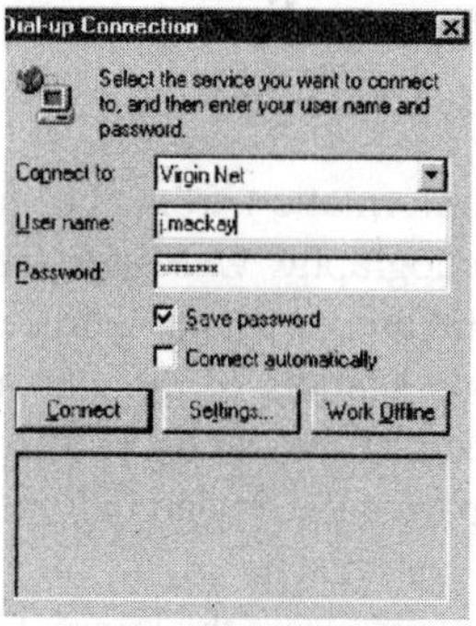

Figure 4.11

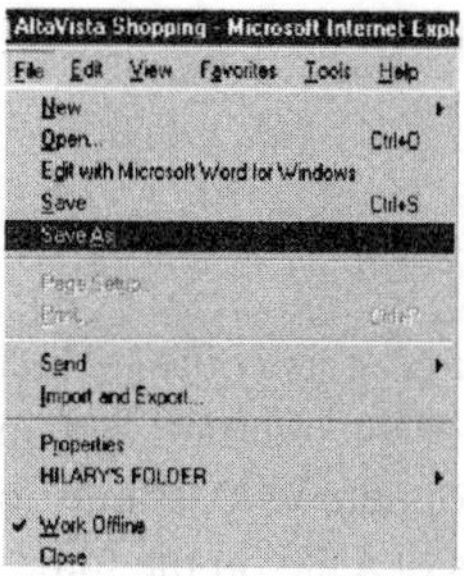

Figure 4.12

read it later, when you will be better placed to reflect on its content and make comparisons.

Your last option is to print the material straightaway. Click on **File** and then **Print** . . . but be careful that you are not about to print 20 pages of a Web site, when all you need is a small paragraph. If you are going to print immediately, it is better to highlight the material you want and click on **Selection** when given the option.

A quick way to save a picture from the Net if using a PC is to right click on the picture and choose **Save Picture As**. If you are using a Mac click on the image button.

When printed you will have the Web site reference printed at the foot of the page, but there may be other detailed information you need if you intend to quote this material in your research.

▶ Referencing online work

Internet

If you have used information from the Internet, this will also need to be entered in your bibliography. Web sites are gradually proving themselves to be more reliable and are a popular source of research information.

There are various schools of thought as to how electronic information should be displayed so it would be best to check with the establishment for whom you are preparing the research. *If you cannot obtain the information you need, adopt the layouts shown.*

Citing references taken from the Internet is essential and should include the following information:

1. Author's or editor's surname, followed by initials
2. Year
3. Title (online)
4. Edition (if available)
5. Place of publication
6. Publisher or printed source, this could include organisations responsible for maintaining the site of the Internet, perhaps a university for example
7. Available from: state URL here (URL stands for uniform resource locator, think of it as the address of a file on the Internet)
8. Last date you accessed the site

See the following example:

> Green, Louise (1999) 'Social Research Issues'. London. Anycity University. Available from http://www.anycity.ac.uk/library/resources (Accessed 2 November 2001)

It is likely that you will have a mixture of conventional and electronic references. Some establishments prefer that you have all citations together in one alphabetical list. If this is the case, you need to show that a particular reference was obtained from the Internet by typing the word 'online'. See the following example:

> Green, Louise (1999) 'Social Research Issues' (online), London. Anycity University. Available from http://www.anycity.ac.uk/library/resources (2 November 2001)

Some establishments prefer that you display your bibliography in two

Bibliography

Brock, David (1996) '20th Century Fox' in Judy Mail and Ron Nelson (eds) *Cinema Today*. London. BBC

Hopkins, David (1985) '*A Teacher's Guide to Classroom Research*'. Milton Keynes, Open University Press.

Huchison, Steven (1999) 'Software in Action'. *Microsoft Advantage*. **1** (10): 15–20

Electronic sources (online)

Green, Louise (1999) 'Social Research Issues'. London. Anycity University. Available from http://www.anycity.ac.uk/library/resources (2 November 2001)

Lucas, P (2001) 'Health Descriptors and Medical Indicators' Birmingham http://www.heal/joss.ac.uk (24 January 2002)

sections as shown in the box above. Don't forget to show the date when you last visited the Web site because the site may not be permanent.

CD-ROM

CD-ROM material, whether an interactive programme or a reference work, is referenced in the same form as non-book media, that is, author, initials, (year), document title in journal details (CD-ROM), CD-ROM title, version and/or date. The access date is not needed when it is a CD-ROM. See the following example:

> Coombes, Richard (1997) Woodcarving – The Vikings. CD-ROM. Encarta 97 Encyclopaedia. Microsoft.

Computer database program

If a computer database has been used for data research or has been referred to as a data source then it should be identified by the data program name or by the data source and cited as follows:

> UK Database of Health Descriptors and Medical Indicators for 1998. London. Department of Health. Available from http://merlihn.lib.glo.ac.uk 24 January 2001

Email

If you need to refer to personal email messages, for example if you have sent questionnaires out by email, the following format could be adopted:

1. Author's or editor's surname, followed by name or initials
2. Sender's email address

3. Day, month and year
4. Subject of message
5. Email to recipient's details
6. Recipient's email addresss

For example:

> Browni, Terry (t.browni@virgin.net) 4 April 2001. Questionnaire Return.
> Email to Nicky Guichi (n.guichi@cecomet.net)

Mailbase discussions lists/email
If you join an online discussion group, you will quickly build up a list of people's email addresses that belong to that mailbase, as usually any emails generated by one member of the list are sent to all subscribers of the list at the same time. Reference to these should follow the format below:

1. Author's or editor's surname, followed by name or initials
2. Day, month and year (this is the date the message was originally sent)
3. Subject of message
4. Discussion list, with the word (online) in italics afterwards
5. Available from: (list the email address here)
6. Date the site was accessed

For example:

> Jancovich, Judie. 23 January 2002. Computing needs of ACCESS
> students. List-links (*online*). Available from
> http://www.mailbases@mail.ac.uk (Accessed on 24 February 2002)

Electronic online journal
The reader of your research work will need to know:

1. Author's or editor's surname, followed by name or initials
2. Year
3. Article title
4. Journal online title
5. Volume number (if any)
6. Part/issue number (usually in brackets)
7. Location within the host (if applicable)
8. Available from: state URL here
9. Last date the site was accessed

For example:

> Coombes, Victoria (2001) Criminology today. Crime & the criminal (online). Volume 2 (14). Available from http://www.gopher/presentations.com/create (Accessed 14 January 2001)

Footnotes and endnotes

If you are using the Vancouver system of referencing, your citations will need to be placed at the end of the passage (or chapter) where the direct quotation/s or summary has been made. For an example of a footnote, see Vancouver style of referencing within text, p. 64. Brief details on how to do this using Microsoft Word follows. If you are using different software, look up footnotes and endnotes in the on-screen help or your software manual.

How to insert footnotes (and endnotes) with Microsoft Word

1. Check that you are working in Normal View (Click on **View** – **Normal**)
2. Type the quotation or summary, for example

> Pleasing the teachers plus the parents may not be in the best interest of the pupils and the children may find themselves in a position where they cannot win; this can cause the child to give-up trying.[1]

3. Immediately it is finished, click on **Insert** and then **Footnote**. The following drop-down menu will appear:

4. Click on the circle beside Footnote or Endnote, depending on which you require.
5. Auto Numbers are easier to use at first, but if you want to customise your footnotes by using a different symbol (for example a *), then click in the circle beside Custom mark and type the required symbol in the blank rectangle.
6. A small raised number (or custom mark if chosen) appears with the cursor

flashing beside it. Type in your reference. If you wish to change the font size or style, highlight the typed text and change in the normal way.

7. If you click on the arrow in the notepane above your typed reference, the drop-down menu will give you the option of separating your reference from the body of the text with a line. Click on **Footnote Separator** and experiment by deleting the line or keying in a longer one. You do not have to do this if you are happy to accept whatever layout is shown eventually.

8. When you click on **Close**, your footnote will be inserted (for example, 1. John A Bloggs. *Education Sociology*. Palgrave, Basingstoke (2001) p. 49), with or without a line depending on what you have chosen.

9. There will also be a small raised (superscript) number alongside the text to which this reference refers (as shown in the text beneath instruction 2 above). If you go on to insert other footnotes the superscript numbers [2] [3] and so on will appear.

Consistency in referencing

Once you are into writing up your research findings, the little details such as whether to use single or double quotes can be easily forgotten. There might well be several gaps, sometimes weeks apart, between the times of putting your thoughts to paper. During this protracted time of writing you may well have forgotten your original adopted style, especially as the main thing on your mind will be the formation and content of your writing. You will be tempted to key references in some kind of fashion, telling yourself you will tidy it up later.

However, it can be extremely time consuming and irritating to have to check your final research document for consistency in presentation. Even though most software has the ability to 'find' key elements (for example search for), imagine how many false starts you will encounter as the computer finds not only each single quotation mark you have keyed in but also each occasion you have keyed in the plural of a certain words (for example child's). It is better to key in references exactly as they should be as you proceed, that way, when your research paper is finished, you will have actually finished and not have to start checking the whole thing for consistency.

To help you to remember your detailed layout, keep a file saved with an example of the exact detail you've chosen, and keep this open on your computer desktop for easy reference whenever you wish. Or tape a printed version to one side of your monitor screen so that you can instantly consult it whenever you need.

▶ Online databases used in libraries

A database is an organised collection of information, categorised under various headings. Common use of interrogating a database can be seen at estate agents. A customer might ask whether there are any bungalows for sale and tells the estate agent that they require three bedrooms, one en-suite and one family bathroom and they would also like a large garden. The estate agent, by keying in the words such as 'bungalow, three beds, en-suite bathroom, garden', will be presented with a list of suitable properties on their books at that time.

Online databases are similar but fall mainly into two categories. The first are *data banks* and these contain numeric and/or factual information such as economic material, or legal texts and so on. An airline ticket desk would use a data bank to discover available flights.

The second database contains *bibliographic files*. These contain abstracts of books, documents, periodicals, organisations, people information and so on. Database information has the advantage of being updated regularly, possibly every couple of days, so you know that the information you download is current.

There are many organisers of and contributors to database information, and you will hear various names of vendors or hosts mentioned in association with database interrogation – DIALOG, ORBIT, ERIC, DIANE, BIDS, SCORPIO to name just a few. Each of them contains a number of various topic areas. For example, if you were interested in social science literature dating back to the 1960s, or wanted more detailed information about international coverage of sociology, you would consult the sociologial abstracts which would be available on the DIALOG host, among others.

To choose the right database to search you need the skill and expertise of a librarian and you will initially need the assistance of trained staff to help you to search for your particular topic area. Normally no charge or only a token charge is made if you are a student at the academic establishment offering the database, but charges are sometimes made if you wish to use the service and you do not have a connection with the university or college. Some larger public libraries now also offer these services but once again there is often a charge associated with interrogation of online databases.

▶ Online databases available on your home computer

You will soon discover that you can tap into a huge source of online databases once you get used to using search engines (see the paragraphs on Internet – searching for information pp. 73–4) but to get you started there follows a list of sites you might like to try.

Biz/ed is a free Internet service for students and teachers and those interested in business and economics. It contains statistics from the Office of National Statistics, data for countries around the world, information on 500 companies including profits, numbers employed and other variables. It also has useful links to many different areas in business and economics. Try http://www.bized.ac.uk/ if you think it might be useful.

If you are interested in education, http://www.education2000.co.uk is worth looking at. This site provides daily updates on educational news from publications such as the *Guardian* and the *TES*. It also publishes the latest educational news from the Department of Education and Science and the BBC.

The BBC Alert service http://www.bbc.co.uk/education/alert will send you free email if you inform them that you would like to receive national or regional listings and dates of broadcast on subjects that interest you. This includes broadcasts on radio channels too. It's a good way to find out what's about to be broadcast that might be of interest to you.

The Central Office for Information on http://www.worldserver.pipex.com is a marketing tool for the government, but you can find marketing and research information that might be useful on this site.

On http://www.statistics.gov.uk you will find the latest range of official government statistics as well as free access to a wide selection of the most recently released publications.

Some statistical information connected with the environment and transport can be found on http://www.open.gov.uk together with other more general information on research areas.

Once you log on to one of these Web sites you are often offered the option of clicking on sites that offer similar information and if you do so you can start a trail that might lead you to exactly the piece of information you are seeking. However, be wary, *it is addictive*. You will sit down for what you think is going to be a ten-minute search and three hours later you will still be sat in front of your computer – but it can be a very interesting and rewarding three hours nevertheless.

▶ Data Archive

One of the most important access points for researchers in the UK is the Data Archive at the University of Essex. It contains the largest collection of accessible computer-readable data in the social sciences and humanities in the UK. You can select data on a wide range of areas from crime surveys to details of personal incomes. Through these Web pages it is possible to search the catalogues of other national archives for computer-readable data and use the services of the Data Archive to acquire these data on your behalf. The Archive is a specialist national resource that is funded jointly by the University of Essex where it is located, and the ESRC (Economic and Social Research Council) and JISC (Joint Information Systems Committee). If you are interested, log on to the Web site (address below), alternatively you could write to The Data Archive, University of Essex, Colchester, CO4 3SQ for more information.

To give you some idea of how easy using this site is, once you have keyed in the web address http://www.data-archive.ac.uk/search/index/asp all you need to do is type in the search keyword/s required and then click on search (Figure 4.13).

▶ Other relevant Internet sites that might be of interest

Once you start searching the Internet you will soon see that there are thousands of Web addresses available. Most new surfers get hooked by the excitement of it all, there is so much available that it is very easy to spend hours in front of your computer screen clicking on and moving between various links.

Table 4.5 lists some site addresses that might be of interest to you, depend-

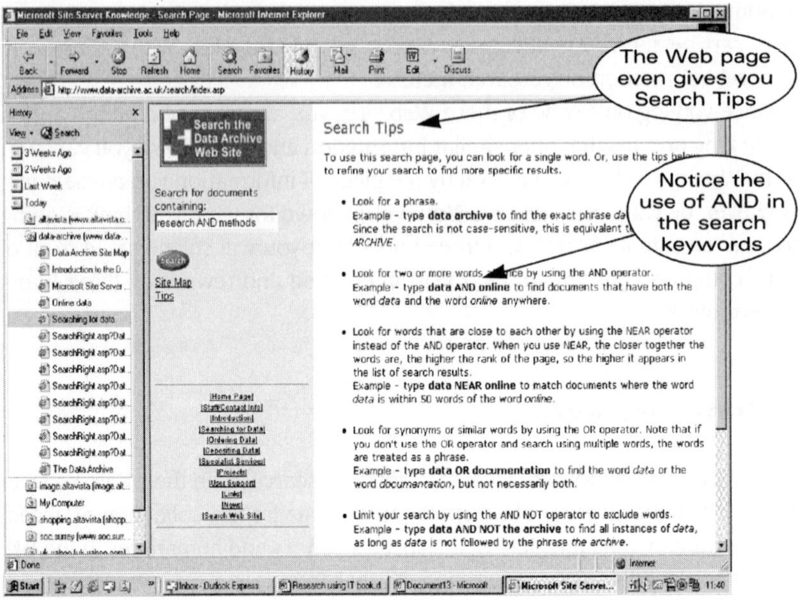

Computer Support

The Web page even gives you Search Tips

Notice the use of AND in the search keywords

Figure 4.13

ing on your research topic; once you log on to the particular sites, you will find links to sites of similar interest.

TABLE 4.5 USEFUL INTERNET SITES FOR THE RESEARCHER

Academic Information on Religion http://www.academicinfo.net	This site houses a large range of educational resources covering a wide area of topics.
Amnesty International Publications http://www.amnesty.org	Reports on numerous themes (women, death penalty, child violations, and so on) arranged by year and continent.
Gutenberg Project http://promo.net/pg	A vast list of library material saved in a wide range of formats that makes it easy for virtually any computer to read or download.
Brunel University Research Groups Centre http://www.brunel.ac.uk/ info/research	Various resources and links to similar sites. The HERG (Health Economics Research Group) is particularly good, and covers a wide range of topics from anthropological research findings through to neotectonic research.
History Learning Resources http://www.warwick.ac.uk/fac/ arts/History/teaching	A large range of very detailed topics ranging from social aspects of industrialisation to major themes in women's history.

http://www.drugtext.org	Scientific reports on drug substance abuse from many countries.
Marx/Engels Archive http://csf.colorado.edu/psn/marx	Electronic versions of Marxist writers including Marx and Engels. The search engine will search through thousands of pages of text to trace specific queries.
National Political Index http://www.politicalindex.com	An index to important substantive political information for voters, political activist, academicians and so on.
http://www.soc.surrey.ac.uk	Sociological research online, this site contains a large searchable database.
The Qualitative Report http://www.nova.edu/ssss/QR	Online journal devoted to discussion and writing about qualitative and critical inquiry. A good forum for researchers.
http://lcweb2.loc.gov	A site focusing on American history that covers a broad range of topics including those of social science research. The site includes audio and motion picture materials.
Social Science Information Gateway http://sosig.ac.uk	Various categories of research findings for practitioners in business, social science and law.
Psychiatry online http://www.priory.com/ otherpsy.htm	A good starting point for a wide range of psychiatry information. The site includes a very wide range of searchable topic areas and useful links to other related sites.

Internet resources – keeping up to date

New Web sites are appearing on the Internet and existing sites are being updated by the minute. It is impossible to keep abreast of all the new information, as the change is too rapid and too great. The site below (Table 4.6) monitors new resources that are added and if you check it regularly you will sometimes find useful information.

However, there is no guaranteed way to keep absolutely on top of new Internet resources.

TABLE 4.6 A SITE THAT MONITORS NEW INTERNET RESOURCES

http://wwwscout.cs.wisc.edu	This report is updated regularly and points out newly available resources. It has separate reports in various subjects, such as Social Sciences, Business & Economics.

▶ Library CD-ROMs

Most libraries will give you a list of the CD-ROMs that they currently hold; some also have a brief guide to the type of information they contain. Often the CD-ROM will have been loaded and networked onto several computers in the library or information technology room and you will not necessarily be given a CD-ROM disc to insert into the computer that you are using.

To give you some idea of the range of information that is available on CD-ROM, look at Table 4.7 below. This list is only a minute glimpse at what is obtainable; there is a huge range of CD-ROMs that covers almost any area that you can think of. CD-ROMs will not necessarily contain the very latest information available, but they are an extremely easy way of finding data on the past history or statistical details surrounding a particular research area.

TABLE 4.7

CD-ROM	Guide to the information contained
F T McCarthy	McCarthy is a database of financial and business articles taken from a number of magazines and newspapers including the *Financial Times*, *The Economist*, *The Times*, the *Guardian*, trade and law journals. It operates on a search icon, where you can refine your requirements with keywords, for example unemployment, redundancy, Wales, women.
Hutchinson's Multimedia Encyclopaedia	Hutchinson's contains all the information that you would find in a normal hardback encyclopedia, only more of it. It also has video and/or audio clips that you can watch and listen to. You simply key in a keyword and click a search icon.
IOLIS Guide	Details of law can be found on this CD-ROM. It is interactive and there are various multi-choice activities that you could take part in if you wished (answers are given if you get it wrong). It is divided into areas, each of which looks at a different area of the law, so if you were interested in punishment and sentencing in the UK you would consult the Concept of Crime chapter.
Times/Sunday Times	This is a dated CD-ROM, for example there is a CD-ROM for the 1992–8 data. You search on keyword/s such as 'prisons' and a matching list of articles will appear that contains the chosen keyword/s. You read them by clicking on individual titles. You can narrow your search by requesting the selection of articles that have the chosen keyword as part of the headline; or

you can choose which section of the paper you want to search, for example business, sport and so on.

World Guide

This is also a dated CD-ROM, for example 1995. It is useful for detailed information, statistics and graphs for the countries of the world. You are presented with a map of the world and you simply click on the country that you are interested in, and narrow this down to specific areas or cities if you wish. You will be presented with options to look in detail at various topics about the chosen city, such as health concerns, for example Aids, cancer or childhood death statistics.

5 Interviews in Detail

PART A

▶ What do you want from the interviews?

Interviews have long been used as one of the major methods of research and there are many different types of interview that you could adopt – structured, oral or life history, counselling, diary or unstructured to name just a few. Interviews can be carried out on a big scale using large groups of people or in a one-to-one small-scale enquiry.

Before you start you need to get clear in your own mind exactly what you want from the interview process. This is the logical way to ensure that any interview-based research is focused and achieves its aims. If you are not organised at the outset, you will gather an enormous amount of unnecessary, confusing and time-consuming data.

Getting to the heart of the information from the point of view of using and designing questionnaires as a form of interview is dealt with in detail in the next chapter. This chapter deals with the basics of the decisions surrounding the administration and sensitive adeptness you will need to foster if you are to be skilled in this method of research.

Hitchcock and Hughes (1992:80) ask four pertinent questions that they believe teachers engaged in research should ask themselves at the outset of any research. These questions apply equally to anyone undertaking research:

1. Why interview?
2. Where do I interview?
3. Whom do I interview?
4. When do I interview?

Can you answer these questions about your proposed research? Try to give detailed answers without being flippant. It would be easy to answer question one with a quick 'because it's the best method' but a really thought-out answer will help you to focus on what you want from interview research.

Perhaps you are looking into whether hospitalised children recover more quickly from their illness if someone they love is allowed to be constantly near them in the hospital. Getting at the feelings of the child and the loved one would be impossible by questionnaire or observation, although you could also use these methods to gather background information and comparisons with other children in the ward. The reason for using the interview method in this particular case would be that it would allow a personal insight into the feelings of those concerned which could not easily be captured in any other way.

The focus of using the interview method, therefore, would be to gain as much information as possible on how the cognitive processes are affected by the secure and comforting atmosphere created by the nearness of a loved one. There is a cognitive form of therapy used as a positive force that encourages patients to change the way they see the world and themselves. A child may see the world in a different way when they feel secure and you may eventually decide to argue that this has a positive outcome in that the healing process is quickened. You may decide in the conclusion to your research to refer to this particular part of your research as the basis for recommending sleeping accommodation provision situated alongside certain patients, recognising that this could have cost-cutting effects in that hospitalisation would be shorter. You can see that if you initially answer the question 'Why interview?' carefully it could have an enormous bearing on your subsequent questions and research outcomes.

▶ The structured interview

The structured interview is frequently used with large numbers of people such as in the case of voting intentions or shopping surveys. The questions asked are usually to the point and short, and the responses are also brief, often a simple yes or no answer will suffice. One of the advantages of brief responses is that they are easier to analyse, compare and collate eventually.

The researcher normally aims to interview either a representative sample from the population, that is, roughly equal numbers of gender and ages and so on, or they decide to interview randomly. There is a belief in some research areas that by interviewing a random selection of people they are bound to represent the population generally in that anyone could have been chosen for interview. This you should question. Generally, busy people are less likely to stop and answer clipboard questions. Also the geographic area in which the interviewer locates the interviews will have some influence on the variety, social standing and age of the passers-by and even the day of the week and time can have some influence. For example, if you interview in the middle of a large city you are less likely to find as many senior citizens walking past compared with interviewing in the suburbs on the day that pensions are paid.

In order to administer structured interviews the researcher needs to decide at the outset the exact data needed. This sounds simplistic, but it does need to be well thought through. If you were conducting an in-house work survey into whether the staff canteen met employees' needs, you would need to think carefully whether it would be useful to know, for example, the department in which the canteen user works. It could be that 'word of mouth' is playing a part and that users will tend to come mainly from a small core of departments. Perhaps some departments are situated a long way from the canteen facilities so that people in those departments can't be bothered to use the canteen and bring sandwiches or use a microwave that someone has brought in instead. This could lead you to think about the location of the canteen, and it may be that you will wish to devise two parts to your questionnaire, one for those who say they use the facilities and one for respondents who don't. Your first question in that case will be – do you use the canteen facilities?

The layout and presentation of the schedule the interviewer is to use needs to be clear with columns or boxes that can be ticked as the questions are answered. The structured interview tends to have very little space for added comments.

Once you have designed your questions and questionnaire layout, it would be wise to try it out on a few friends before launching it on your target audience. Check with them whether they found that the questions you asked were precise and not misleading. Their constructive criticism at this early stage will be invaluable.

The structured interview is a useful research tool where straightforward data is needed and, once the questions are formulated, it has the added advantage that more than one person can ask the pre-arranged questions. An example of a typical structured interview questionnaire is given in Figure 5.1.

▶ Unstructured interviews

In-depth unstructured interviews allow an enormous scope and free flow of information between the interviewer and interviewee. Because of this it offers a greater flexibility and questions can be spontaneous and responsive to the latest thing that the interviewee has said. A wealth of valuable research information can be obtained in this way; however, do not mistakenly believe that it is just like having a talk with a friend, it is far from that.

Unstructured interviewers are best left in the hands of experienced researchers. They require a great deal of expertise in order to get at the data that is needed. They also require deft control of the conversation if they are

Questions to be asked regarding canteen use

1. Do you use the staff canteen?

YES	NO
IF YES, ASK Do you use it:	IF NO Continue to question 2

Every day	☐
2–3 times a week	☐
Once a week?	☐

Do you tend to eat in the canteen
on certain days of the week?

Mon	☐
Tue	☐
Wed	☐
Thu	☐
Fri	☐

2. Which of the following foods do you buy regularly?

Would you use the canteen if it offered a wider variety of food choice?

Sandwiches	☐	
Filled rolls	☐	YES
Hot toasted snacks	☐	Continue to question 3
Pasta	☐	
Curry	☐	NO
Fried breakfast	☐	

. . . And so on

Figure 5.1 Example of a typical structured interview questionnaire

not to become a general chat which, although may be of interest, will prove to be of little use to the research in hand. They also have the disadvantage of being very time consuming and difficult to analyse.

They are useful to the person who is new to research, however, in that they can be used as a 'sounding board' or pilot for ideas. If you are unsure of what is really important in your research, what questions to ask or what area should be looked at first, an unstructured interview with a knowledgeable and supportive colleague can be invaluable. You will need to prime the person beforehand, let them know your basic ideas and what initially you are hoping to get from the research. At this point you could give them a few days to mull over what you've said before requesting that you spend a pre-arranged time in order to discuss matters in a little more depth.

You do not need to keep copious, detailed notes of what has been said, just one-line headings to remind you of pertinent areas to think about would be enough. The information and ideas you gather at this stage would eventually be incorporated into your final research document, when you will highlight the avenues you explored before deciding on the eventual pattern of your research.

▶ Semi-structured interviews

Semi-structured interviews probably enjoy the best position as far as interviewing goes. They are a much more flexible version of the structured interview and, while having a framework (the written questions) to guide the researcher, they also allow for additional comments to be noted and other avenues to be briefly explored. These additional bits of information are often useful when the questionnaires are analysed. Comments sometimes lead the researcher into considering a previously unthought-of area connected with the research.

It can be useful to grade responses or ask supplementary questions and if this was carried out with the canteen questions used as an example for the structured interview section, then the questions might be as shown in Figure 5.2 (the supplementary questions are ringed for quicker reference).

You can see that the supplementary questions could open up new avenues of exploration.

At the time that the schedule is being devised, a summary sheet should also be prepared. This will help smooth the eventual analysis of the data collected. For more detail see Coding questionnaires using summary sheets, pp. 159–60.

A short summary of the advantages and disadvantages of the various interview structures can be seen in Table 5.1.

Questions to be asked regarding canteen use

---

1. Do you use the staff canteen?

YES   NO

IF YES, ASK   IF NO, ASK
Do you use it:

  Every day   ☐   *Is there any reason why you*
                                                don't use the canteen facilities?
  2–3 times a week   ☐

  Once a week?   ☐

Do you tend to eat in the canteen
on certain days of the week?

    Mon   ☐

    Tue   ☐

    Wed   ☐

    Thu   ☐

    Fri   ☐

Is there any reason for
for choosing certain days?

---

2. Which of the following foods do   Would you use the canteen if it
   you buy regularly?   offered a wider variety of food
                                             choice?

  Sandwiches   ☐

  Filled rolls   ☐   YES   NO

  Hot toasted snacks   ☐   *What food/s*   Continue to
                                              would you like   question 3
  Pasta   ☐   *to be available?*

  Curry   ☐

  Fried breakfast   ☐

. . . And so on

Figure 5.2 Example of a typical semi-structured interview questionnaire

TABLE 5.1 SUMMARY OF SOME OF THE ADVANTAGES AND DISADVANTAGES OF INTERVIEW STRUCTURE METHODS

	Structured	**Semi-structured**	**Unstructured**
Can be used with large numbers of people	Yes	Yes, but a little more time consuming	No
Useful for obtaining a large amount of straightforward data	Yes	Yes, plus added data will be generated	No
It is possible for more than one researcher to carry out interviews	Yes	Yes	Data can be more valuable where trust is built between two people
A free flow of spontaneous information gathering is possible	No	Yes, but only in a controlled way and to a limited extent	Yes, but it usually needs guidance otherwise too much data is generated
It is easy for inexperienced researchers to carry out	Yes	Yes	No, deft control of conversation is needed
It is fairly quick to complete individual interviews	Yes	Yes	No
You need to keep detailed notes	No, tick boxes are usually sufficient	No, but some added data may need to be noted	Yes
In-depth information can be obtained	No	No	Yes
A pilot version of the proposed questions should be tried out on a friend for their comment	Yes	Yes	Yes
Analysis is straightforward	Whatever method of questioning you use the analysis will be straightforward if you keep records and work methodically. Follow the advice given in this book.		

▶ Who should be interviewed?

Not everyone makes a good interviewee. I am sure you know people who find it very difficult to articulate their views and feelings and there are others who are very dogmatic and have unshakeable views that they are determined to share with anyone who will listen. Ideally the people you interview should be a balance between these two types of personality, if you're lucky enough to have a choice, but sometimes you need to interview someone because of the position they hold within an organisation and then you have no choice in the matter. Reread the section on Life history research (including interviews) on pp. 35–7 if you are planning to interview only a handful of people as it contains useful tips on the ideal interviewee.

If you plan to interview a large number of people, you need to decide whether to choose a representative sample from the population (that is, choose people because of age, gender or social standing and so on) or whether to interview randomly. Your decision will depend on the research you have chosen. If you have decided to investigate why more men than women take up evening classes in computing, you might target female respondents to find out why they don't join or you might target men to find out why they do; probably in a case like this you would need to target both groups independently.

▶ The skills needed to be a successful interviewer

The interviewee has been discussed, but the interview method of research needs two people and the personality and personal attributes of the interviewer is equally important. Even if the interviewer is standing on the street corner carrying out structured or semi-structured interviews, the way they are dressed plus the way they initially approach the passer-by will influence whether or not an individual will stop. Would you give your time to someone whose appearance frightened or confronted you? This is not the time for the all-black confrontational battledress look, and a smile goes a long way towards persuading someone to give you a few minutes of their time.

If you intend to conduct a more personalised interview, then you need good communications skills. You send information about yourself immediately you open your mouth to speak – after all it isn't what you say it's the way that you say it. 'Can you please stop for a minute' can be received by the listener in two different ways. It depends whether the words are said in a friendly manner with the voice raised in question at the end of the sentence, or whether they are uttered at a fast pace with a rather bored, single pitch tone.

You can send body communication without you even realising that you are doing so. Consider the list in Table 5.2 and ask yourself whether you do any of these things. They can in some instances be off-putting to the recipient, and also send out messages about you that are not always the true picture.

TABLE 5.2

Expression	Are you ever guilty?
Body position	Turning away from the person? You're not signalling a friendly welcome
Breathing	Breathing heavily, noisily, sniffing or snorting? It's off-putting
Eye contact	Staring, looking away, looking down? All signalling disinterest or boredom
Facial expression	Frowning, grimacing, looking hostile? Not very welcoming
Fiddling	With hair, clothes, etc? It's very irritating to watch you
Grooming	Untidy? You don't care, they'll have to accept you as you are
Perspiration	Body odour? Shame on you, have you never heard of deodorant? It's not very nice for other people, don't you care?
Speech repetition	Repeating the same point over and over? Boring!
Speech	Too fast/slow, loud/quiet, mumbled? Your audience has to listen carefully to understand you. They might not bother
Voice pitch	High pitched, low pitched, shrill? Listening to you for a long time can be quite a strain

Nelson-Jones (1986:82) sees the importance of how you look and how you sound as being as important as what you say. He points out the need to communicate:

- Liking of the other
- Absence of threat
- Interest in the other
- Some initial definition of yourself.

This is as true for the structured street corner interview as for an in-depth one-to-one life history interview.

You need to explore your own interrelationship skills even more before embarking on one-to-one interviews. In the many years' experience I have had interviewing students in a supportive role as their tutor and in the interview research I have carried out, I have made myself a golden rule. I consciously *try to listen and not interrupt people when they are trying to explain or tell me something important to them.* It is tempting sometimes to help them out – they may be slow, I may not have a lot of time to spare, I sometimes feel I could finish the sentence for them. I may be tempted to impose my interpretation of what they are saying in a much more succinct way, but my interpretation could be completely wrong, and so I strive to be patient and listen. I have found the following checklist (Table 5.3) helpful in reminding me of my part in interviewing.

TABLE 5.3 INTERVIEWER CHECKLIST

Strive to be non-judgemental	You don't know anything about them and haven't lived their life experiences
Choose the right vocabulary	If someone can't understand what you are asking, how on earth are you going to get a meaningful answer?
Express an interest in what they are telling you	The occasional nod of the head, smile of understanding, or verbal interjection of encouragement shows you are listening
Be aware of non-verbal communication	Encourage the interviewee with the right body language – see Table 5.2
Be silent when the interviewee pauses – they may need time to gather their thoughts	You don't need to quickly get in another question just because there is a pause. Give your interviewee time to think
Really listen to what they're telling you	Don't attempt to rephrase their words with your interpretation

▶ Helpful questioning

Wrongly used questions can lead interviewees along a path that might be at odds with what you are trying to achieve. For example, they might be telling you something about their life history that is very interesting but not directly relevant to the research you are undertaking. Sometimes letting interviewees stray from what you're trying to discover will give you unthought-of useful information and may lead you along another research path. However, unless you rescue the situation at some point by asking the right questions that will gently lead the interviewee back to the information you need, you will find that interviews will take up a lot of time and you will record an enormous amount of unusable data.

You may find the following type of comment helpful in getting you back on track.

'That's really interesting, for some reason it reminds me of what you were saying earlier about . . . On that earlier topic, what was your view on . . . ?'

'Can we backtrack a little, can you tell me a little more about . . .'

'It's amazing what happens in life. I'm really interested in what you were saying last time we met about . . . Is there anything more you could tell me about that?'

Be careful not to use *leading questions*. You don't want to put words into the other person's mouth. If you mistakenly assume that the interviewee shares your view about a certain matter, your questions might reflect this. For example, if you like the new library booking-in system and ask 'What do you like best about the new booking-in system?', you are assuming that the respondents thinks that the new system is good by using the words *like* and *best*. They may think the new system is not as good as the old one, but you haven't given them the opening to tell you that, you've simply asked for positive points. It would have been far better to ask, 'What do you think of the new booking-in system?', then they could have given their opinion.

Questions that are too *probing* or ask *too many questions* might lead to the respondent becoming defensive. Trust between the interviewee and interviewer takes a long time to develop. So, unless your research schedule timing enables you to devote a lot of your personal time to developing this kind of relationship, or unless you already have this kind of relationship with your proposed interviewee/s, perhaps the focus of your research should be a topic which does not require such in-depth information.

Open and closed questions

A *closed question* reduces the other person's options for responding. If you ask 'Do you enjoy your work?', you are inviting a yes or no answer, which closes down your option to expand the question further. Had you asked an *open question*, such as, 'Which part of your work do you enjoy the most?', then you would have been given an answer (for example the person may have said 'working with others') that would enable you to ask 'Why?' In this way you can expand and develop a better understanding of the situation.

Open questions are those that use the words how, what, why, where, which and so on, and if you are considering using semi-structured interviewing in your research, their use will be essential. This topic is covered in more detail in Chapter 6.

▷ The ethics involved

Most universities and many professional bodies have developed codes of ethics to guide would-be researchers. Once you have identified where your research is to take place, ask whether that company or educational establishment has drawn up a relevant code of ethics. Whether or not you are given official guidelines on how you should properly conduct your interviews, you should define your own guidelines with due consideration to your code of behaviour and the moral value you place on those involved in the interview process.

The following is a list of guidelines for your consideration. Always remember that the interviewee is a person with feelings and rights just the same as you. They deserve your respect and consideration.

- Always inform the interviewee of the objectives and eventual results of your research. You owe this to them.
- Consider the psychological consequences of the questions you ask. I have a very elderly relative who suffered dreadfully in a prisoner-of-war camp during the Second World War. Reminders about the war send him into a deep depression for many weeks.
- If your advice is sought, extreme caution should be exercised. If the problem is serious, seek the advice of a professional in that area.
- Do not encroach into the privacy of the interviewee if it is obvious that your questions are unwelcome. Offer at the outset the choice of refusing to answer any question without feeling obliged to give a reason.
- If your research involves children, you should obtain the consent from the parents or from those *in loco parentis* (acting in the role of a parent). Also be careful if you discuss the results of your research with the parent or teacher, as sometimes the unguarded comment carries unintended weighting and importance to the recipient. You have a moral duty to the child not to disclose anything that they regard as personal to them. If they reveal something that you think is serious, discuss it first of all with a trusted colleague or professional in that area, before tackling the parents.
- Treat all information that you are given as confidential and let the interviewee know that you are doing so.

- If possible and if the interviewee prefers, strive to conceal the identity of your informant.
- If a situation proves to be more stressful or upsetting than imagined, stop the investigation and seek the advice of an experienced colleague before deciding whether to continue.

▶ Using diaries for research

At some time during their lives most people have kept a personal diary. Their entries may be of an emotional nature, how they felt about something, what they said and so on. This is frequently interspersed with factual information on what they did that day – went to the cinema, went shopping and so on. The research diary is the professional equivalent to this and it can provide valuable information to the researcher when the respondent records the timing and patterns of activities in the workplace or educational environment.

Sometimes it can be useful to keep a diary for a short time as the first step in the research process. It will give you pertinent information on which to base subsequent interviews.

Filling out diaries is very time consuming for the respondent and not everyone has the written ability or inclination to record events. You need to choose carefully the people you ask to keep research diaries, for unless they are enthusiastic and supportive, the diary method of gathering data is not likely to succeed. It is important to explain to proposed respondents exactly what you are doing and how valuable their contribution would be and in what way it would help. If you are lucky enough to find several people who are supportive and willing to complete a diary, you can eventually engage in a comparative exercise when differences, similarities and patterns could be established across the recorded material.

Slimming clubs often ask their members to keep a factual diary of every item of food they consume each day. They do this to highlight the forgotten, unaccounted for morsels of food that are eaten without thought and which prevent weight loss. A research diary could reveal areas and events that are also generally unaccounted for by the individual concerned, but they could throw light or have a significant bearing when viewed from a research angle.

A diary for research purposes generally covers a specific, agreed period of time, ranging from half a day to several weeks. It could take the form of asking the respondent to record every time that they performed a certain action, such as sorting the post. It may be that your area of research is investigating whether computer training would benefit social workers. You might have gained permission from your local social services to talk with practitioners in that field of employment and perhaps a group of social workers have agreed to keep a diary of the occasions that they could have used a computer effectively had they been given the appropriate training.

Instructions for the completion of a diary need to be clear. If you were designing a diary page for the use of social workers in the above situation you could follow a when, what, where, how type of format. This could look something like Table 5.4.

Care needs to be taken when you design diary questions. The information given will eventually need to be analysed, so you do not need unnecessary information that will only cause problems later; also the person completing the diary will find it easier and less time consuming if the questions are short and to the point.

▶ Telephone methods of interviewing

Using the telephone to conduct small-scale research may not be a method that you have considered, but it does have many advantages. It enables you to collect data and complete interview schedules quickly as it is much less time consuming than interviewing on the street corner (field interviewing). You can avoid the unpleasant experience of trying to entice people to answer your schedule while standing in the cold or the rain, a chance element that you cannot control. You can also target a specific geographic area or choose a more random search area, whichever best suits your specific research topic. Initially it is also easier to administer than posting questionnaires because you have no envelopes to address, stamped addressed return envelopes to prepare, or covering letter to compose.

On the other hand there are disadvantages. Some people do not like to answer questions over the telephone, some might hang up the phone once you begin to explain the purpose of your call. Most people now have a telephone, although a number of them are ex-directory, and some people only use mobile phones. However, you could compare this with the limitation of people available to you through the postal system or field interviewing.

The possibility of bias needs to be addressed if you decide to conduct a telephone interview. You will exclude that part of the population without a telephone, for example people on the move, and poorer people within our society; as well as those who are ex-directory, who are likely to be living in larger cities, could be female and living alone or busy professional people. Immediately you will have minimised the opportunity for the unattached female or busy professional living in the city to express their views.

To move some way towards minimising this bias, telephone interviewing

TABLE 5.4 TYPICAL DESIGN OF A DIARY PAGE FOR SOCIAL WORKERS

Day and date	Time	What was job?	How could the computer have helped you?	What did you do?	Time taken	Comments
Monday 1 December	1.15	Completing similar information about a client on three different forms.	Had the form been saved on computer it would have been quicker and would only have to have been keyed in once.	Wrote the information three times on the notification forms.	25 mins	A form needs to be devised that can serve the purpose of the existing three separate forms.
Tuesday 2 December . . . and so on						

could be used alongside some other method of research such as field interviewing. When the eventual analysis of the findings of each method are compared, it might throw a different light or highlight some unthought-of area within the research undertaken. However, both methods will form part of the written presentation of the eventual findings.

▶ Access

Access to informants and premises is a major issue in interviewing. There are two main approaches, either boss down or employee up. If you are using the boss down approach, it is likely that you will need to spend some time in the first instance trying to find out whom to approach for permission to interview. If you wish to interview within a large company and you have no initial contacts, you could start by telephoning the personnel department who should be able to tell you the name of the person to contact.

Often a letter explaining your aims and the value of your research is a good method of approach. This can be followed up a week or so later by a telephone call if you have had no reply. Giving your contact the time to mull over your request is not only polite but you are less likely to be given an instant no. If you telephone without notice and your contact is too busy to listen to your request, the quickest way to get rid of you is to say no.

Be prepared for your request to be turned down. You may have to make several approaches to different organisations before you gain permission. This can be time consuming, so as soon as you have decided that you want to carry out interviews within an organisation, make the initial approach as quickly as possible.

If you are using the employee up approach, you may be in a better position to get things moving a little quicker. Your inside employee contact is probably already supportive of what you are trying to do, otherwise they would not have taken on the job of seeking permission on your behalf. You can best help them by being prepared and ready to write, telephone or submit a copy of your proposed research or questionnaire as soon as requested. In this way you will also give the recipient the impression that you are organised and efficient.

Initial contacts
Once you have gained permission to interview staff, if possible you will need to speak to the people that you hope to interview or ask to complete questionnaires. Building rapport with your proposed informants will help you to gain their support. It may be that all you can do is put an introductory letter

in their internal pigeon-hole or send it via the internal email system. This communication needs to be carefully worded, as you need to explain not only what and why you are researching but also to persuade them to give up their time to help you. Explain the way in which your study will proceed, what you will do with the information they provide and promise anonymity and confidentiality at the outset. Although writing and distributing an initial explanatory letter is time consuming, you are likely to get a better response in the long term if you make this initial contact before approaching people for individual interviews or sending the actual questionnaires.

Never make promises that will be difficult to keep. For example, if you are undertaking one-to-one semi-structured interviews, it would be ideal if you could let the respondent see your first draft in order to check that you have interpreted correctly what they have said, although time constraints might make this impossible.

You must decide whether you are going to let participants see a copy of the finished research, or at least the statistics or conclusions that the information they give you will generate. Think about this carefully because it could be expensive to photocopy and distribute to everyone involved, so perhaps you will decide to pin one copy on the noticeboard, or send one to the department manager. Whatever you decide, it is best to let people know at the outset.

The participant has far less to gain from your research than you. You might hope that your research will change something for the better within the participant's world but you cannot guarantee this. It is they who are doing you the favour, so act accordingly.

Organising the how and where

To gain support and foster a good research relationship with your respondents, you need to prove to them that you are reliable and aware of their difficulties. Always arrange to see them at a time convenient for them, arrive on time and minimise their inconvenience by travelling to a meeting point that is suitable for them. If you arrange that an interview will last an hour, then after 55 minutes start to bring the interview to a close. If you remember that they are giving up their time to help you, your attitude and consideration will help you to build a relationship that will foster the best from your research enquiry.

▶ Recording the spoken word

How you record what is said is a decision that you need to make early in your research because you will need to negotiate your intentions with your interviewee. There are three main ways of recording the spoken word:

1. taping everything that is said
2. jotting down important points (summarised by two or three words) as they arise
3. taking notes word for word.

None of these systems is without problems.

Tape-recording

If you tape everything, there are two big disadvantages. First you will have to listen to the recording later and transcribe what is said. This is extremely time consuming and if your respondent's speech does not record clearly or if your equipment is not sound, you may find yourself replaying parts of the interview over and over in an effort to work out what was said. You will also have to listen through again parts of the conversation that were not particularly relevant to your research, as you search for the pertinent parts. Also, for every hour of tape-recording you will need at least another two hours outside the interview time to key in what was said.

The second disadvantage is that the very presence of the tape machine will play a part. Recording verbatim what people say on tape may affect what they tell you. Also you will need their permission before you embark on this method of recording the interview.

Jotting down pertinent points

Jotting down pertinent points is an option open to the interviewer. Keeping notes during the interview to the minimum has the advantage of allowing the interviewer to be attentive to what is being said. It allows for a more relaxed approach with minimal intrusion by the act of writing. However, there is a risk that when writing up the interview later the interviewer might recall bias or false statements because their jotted heading leads them to remember only certain things. If time constraints are sorted out and the interviewee is given an opportunity to read the first draft and check that the interview has been interpreted correctly, this problem would be alleviated.

If you work out in advance some kind of shorthand shortcut of your own, you may be able to write a little more than just the pertinent headings, but this would be your personal choice. If you have a good memory and are in the position of being able to leave the interview and write up your notes almost immediately, this method can be well worth considering.

Taking notes verbatim

To struggle to write down every word that your interviewer says is daunting unless you can write shorthand. The very act of constantly scribbling will be off-putting to the interviewee and they may feel in some way threatened because you are recording their every word. You will also have to write down your questions, otherwise it will be difficult to transcribe the answers in context. If your interview is semi-structured, you could write the questions in advance and leave space for the reply. This is not as straightforward as it appears however; inevitably an answer will prompt you to ask a supplementary question that is not written down, or you will not have allowed enough space to write the answers.

You will also need to decide whether you are going to write the words exactly as said, for example in the present tense, with slang or grammar errors. You may lose some of the importance of what is being said if you try to rewrite it as you listen. For example, if you were interviewing teenagers about their perceptions of school and one of them said: 'I reckon you get yer 'ead messed up fur good if you get put with the dickheads early on like', this tells you a lot about where the teenager was coming from, their ability to express themselves and their built-in opinion. Compare it with a watered-down, tidied up version, 'I think that you never catch up if you're put in the lower ability classes at first'. It can also be easier to write exactly what is said, as the art of paraphrasing on the spot isn't easy.

You may find it helpful to work out in advance some abbreviated forms that you can use as you write, perhaps using initials for frequently repeated jargon-type words, or just the letter 'w' for commonly repeated words, such as 'what'. It's worth trying to interview a friend beforehand just for the experience and you will soon learn the commonly repeated words.

Taking verbatim notes can bring a feel of formality to the interview, but this is also governed by the previous relationship between the participants. Depending on the type of research you are doing, you may not wish to foster this formality.

Summary of recording methods
The best method of recording what your respondents say must be decided before you embark on interviews. It is no use deciding on the day of the interview, as this may be too late to familiarise yourself with the equipment or skills needed. Table 5.5 compares the various methods to help you with this decision.

TABLE 5.5 ADVANTAGES AND DISADVANTAGES OF THE VARIOUS RECORDING
METHODS

	Tape-recording	Jotting down important points	Writing word for word what is said
Respondents may feel inhibited	Yes. Some people will not wish to commit their spoken words to tape	Less so. Respondents can always say that the interviewer misunderstood what was said	Less so. Respondents can always say that the interviewer misunderstood what was said
The method is off-putting to the respondent	Yes, for some people, they cannot forget the presence of the equipment	Less so, especially if the interviewer is able to still be attentive to the respondent	Yes. The interviewer will be writing for most of the time
Transcribing is straightforward	Yes, but it can be time consuming if the recording quality and equipment is not good	Yes, providing the interviewer has a good memory that is nudged by pertinent headings	No, it is usually very time consuming, especially when the handwriting becomes difficult to read
The data gathered will be accurate	Yes	If the interviewer is efficient and has written down accurate headings. There is a possibility that biased statements will be falsely recollected later	Yes, if the interviewer is well prepared
The method is quick	No	No	No
Analysis is uncomplicated	Whatever recording method you use, the analysis will be less complicated if you keep records and work methodically. Follow the advice given in this book		

▶ **Paying respondents**

You probably have received an unsolicited questionnaire in the post that contained a free biro and a prepaid return envelope as an incentive to encourage you to complete and return it. Sometimes this type of mail offers you the chance to be entered into a free draw that offers the glittering prize of a new car or holiday. The commercial world advocates this successful method of offering nominal payment or free gifts and samples as an incentive to participants when information is required. Outside the commercial world of research, direct or indirect payments have never become commonplace, as it is thought to increase the possibility of bias and contamination in the research material.

Payments are rarely considered in qualitative research. Sonia Thompson (http://www.soc.surrey.ac.sru.Sru.html), an experienced lecturer in the field of youth and community work, highlights the issues around research payment and points out that it may be because the researched are often those lacking the power to insist on being compensated for their time. She further points out that it would be undesirable to pay socially powerful people, for example interviewees selected because of their specialist knowledge or position of authority. She cites the impossibility of paying recompense to a managing director of a multinational company at a level that would not seem derisory.

With small-scale research, payment is not usually even considered. However, if interviewees have been kind enough to give up their time to help you in your research, it would be courteous if you showed your appreciation in some way. Perhaps a bouquet of flowers, tickets for the theatre or a bottle of wine; after hours spent talking to your interviewees you will know their preferences. The same idea could be applied if you have been lucky enough to gather research material or have your questionnaires completed within a company. A 'thank you' box of chocolates or tin or biscuits to the department will show that you have appreciated their assistance; and if you gained access to the department via an internal employee (employee up approach), you will put that person in an agreeable position.

▶ Pilot study

Whichever interview method you choose, it cannot be stressed too strongly that you should pilot a sample before plunging headlong into the real thing, rather like a dress rehearsal before the opening night.

If your chosen method/s involve/s life history, interviews or questionnaires, write out your proposed questions and try them on a willing friend or compose your structured interview questionnaire and give it to several friends to complete. It is only when you have conducted a trial run that you will find out which questions are ambiguous or too personal. Your friends may even have suggestions for additional questions that would be useful and informative to your research.

When you are satisfied with the composition of the questions, a second pilot study with the general public has the added advantage of training those who are going to ask the questions. When Rex and Moore piloted their questionnaire into immigrants in the inner-city area of Sparkbrook, near Birmingham, Moore wrote that 'this gave our first batch of student interviewers an opportunity to try out their own skills as well as to test the efficiency of the schedule' (quoted in Bell and Newby 1977).

Piloting any empirical research is a good idea but there are some facets of case study research where piloting is difficult. It could be that you wish to study one particular case, and it would be difficult to find a sensible equivalent to use as a pilot study. In a situation like this, full details of the way that you formulated your case study research need to be explained when you eventually write up your findings, perhaps using the word 'exploratory' when discussing your case study.

▶ Which interview technique to choose?

It is not carved in stone that you can only use one interview technique and which one you choose will depend on what you require, how much time you have and whether you need to sample a large audience or just a few respondents. It is well worth considering the unstructured interview with colleagues to develop the path your research will take. You may then wish to use one of the other interview methods if you believe it is the best way to generate the data you need.

PART B

▶ Email

International connection via the computer provides you with a cheap and effective vehicle for collaboration with your colleagues. Long distances and time zones have no effect on your communications and it is easy to share resources with other researchers anywhere in the world.

Once you have found your way around your computer you will find discussion groups that will have relevance to your work. As you begin to build up links, not only with your immediate correspondents but also through them to other academic discussion groups, you will discover connections to research material that perhaps you did not know existed. There are many academic discussion groups in the UK and many thousands of groups worldwide

Computer Support

(sometimes the word 'list' might be used instead of group, but it has the same meaning).

▶ Finding your interview audience online

Using the computer to conduct interviews is not as difficult as it might at first appear, but you will need time and patience to find ideal recipients who are willing to take part in your project.

Joining an email discussion group (sometimes called subscribing to a group, but you don't have to pay) is one way of fostering links with people who may have similar interests or are employed in a relevant area.

Discussion groups are often linked to a theme, for example I have a friend who helped her son find online information about the Vietnam War for a school project. One of the sites they visited had an email discussion group where messages or questions could be left. She subsequently learned that many of the members on the list were ex-helicopter pilots and so they were well placed to answer questions. Through this tenuous beginning my friend became more interested and involved in the Heli-vets discussion site; discussing the present lives of the pilots and their past Vietnamese experiences.

To join an email discussion group you normally send a specific message to the person running the group. Messages are then distributed to all the group members. In time you will build up links with others in the group and will hopefully be in a position to ask if any of them would be willing to complete an online questionnaire, or answer questions relating to your research project. It is far better to build up links before you request information.

One particularly useful email discussion group is called mailbase. Mailbase provides electronic discussion lists for the UK higher education community. They currently have 1,913 discussion groups and 134,603 members worldwide. It is a JISC (Joint Information Systems Committee) funded service based at the University of Newcastle and receives additional support from Sun Microsystems.

The JISC is funded by the Scottish Higher Education Funding Council, the Higher Education Funding Council for England, the Higher Education Funding Council for Wales and the Department of Education Northern Ireland, and the mission of the JISC is: 'To stimulate and enable the cost effective exploitation of information systems and to provide a high quality national network infrastructure for the UK higher education and research councils communities.'

There are discussion groups on a wide range of topics that are available to anyone with an email address. For example, if you are interested in geriatric medicine and you key in http://www.bgs.org.uk/bgstrg.html, you will be linked to a discussion site, the aim of which is to encourage open and interactive discussion, particularly between trainees and trainers, on a wide variety of issues related to training, evidence-based practice, research and new developments in geriatric medicine.

The mailbase discussion group covers a vast range of topics, psychology, physiotherapy, nutrition, even fish diseases to name but a few. It is easy to use and if they don't have a discussion group which interests you they might even help you to set one up if they feel it will be of interest to others. Search for 'mailbase' in your search engine.

Once you begin to browse the Internet you will notice that there are millions of general chatlines available to you. These are lines dedicated to particular topics, health, comedy, addiction, teenagers, sex, entertainment and so on. People log in and out of these lines as they wish; sometimes they join in with the discussion afoot by typing in a comment and sometimes they just read the 'chat' between other people using the 'chatroom'.

It is very easy to use a chatline. You simply click on a picture (or word) of an area in which you interested, and the chatroom page will appear. Sometimes you have to fill in your details (which do not appear on the chat screen) and a pseudonym that you wish to be known by. The pseudonyms that people choose can range from a simple 'Jane' to something quite sublime, for example 'Truly, madly, deeply'. The next step is to click on a button named 'connect' (or something similar) and that's it – you're away and chatting. Using a chatline can sometimes be interesting, but often quite boring or irritating depending on the people involved at the time. With persistence you will find favourite ones where the contributions are interesting and meaningful and you will enjoy 'chatting' with others.

Chatrooms have their own jargon and the terms or abbreviations that you see sprinkled among the conversations, such as IMO for 'in my opinion', will quickly become familiar.

▶ Computer-assisted personal interviewing (CAPI)

Although the history of CAPI goes back to the 1970s, it is only recently with the advantages of the latest technology and laptop computers that it has become an acceptable form of personal interviewing. Interviewers in face-to-face interviews record respondents' answers directly onto a computer rather than onto a paper questionnaire. A CAPI questionnaire is a computer program designed especially for a research purpose.

The written text question appears on screen with possible response categories, the interviewer reads out the question and enters the answer given; immediately the computer responds with the next question. The pattern of questions asked sometimes runs in relation to the type of answers given. One of the biggest advantages of this type of interviewing is that subsequent analysis of the data is very quick, in some cases almost automatic.

CAPI has been used for many years in telephone surveys, when the person asks the questions via the telephone and records the answers on their computer. Banks, building societies, insurance companies, catalogue clubs, and those unwanted marketing-type telephone calls all use this method. CAPI has also been used for customer satisfaction-type surveys on behalf of large organisations such as British Telecom or government departments. However, recently CAPI is being used more and more for one-off small-scale projects and could be a valuable tool to the research process.

In 1994 the Social Policy Research Unit commissioned Research Services Limited of Harrow to survey over 1,100 income support recipients by this method. They sought to identify and investigate, over a six-month period, changes in claimants' circumstances and the resulting impact on their lives and social security benefits. Sainsbury et al. were involved in this survey and have highlighted the aspects of CAPI which need to be weighed against traditional paper and pencil techniques, including the quality of the data, speed of delivery and costs. First they summarised their experience against claims that CAPI enhances the quality of survey data:

> Interviewing is made easier by the 'customising' of questions. The computer program can recall a piece of data from its memory, such as a name or date and insert it in the appropriate place. For example, it is common for a paper questionnaire to include questions such as 'How often do/does (you/NAME) use (TYPE OF TRANSPORT)?' Using CAPI interviewers would not have to keep a check on which member of the household and which type of transport they are asking about. Instead they would be faced with a series of questions like 'How often does Bill use the train?' In this way the accuracy of the question and the smoothness of the interview are improved. (Sainsbury et al. 1993, online)

Without the specialist software it will not be possible for you to administer a questionnaire using the above techniques, but some companies and academic organisations might have access to specialised software. The most common packages in the UK are BLAISE, QUANCEPT, MICROTAB, and BV

Solo, all of which offer software for one-off surveys. For the more ambitious who would like to design their own CAPI programmes, it is possible to buy some basic packages direct from the suppliers (eg Blaise, Central Bureau of Statistics, Hoofdafdeling M3, PO Box 959, 2270 AZ Voorburg, The Netherlands. Tel +31 70 6994341). Although designing your own CAPI programme is not something for the consideration of total beginners, it might be worthwhile consulting your company or university and also befriending the computer staff who may well be interested in acquiring and setting up the software.

If your own computer is not portable, you might be able to borrow a laptop computer from your company or academic organisation, which would enable you to load your designed questionnaire or questions beforehand, and transport the machine with you. I once worked in a university that had a limited number of computers that students could loan for a fixed period for a small charge, but it was not generally advertised, because it was felt that demand would outstrip availability. So do ask, otherwise you'll never know whether there is a laptop available.

The process of converting the information you have handwritten from paper to computer can be quite time consuming. If your information is saved straight to computer, you will find it extremely useful to copy and paste information from questionnaires directly into a spreadsheet programme in order to produce bar or pie charts. Also copy and paste will again be useful when you want to quote directly from personal interview information.

You will also be able to search and find keywords within your saved work. For example, perhaps you would like to know how many times interviewees said they could not answer a particular question, or maybe you would like to know on how many occasions an interviewee referred to their 'workload' or their 'mother' or whatever. It will simply be a matter of pressing a few keys if your text is saved straight onto computer.

The design of the computer questionnaire is extremely important, however this is covered in much greater detail in Chapter 6, which deals solely with questionnaires.

▶ Using email to aid interviews

The use of email is increasing rapidly as a means of communication. Given its growing importance within our society, it is odd that its use as a research tool seems to have been largely overlooked. One of the advantages of using email for research purposes is that it is fast, and almost instantaneous communications between researcher and subject can be organised. One of the main disadvantages is that it has a biased and limited population of users (in terms of age, income, computer ability, race and gender); although as time passes this will diminish as more people become part of the electronic age.

Encouraging response to your research questions needs careful planning. The recipient of an unsolicited email is more likely to ignore it as part of the ever-increasing 'junk' mail that is delivered via his computer. Mehta and Sivadas's (1995) study found that email response rates increased by 23% when an initial email was sent requesting participation in their study. You could browse the Internet's specific discussion lines searching for people who may have an interest in your research topic (although you should consider whether this would give your research an unwanted bias). Or if you search the Internet for related topics you will be surprised how quickly a list of potential email contacts that might be useful to your research can be compiled.

Early reports indicate that email has a very favourable response rate when compared to conventional mail. Anderson and Gansneder (1995) report a 65% response rate to their 72-item email survey (with 76% returned via email, only 24% returned conventionally). So you have a better chance of response if you use email compared with pushing your request for information through doors. You also have an opportunity of utilising a global response rather than localised information if this suits the needs of your research project.

If you are researching within an organisation, you might be able to use the *internal* email system as a tool to gain the answers to your questions. Sending the same email to many computers within one mailshot is relatively straightforward, but you should first negotiate permission to do so from the relevant person. Some companies are not willing to allow you online time because (a) they do not wish their employees to be distracted from their work, and (b) they fear that your email communication prepared away from their computers may cause them technical problems. You are more likely to be allowed this kind of access if you are an insider, or have an inside contact, or if your research is relevant to the organisation.

Anonymity is difficult to guarantee using email and this could be an important issue. It is very difficult to hide the name of the email respondent, because the respondent's email address is automatically added to their reply. However, there is nothing to stop you promising absolute confidentiality, which might go some way to reassuring participants.

Using email as an interview technique has the advantage of reducing visual or non-verbal cues. For example, an interviewer with an annoying habit (for example sniffing, rubbing his chin and so on) can be very off-putting to the interviewee, as can the interviewer who nods constantly and looks expectantly at the interviewee, almost forcing them to formulate an answer quickly.

Also the negative effects of shyness are easier to overcome when communicating via the computer. However, the email technique is not without problems. If used for personal interview purposes, it might not be easy to 'read between the lines' the hidden agenda that the interviewee would like to explore, but doesn't like to raise directly. Reading the written word without seeing the facial expression, or hearing the audible pause might lead the researcher to miss an important cue. For some people expressing themselves using the keyboard may not be their strong point, and typed replies may be a poor alternative to the richness of the spoken language.

It is worth giving serious consideration to using email to support part of your research, especially if you wish to use questionnaires in the research process. As with CAPI, you will at least have all the replies immediately electronically stored on computer, which will be of enormous benefit to you when you begin to analyse the data. Internet interviewing is not a direct substitute for the more traditional research methods, but can be a very helpful associate.

▶ Pros and cons of online interviewing

The Internet is continually evolving. As technologies develop, the convergence of telecommunications, television and the Web will improve this method of research. As with any medium of obtaining information, there are advantages and disadvantages. There are a number of methodological and technical difficulties but these must be balanced with the clear benefits that this method can bring. Qualitative Internet interviewing is not a direct substitute for more traditional methodologies but it is a supporting partner well worth your consideration. Table 5.6 will help you to consider whether online interviewing might be suitable for your research.

A touch of caution before you begin

If you are planning to use a form in your interview research or a list of questions for your respondent to complete, you need to ensure at the beginning that the research does not get too big and unwieldy. Before you embark on Internet interviews read the section in Chapter 6 A touch of caution before you begin, pp. 148–50. It is better to be forewarned.

Computer Support

TABLE 5.6

Advantages	Disadvantages
It is easy to reach respondents	Your respondents will be limited to computer owners
It is ideal for overcoming 'time' and travelling problems	There will be a bias towards the technically able person
It is still comparatively new – people are more enthusiastic to participate	You will not be aware of non-verbal communication or body language
There are no geographical boundaries	Respondents will have time to consider responses – loss of spontaneity
You can seek out people with specific interests if useful	Lack of keyboard skills may mean shorter answers
Some people are more likely to reveal certain information if not in a face-to-face situation	It is more difficult to create a rapport or feeling of confidentiality with the respondent

6 Questionnaires

PART A

When you read this chapter you should look also at Chapter 5 because the two topics are linked and there are areas within each that interrelate. A good questionnaire is not just a list of questions. It will have been carefully planned, drafted and piloted with a few colleagues, have taken into account the likely respondents and throughout the whole process the eventual method of data analysis will have been borne in mind.

In the construction of a questionnaire several stages have to be worked through. Ann Lavan (1985) laid these down as being:

1. Selecting the population to whom the questions will be addressed
2. Designing the questionnaire:
    Preparatory work
    Questionnaire format
    Question content
    Pre-testing
3. Training the interviewers
4. Coding the data
5. Analysing the data

A well-designed questionnaire should translate the broad objectives of your study into questions that will obtain the information you need. Using and completing your questionnaire needs to be as effortless and simple as possible and the questions should have a direct bearing on the data you need and the analysis of that data. This sounds simplistic but it is amazing the number of questionnaires that are either confusing, ask the wrong questions or omit to ask crucial questions. A badly designed questionnaire will give meaningless data and be misleading. A sound awareness of good questionnaire design will enable your research to be valid and meaningful.

▶ Open or closed questions – designing the questionnaire

At the outset you need to decide whether the questionnaire is to be used fairly quickly with many respondents or whether it is to be used with just a few people in a longer, in-depth, one-to-one situation. If you are planning to use the questionnaire with many people, using too many open-ended questions could make it too long and laborious to administer and eventually analyse.

Open or closed questioning was very briefly looked at in Chapter 5, but, as you begin to design your questionnaire, you need to look at the importance of question structure in more depth. The answers to open-ended questions that allow the respondent to give a personal opinion (for example What do you think is the most important role of computers in the workplace today?), will need to be coded in some way prior to analysis. Analysing questionnaires is covered in full in Chapter 7.

Sometimes the answers given to open-ended questions will be irrelevant to the intent of your question. Unless you plan to stand on a street corner personally to administer the questionnaires, the people helping you to ask questions will need to be completely familiar with your intentions. They will then be in a position to ask supplementary questions if they realise that the answer given will not be helpful to your aims. If you are posting question-naires, you will not even have this opportunity to develop a given answer.

Open-ended questions are also more time consuming to ask, listen to and write the answer. This will make the process of questionnaire completion longer and if your questions are too laboured, the respondent may give you quick answers just because they want to get away.

Closed questions are very popular in survey research since the respondents are asked to select their answer from a list provided and this is quicker than allowing the respondent the freedom to create their own reply. The respon-dent is rarely given the opportunity to express an opinion other than choos-ing from one suggested, which makes the questionnaire easy to administer, uniform in answers and easily processed and analysed. One of the main disadvantages of closed questioning is that misleading conclusions can be drawn because of the limited range of options available. Babbie sees this as the chief shortcoming in using closed questions:

> In cases where the relevant answers to a given question are relatively clear, structuring the responses might present no problem. In other cases, however, your structuring of responses might overlook some important ones. In asking about 'the most important issues facing the Unites States,' for example, you might provide a checklist of issues but

in doing so might overlook certain issues that respondents would have said were important. (Babbie 1990:123)

Babbie advocates two guidelines to overcome this shortcoming. First he suggests adding a category labelled 'Other (please specify)' which would give the respondent an opportunity to express a personal opinion. He points out that researchers should be aware that in offering this option respondents often try to fit their personal answers into one of the categories provided even though the fit might not be perfect. This will not make for easy analysis.

His second guideline involves mutual exclusiveness, which is involved with respondents answering more than just one question:

> in some cases, the researcher might want to solicit multiple answers, but such answers will create difficulties in processing. You can ensure mutually exclusive answers by carefully considering each combination of responses and asking whether a person could reasonably give both. Often you ask the respondent to 'select the one *best* answer,' but this technique should not be used to make up for a poorly thought out set of responses. (Babbie 1990:123)

In using closed questions only, it is necessary to examine whether the researcher is pointing the respondent towards a certain answer just because it is offered. Would they have thought of it themselves? For example, a questionnaire on crime might ask respondents to consider whether they believed crime to be a personal problem. Perhaps they would be asked to choose the category they believed to be the most serious from a list suggested. Would they think of, say, arson, being assaulted, robbed or walking alone in the dark as a personal problem unless it had been suggested? In sensitive areas such as this the researcher also has an obligation not to unduly worry their respondents especially if they are dealing with an elderly population.

Whether you use open-ended or closed questions will be a matter of personal choice and the needs of your research; however, to help you to decide a summarised list (Tables 6.1 and 6.2) of advantages and disadvantages in both systems follows.

TABLE 6.1 OPEN-ENDED QUESTIONS

Advantages	Disadvantages
Greater freedom to express opinion	Time consuming to analyse
Bias reduced because response is not limited to certain answers	It takes longer to carry out each questionnaire interview if compared to a closed questionnaire
Respondent can explain their answer	The field workers need training as they may misunderstand the answer given by the respondent and therefore misclassify it or not realise what supplementary questions to ask to meet the aim of the research.
Researchers can ask supplementary questions in order to clarify information	Busy people may not have the time to answer questions fully and might therefore give the interviewer the quickest answer in order to get away
Respondents express their own opinions and will not be influenced by a ready-made answer just because its offered	

TABLE 6.2 CLOSED QUESTIONS

Advantages	Disadvantages
Quick to administer	Misleading conclusions may be drawn because of the limited range of options
Easier to code and analyse	Respondent unable to express personal opinion and may choose the nearest answer to what they really think
Articulate people and those who are less able to express themselves are on an equal footing	

▶ Problem questions

Often the researcher is so involved in the subject that questions which are perfectly clear to them become ambiguous or unclear when read by somebody outside the research area. A good questionnaire will be clear and explicit and leave no room for ambiguity.

Double-barrelled questions

If you ask your respondent for a single answer to a double-barrelled question, then they may agree with you on one point but not another. For example, you might ask the question:

Should the UK spend less money on defence *and* more on the National Health Service?

Some people will unequivocally agree with the first part of the question but disagree strongly that the money should be reallocated to the NHS and wish it to be allocated elsewhere. Others may wish to continue spending on defence but at the same time find money from elsewhere for the NHS. Whether your respondent answers 'yes' or 'no', it is impossible for them to answer your question meaningfully.

Tip to avoid double-barrelled questions. If your question contains the word *and*, check whether you are asking two questions in one.

Leading questions

Leading questions are often emotive. The question might be:

Would you say that animal welfare charities are a good thing?

Most people would feel that they had to answer yes to this question, but if you look at the question closely the use of the words 'would you say' is involving the respondent at a personal level. If they answer no they may feel that you, as the interviewer, would consider them harsh and cold towards animals. Remember that the questions will be asked fairly quickly and the respondent will not have a lot of time to consider the ramifications of the statement. Had you asked, 'Should animal welfare be provided by charity?', you would probably have had more respondents saying no, some of who would have wished to clarify the answer by adding that the government should play its part.

Do not presume that everyone will agree with your opinion because this attitude often leads researchers to write leading questions.

Tip to avoid leading questions. Make sure that your questions don't begin with statements such as 'Do you agree that . . .', 'Do you think that . . .' or 'Would you say that . . .' and so on.

Hypothetical questions

Try to avoid asking questions where the respondents have to imagine themselves in a particular situation. If you are researching people's attitudes it may be difficult to avoid, but it will be difficult to analyse the answers if you use open-ended questions and it could also give rise to unreliable data. Such a question might be:

> If you won the lottery would you spend the money on (a) a new car, (b) a new house, (c) clearing your credit card debts, (d) paying off the mortgage, (e) helping others, (f) a holiday?

The respondent might think there is absolutely no point to this question and view your whole research questionnaire accordingly.

> *Tip to avoid hypothetical questions.* Check whether you start your question with the word *if*. Never base your question on imaginary circumstances.

Memory questions

Problematic questions that ask the respondent to recall events, information or dates are likely to lead to inaccurate replies, which in turn will make your research meaningless. If you asked your respondent to list the illnesses that they have had, it is unlikely that they will remember everything especially if they have had a long and full life. Remember that you are asking them 'on the spot' to recall information that may go back over many years. Ask yourself could you answer this question? You could gain this information by presenting them with a list of possible illnesses and asking them to say which ones they have had.

> *Tip to avoid memory questions.* Consider whether a list provided by you would be better if your question begins with 'Can you please list . . .' or is a 'What subjects did you study at college?' type question.

Sensitive questions

Asking a sensitive question is usually best left towards the end of your questionnaire, then people will, hopefully, have warmed to your research, or feel that as they've answered so far they might as well continue. If your first question was 'How old are you?' or 'How much do you earn?', you might lose half of your would-be respondents in the first ten seconds. Many people do not wish to tell you their age or other personal details and one way of overcoming this is to give them a choice of banded answers (Figure 6.1).

Some face-to-face researchers prefer the use of show cards. A show card

What is your age?	(please tick)
Under 20	☐
21–30 years	☐
31–40 years	☐
41–50 years	☐
51–60 years	☐
61–70 years	☐
71 or over	☐

Figure 6.1

is simply a card with a list of banded answers that has a key, for example a number beside each answer. If we were using the above 'What is your age?' question, the show card would look like Figure 6.2.

The interviewer would ask the question and ask the respondent to choose one number from the show card, which they would immediately hold up before them. The interviewer would then write down the number chosen.

In theory field workers are less likely to know the exact answer being given by the respondent if show cards are used, and this is supposed to encourage

What is your age?	
Choose the appropriate *number*	
1	Under 20
2	21–30 years
3	31–40 years
4	41–50 years
5	51–60 years
6	61–70 years
7	71 or over

Figure 6.2

the respondent to answer. However, I have found that when show cards are used over and over the interviewer very quickly gets to know what the numbered categories stand for, but perhaps the respondent doesn't instantly realise this fact.

People are more likely to answer sensitive questions in face-to-face interviews if some rapport has been developed with the interviewer, which is another reason to keep sensitive questions for the end.

Long questions

If your questions are too long or complicated then your respondent may get lost and their responses are likely to relate only to the first part of the question, which is the part that they will remember. Some researchers advocate the use of show cards (see above) to remind the respondent of the questions and the choices available. However, I think it is far better to rework the question and reduce its length or make it two questions if it is necessary to obtain the information.

> *Tip regarding long questions.* Look at your draft questionnaire carefully, do you have any question longer than one sentence? If so, reword it or split it into two questions if you need all this information.

Questions requiring prior knowledge

If your respondents have to look up information in order to answer your questionnaire then they may abandon it altogether. If you ask a question such as 'What is your driving licence number?', 'What is the sum total of your department's annual budget?' or 'What is the name of the medication you use?', respondents may not know or be able to spell the answer and will have to search for the information.

Before you ask for this type of information be very sure that you really need it to complete your research. If you really must ask prior knowledge questions, prune down their number by prioritising importance. If you overuse your request for prior knowledge answers, your respondent will either leave blanks at these questions or abandon completely the whole questionnaire.

An alternative might be to provide a list that the respondent can tick. If, instead of asking the question 'What is the name of the medication you use?', you provided a list of the generic name of medications, such as headache remedies, water-retention tablets, and so on, and asked the respondent to tick as applicable, you would still gain some information. Whether of course you needed the actual name of the medication used would depend on your research.

Tip to avoid prior knowledge questions. Attempt to answer your own draft questionnaire. If you cannot instantly answer a question, consider whether it is really necessary or whether it could be reworked.

Confusing questions

If you earned £20,000 and were asked to tick your income group on the form below, where would you tick?

What is your income group? (please tick)

Under £7,000 pa ☐

£7,000–£10,000 ☐

£10,000–£15,000 ☐

£15,000–£20,000 ☐

£20,000–£30,000 ☐

Above £30,000 ☐

Figure 6.3

It is very easy to write ambiguous questions without realising and that is why asking willing colleagues to complete (pilot) a draft copy of your questionnaire is essential. If you can't see what is wrong, look at Figure 6.4.

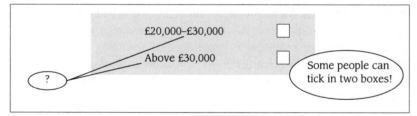

Figure 6.4

Specific questions

When giving people a choice of answers from which to tick, you need to formulate the tick boxes very carefully. If you were presented with the tick box below (Figure 6.5) how would you respond?

If you visited your doctor once during the past six months, would you regard that as 'infrequent' or 'hardly ever'? You might have two patients who attend the doctors about once a month but one would tick this as being 'often' and the other 'regular'. It is far better to be explicit so that everyone understands exactly what is meant. Had the tick boxes been offered as Figure 6.6 below then you would have had no doubt where to tick.

How often do you visit your doctor? (please tick one)	Often	☐
	Regularly	☐
	Infrequently	☐
	Hardly ever	☐

Figure 6.5

How often do you visit your doctor? (please tick one)	Every week	☐
	Once a month	☐
	Once every 3 months	☐
	Once every 6 months	☐
	Visits are more than 6 months apart	☐

Figure 6.6

▶ The layout of the questionnaire

Presentation of your questionnaire is important. If it is badly designed then interviewers and respondents can lose their way and miss important questions. The layout can be almost as important as the wording of the questions themselves. It should be clearly printed, consistent in display and presented logically with plenty of space for replies. All instructions should be easy to understand and unambiguous.

On the following pages there are two copies of a similar questionnaire. The first, Figure 6.7, is confusing to the eye, it looks as though there are more questions than there actually are, and the layout is not easy to follow. In the second, Figure 6.8, consideration has been given to the clarity and spacing of the questions and the overall appearance is pleasing to the eye. The recipient of this questionnaire would find it fairly easy to work through. Compare the question composition of these two figures. Which is the easier to answer and which, in the long term, will be easier to analyse?

When you have compared the two questionnaires, look at Figure 6.9 and the highlighted points.

HONEYFIELDS YOUTH CLUB SURVEY

YOUR YOUTH CLUB COMMITTEE WANTS TO IMPROVE YOUR CLUB. PLEASE HELP US BY
COMPLETING THE FOLLOWING QUESTIONNAIRE. DON'T SPEND TOO LONG OVER ANY
ONE QUESTION, JUST TICK YOUR FIRST REACTION.

1) Are you a member of the Youth Club?	Yes	☐ (if you tick here see 3)
	No	☐ (if you tick here see 2)
2) Are you the guest of a Youth Club Member?	Yes	☐
	No	☐
3) IF YOU DO NOT FALL into category 1) or 2) above then please state in what capacity you are here tonight.	_____	
4) Do you think the weekly subscriptions should be:	40p	☐
	40p–49p	☐
	50p–75p	☐
	75p–£1	☐
	Other (please give amount)?	————
5) The club is open Tuesday and Friday evenings. How often do you attend?	Once a week	☐
	Twice a week	☐
6) Which evening do YOU prefer to attend?	Tuesday	☐
	Friday	☐
7) What has influenced YOUR choice of evening in question 6?	It is not as crowded	☐
	My friends come that night	☐
	It is easier to book the sports facilities	☐
	Other reason (please state)	————

Figure 6.7

HONEYFIELDS YOUTH CLUB SURVEY

Your Youth Club Committee wants to improve your Club. Please help us by completing the following questionnaire. Don't spend too long over any one question, just tick your first reaction.

1. ARE YOU ATTENDING THE YOUTH CLUB TODAY AS A:

Paid-up Youth Club Member ☐

A weekly paid Member ☐

The guest of a Member ☐

Other (please explain)? _____

2. DO YOU THINK THE WEEKLY SUBSCRIPTIONS SHOULD BE:

Under 40p ☐

41p–50p ☐

51p–75p ☐

76p–£1 ☐

Other (please give amount)? _____

3. DO YOU ATTEND

Mostly Tuesday evenings ☐

Mostly Friday evenings ☐

No pattern of attendance? ☐

4. WHICH EVENING DO YOU PREFER TO ATTEND?
(TICK ONLY ONE BOX)

Tuesday ☐

Friday ☐

No preference ☐

5. WHAT HAS INFLUENCED YOUR CHOICE OF EVENING IN QUESTION 4?
(if applicable)

It is not as crowded ☐

My friends come that night ☐

It is easier to book the sports ☐
facilities

Other reason (please state) _____

Figure 6.8

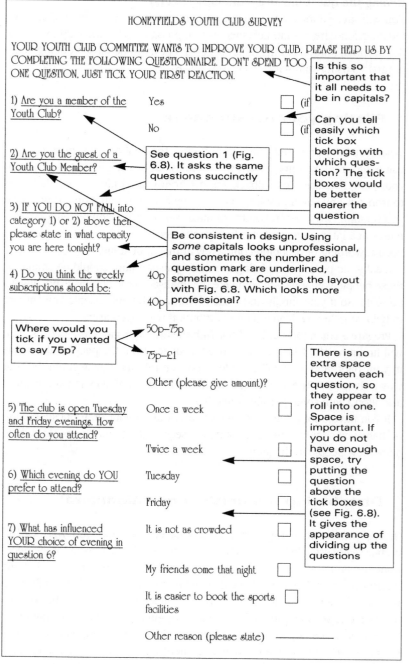

HONEYFIELDS YOUTH CLUB SURVEY

YOUR YOUTH CLUB COMMITTEE WANTS TO IMPROVE YOUR CLUB. PLEASE HELP US BY COMPLETING THE FOLLOWING QUESTIONNAIRE. DON'T SPEND TOO [Is this so important that it all needs to be in capitals?]
ONE QUESTION. JUST TICK YOUR FIRST REACTION.

1) Are you a member of the Youth Club?   Yes   ☐ (if

[Can you tell easily which tick box belongs with which question? The tick boxes would be better nearer the question]

No   ☐ (if

2) Are you the guest of a Youth Club Member?   [See question 1 (Fig. 6.8). It asks the same questions succinctly]   ☐

☐

3) IF YOU DO NOT FALL into category 1) or 2) above then please state in what capacity you are here tonight?

[Be consistent in design. Using *some* capitals looks unprofessional, and sometimes the number and question mark are underlined, sometimes not. Compare the layout with Fig. 6.8. Which looks more professional?]

4) Do you think the weekly subscriptions should be: 40p

40p

[Where would you tick if you wanted to say 75p?]   50p–75p   ☐

75p–£1   ☐

Other (please give amount)?

[There is no extra space between each question, so they appear to roll into one. Space is important. If you do not have enough space, try putting the question above the tick boxes (see Fig. 6.8). It gives the appearance of dividing up the questions]

5) The club is open Tuesday and Friday evenings. How often do you attend?   Once a week   ☐

Twice a week   ☐

6) Which evening do YOU prefer to attend?   Tuesday   ☐

Friday   ☐

7) What has influenced YOUR choice of evening in question 6?   It is not as crowded   ☐

My friends come that night   ☐

It is easier to book the sports facilities   ☐

Other reason (please state) ——————

Figure 6.9

Coding the questionnaire (summary sheets)
You will save yourself an immense amount of time if, at the time of devising the questionnaire, a summary sheet is also prepared. This will help to smooth the eventual analysis of the data collected. For more detail see Coding questionnaires using summary sheets, pp. 159–61.

▶ Piloting your questionnaire

When you have prepared your questionnaire, try it out on a few people before using it for real. You may be tempted to miss out this stage – but you do so at your peril, because the feedback you get from your volunteers will help you to iron out any small problems before they become mountains. It will save you hours of work when you try to make sense of the completed questionnaires at a later stage, and also help you to decide whether certain questions need rewording or dropping completely at this draft stage.

Ideally the people completing the draft questionnaire should be similar to those people you hope will complete the finalised copy, but this is not always possible. So if your family and close friends are the only people you can get to help you, then welcome their contribution with open arms.

Prepare a small form to hand out with the draft questionnaire because you will find it helpful to have the focused feedback from the people taking part in your pilot, and they will be able to concentrate their answers in the best way to help you. The following box shows the kinds of question you need to ask, along with some possible remedies.

If you have a lot of amendments to carry out on your draft questionnaire, perhaps you should consider piloting the second draft and if possible include a few new people in the pilot.

▶ Distributing the finished questionnaire

Unless you are meeting your interviewees face to face, you will need to prepare a covering letter in which you explain briefly the reason for the questionnaire and assure the respondent that you will treat as confidential all the information that they give. You should point out that, although you will strive to conceal the identity of all the informants, in some cases it may be possible for people to second-guess who provided certain information. For example, if there is only one department manager but 50 other staff completing a questionnaire, and you compare the management view with the employees, then the staff can easily guess from where the management view is coming.

How long did it take to complete the questionnaire?	If it's too long, you need to prune the questions or layout. People will not wish to spend more than a few minutes answering your questions.
Were the questions clear? (Did you have to read any question twice to make sense of it?)	Each question should be understood on first sight. Reword any question that fell short of this.
Were the instructions clear?	This is essential, especially if you are using filter techniques (that is, telling them to miss the next question, or go direct to page 2, if they answered in a certain way). Any confusion reported should prompt you to rewrite that instruction.
Did you find any question ambiguous?	Amend any question that could not be answered without confusion. Remember that every piece of information given will need to be analysed and probably counted. Ambiguous questions will cause you a major headache at the next stage.
Did you object to answering any question?	Do you really need this information? If you feel it is essential, ask it towards the end of your questionnaire, and also give a 'get-out' clause and tell your respondents that they do not have to answer if they would prefer not to. Sometimes people will answer if they do not feel pressurised.
Did you find the layout easy to follow?	You are more likely to get questionnaires returned if you pay attention to this detail.
Did you like the initial appearance of the questionnaire?	Once again, if people like the look of it, they are more likely to complete it.
Any comments?	

Compose your letter so that it is friendly and to the point. Long letters are seldom read all the way through. However, don't be so brief as to appear curt.

Return date

It is essential to give a date by which the questionnaire should be returned, as if you don't, it is likely to be put to one side to be completed when there is some spare time, in which case you may never receive it. Somewhere in the region of two weeks is about the right amount of time to allow. If you make the period too long, people are likely to put it to one side believing that they have ages to fill it in, and then they are likely to forget it completely.

Questionnaire return arrangements

Whether you enclose a stamped addressed envelope will depend on how you have arranged to distribute the questionnaire. It may be that you are arranged to leave them at a workplace or college with the agreement that you will return within an agreed time to collect the completed forms. If you do this, it's a good idea to call in a day or two before the appointed pick-up day and remind people that you will be calling the next day to pick up the completed questionnaires. A small reminder note given out at this stage might also help jog the memories of those taking part.

Consider the costs involved if you are relying totally on the postal system:

1. If you are wish to receive a reply, a stamped addressed envelope is a necessity.
2. You may also need to send out a reminder letter a couple of weeks later if you haven't received many replies.
3. Following this, you may receive requests from some people for a second questionnaire because they have lost the original one. You could have automatically sent a second questionnaire out at the 'reminder letter' stage but this would have involved extra photocopying costs, and, depending on the weight involved, extra postage costs.
4. Finally, there would be a letter of thanks.

Whether you have the time or inclination to go to these lengths is a personal matter; there is also the consideration of the costs involved. You need to decide whether it is worth the time and trouble of following the second, third and fourth stages advocated above. If you word your covering letter carefully, you could thank your respondents in advance for their help and add that, unless specifically requested, you did not intend to send out thank you letters in order to save postage costs.

Comparison between different methods of questionnaire distribution

The method you use to distribute your questionnaire will be personal to your research, but to help you to decide whether an electronic questionnaire is right for your research and give you some idea of average response rates and other related issues, Table 6.3 might be useful. Part B of this chapter provides details on how to produce an electronic questionnaire.

Various researchers, depending on the research programme being undertaken, judge the success or otherwise of the response rate differently. For example, it is difficult to compare the return response rate of a captive, interested audience, such as one that is sitting in a hospital waiting room being

TABLE 6.3 RESULTS OF RESPONSE RATE STUDIES USING ELECTRONIC
QUESTIONNAIRES

Studies seem to indicate that 'electronic' questionnaires have a very favourable reponse rate when compared to average response rates usually achieved by conventional mail surveys. Frankfort-Nachmias and Nachmias (1995) have found that the typical response rate to conventional mail as being 20–50%. Compare the typical response rate of 20–50% of conventional mail to the findings of various researchers below.

Walsh et al. (1992) carried out an online survey using self-selected and randomly selected respondents in a computer network survey	Randomly selected sample: 76% response rate	Self-selected sample: 96% response rate
Anderson and Gansneder (1995) undertook an electronic mail survey and computer monitored data survey for studying computer dedicated communication systems	76% response rate (of the overall 68% return) obtained by email	24% response rate (of the overall 68% return) obtained by conventional methods
Mahta and Sivadas (1995) compared the response rates to a conventional questionnaire with an email equivalent	The unsolicited email achieved a 40% response rate. However, the response rate increased to 63% if an introductory initial email was sent requesting participation in the study	45% response rate to the unsolicited mail questionnaire

Source: adapted from Walsh et al (1992); Anderson and Gansneder (1995); Mehta and Sivadas (1995)

asked to complete a one-page questionnaire on 'hospital waiting times' against the response rate of a field worker standing outside a supermarket trying to complete four-page questionnaires with passers-by. However, McNeill (1985) sees response rate as one of the major drawbacks of the postal method, in that it is usually around the 30–40 per cent, compared to the 80–90 per cent response rate that can be achieved in face-to-face research.

Comparisons of the work involved between questionnaire and face-to-face interview techniques are different depending on the research undertaken. Whether the questionnaires are administered in depth with just a few people, or are undertaken by someone standing on a street corner and asking passers-by to spare them a few minutes makes quite a difference. At a practical level, interviews are time consuming, inconvenient and, if much travel is involved, can be costly, but you will obtain a good response rate. Self-completion questionnaires, on the other hand, can be sent easily to a much larger number of people and will not take up as much personal time, but be prepared for a lower response rate.

Glastonbury and MacKean offer excellent advice on which method to choose:

> A rule of thumb guide is that if you are more interested in the depth and quality of your data than in having a large number of responses, then look carefully at interviewing. If your questions are fairly easy to answer and you want a lot of responses to facilitate statistical analysis, then self-completion may be for you. But, and it is an important reservation, keep practical issues well in focus – the time and resources you have for the data collection sequence, the accessibility of your sample, the administrative tasks surrounding the questionnaire, and your own interests and aptitudes. (Glastonbury and MacKean 1993:228)

Pre-coding questionnaires

The words 'analysing data' and 'computer' go together, as computers are extremely good at analysing information. Once you have successfully gathered the data, you will be faced with its analysis. If you only plan on gathering a small number of questionnaires, it is relatively easy to count up all the 'yes' replies, or the number of people who are under 20 years of age or whatever.

Whether it would be useful for you to introduce some kind of coding plan for your questionnaire is debatable. It is unlikely that you will be seeking a very large response rate and the time involved in setting up codings may not be of benefit to you. However, you should be aware of the use of pre-coding in questionnaires because, if you do decide that it would be useful for you, you need to incorporate coding into the questionnaire at the planning stage. Full details of pre-coding can be found in Coding data, pp. 157–9.

Analysis of data obtained

Chapter 7 deals in detail with analysing the data from your completed questionnaires and you should read this before you structure and pilot the questionnaire. The formation of the questions and presentation of various tick boxes will be important when the time comes to analyse the data.

PART B

▶ **Using a computer to lay out a questionnaire**

As you know, the layout of your questionnaire is extremely important. If you come to grips with your software early in the research stage, then using tables to prepare questionnaires effectively will not be daunting to you at this point.

Designing the layout of your questionnaire, where you can use plenty of space for ticking boxes or writing replies, is easy using your computer. The use of lines to separate various areas of the questionnaire can be effective, while shaded borders, line thickness, specific design styles or drop-shadow boxes can enhance the layout and help your questionnaire to look professional and appealing to the eye and hopefully entice the respondent to complete it.

Individual software packages are slightly different in their approach to table design, but the keywords to search initially in your online help facility or paper-based textbook are tables, borders and shading. If you are using Microsoft you can use the table toolbar to insert a table.

If you cannot see this toolbar on your screen, click on the word '**View**' (near the top left of your screen) followed by the word '**Toolbars**'. A drop-down menu will appear – click on the words '**Tables and Borders**'. Once you have the toolbar, it is simply a case of pointing to the pencil, clicking the left mouse button and drawing the table shape that you require.

Alternatively, if you do not feel confident in drawing a table layout, you can achieve the same aim by clicking on the word '**Table**' (nearer to the top centre of your screen), followed by '**Insert**' and then '**Table**'. The following dialog box will appear (see over); all you need to do is key in the number of columns and rows that you require. Do not worry if you're not sure of the number at the outset, you can always add more when you have completed the last row by tapping the **tab** key on your keyboard. In fact, tapping the **tab** key after inserting text in a column or row is the best way to manoeuvre around the table.

Table 6.4 (p. 145) gives you some idea of a typical 'table' layout that you could formulate using either of these methods.

Computer Support

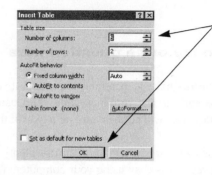

Simply fill in the numbers of columns and rows and press OK, and you will have the outline of a table that is ready for you to key in your data

▶ Creating a questionnaire to be distributed on the Internet

Using word-processing packages and email

If you have decided that you are going to distribute your questionnaire on the Internet to a specific discussion group, it is important that you design your questionnaire using specific formats, otherwise your finished questionnaire, that looked great when you sent it, will arrive at the other end looking rather scrambled. Another disadvantage of designing a questionnaire using just word-processing software is that it is difficult to ensure that your respondent can tick or put a cross in the box provided if it has been drawn in certain ways.

If you have inserted a box similar to this ❏ using the 'symbol' sign in your software, try to insert a cross into it. Not possible? If you must use boxes, you are better advised to draw boxes with the drawing rectangle icon, although this could be problematic in that the box might move out of alignment when viewed on the recipient's PC. To overcome this shifting of alignment, you need to constrict carefully text or objects into tightly drawn tables.

Another problem can be leaving space for your respondent to key in an answer. Just leaving space doesn't always work well. Once more the questionnaire layout can move out of alignment to a greater or lesser degree.

These problems do not always occur, however, and, if you haven't time to learn about Web pages before you send your questionnaire, you could always trial a dummy run of your proposed questionnaire by sending it to several email friends. Don't be surprised if some of them receive a perfect questionnaire and can reply with no problem, while others receive a copy of the questionnaire that does not look quite as intended, and inserting their replies (especially as regards to typing in blank spaces) causes slight problems.

Do not think that it is impossible to send out a questionnaire using word-processing software. Explain to your recipients that there might be a slight display problem, especially connected with alignment of items, and providing the problem is not so bad as to make the questionnaire unreadable the recipients will hopefully ignore the rather less than perfect layout.

If you are using Microsoft and wish to work with tables over the Internet, avoid using the **Insert Table** icon when you initially draw your table. It is better to use the **Draw Table** tools (click on **View**, **Toolbars**, **Tables** and **Borders** to get started) because there are some differences in how borders are applied and cells formatted by this method, and it is more compatible as a layout tool on Web pages.

▶ HTML and XML – what are they?

The World Wide Web is the fastest growing Internet resource and HTML (HyperText Markup Language) is the most common language that it understands at present. Almost all computers can view documents written using HTML, so if you learn the basic formatting commands, your questionnaire will be able to be read and completed easily by its recipient. It is also possible to convert documents created in other computer languages into an HTML document.

There are many books written for all the various computer systems that explain in great depth about the WWW, Web browsers and their relation to HTML. Many of these books explain in great detail how to produce your own Web page and place it on the Internet. Some include a CD-ROM disc that will enable you to produce quite complicated HTML documents and launch them on the WWW. However, this is not the remit of this book. This book is about research, but what could form a useful part of that research would be to send a simple questionnaire to various would-be respondents over the Internet. If, as part of that exercise, your appetite to learn more about HTML is whetted, do visit your local bookseller and see what is available for your computer system. It could be the start of a fascinating journey into the world of computers.

There are lots of online browsers and help about HTML that you could download from the Internet to your computer. If you decide to go down this route, do be sure that you (or a friend) can put right any default settings that might be affected by this. Downloaded Internet programs can (albeit infrequently) cause repercussions elsewhere and, unless you have an expert computer technician on hand, these could be frustrating.

XML (Extensible Markup Language) is another language much like HTML used to create Web pages, however, it is much more versatile than HTML. Both languages use a system of tags that describe components of a document, and both are subsets of something called 'Standard Generalised Markup Language' (SGML). The HTML 'tags' instruct a browser to do certain things with a document (usually involving aspects of presentation – font styles, sizes, spacing and so on), some tags also identify links to other Web pages, drawings and so on. Since these tags are mainly concerned with data presentations they cannot be used to describe the structure of data or the contents of a document.

XML allows tags to be defined by users. This gives users the ability to describe the structure of document information. However, this means that standard browsers will not be able to do anything with these extensions. This makes the software environment for XML more complex since it needs to use an associated language (XSL – Extensible Style Language) to do this.

Unless you have some overpowering urge to learn about the make-up of computer languages you really do not need to know a great deal more, but now when you see the acronyms HTML or XML you will have some idea what it is all about.

▶ Converting word-processed documents to HTML documents

It is possible to design your questionnaire in a word-processing format and then save it to a Web page format by deleting its file ending, for example **.doc** and inserting **.HTML** in its place. This has the effect of closing the word-processing document and reopening it in a format that can be published on the WWW. Keep an original copy when you try this, in case you need to rethink strategies. When conversion takes place, some elements of your word-processed document might change and it can be useful to see this before you email the questionnaire. It might be just a superficial change, such as a font size that hardly notices or it might be something that renders a specific question meaningless.

Set out below (Table 6.4) is a brief list of the main changes that can happen when you save a word-processed document as a Web page (that is, changing the **.doc** to .HTML when using 'Save As'). This does not mean that they *will* happen.

If you bear in mind these possible changes and modify the original design of your questionnaire as you proceed, you are less likely to spend time redesigning the first attempt because of conversion alterations.

If you're wondering whether it's worth the fuss, let me assure you that if

TABLE 6.4

FORMAT USED	POSSIBLE EFFECT WHEN THE FILE IS CONVERTED TO HTML
Bold, italic and underline effects	Usually successful, but some special underline effects, such as dotted underline, will not convert or will be changed. Using this method to produce dotted lines indicating where the reply should be keyed in is not successful
Drawing objects, such as text boxes, shadows, autoshapes	These will not be retained. You can use drawing tools in the Web page authoring environment by inserting Word Picture Objects
Drop caps	Drop caps are not successful and are lost in conversion. In the Web page environment you can increase the size of one letter by selecting it and clicking on Increase Font Size A. Alternatively if you have a graphic image of the letter you can insert that instead
Embossing, shadow, all capitals, small capitals, double strikethough and outline text effects	Usually these formats are lost, but the text remains
Font sizes	The font sizes that you have used will be mapped to the closest HTML size available, which ranges from 1 to 7. These numbers are not point sizes but are used as instructions for font sizes by Web browsers. This could change your layout
Footnotes and endnotes	These are lost in conversion
Headers and footers	These are lost in conversion
Highlighting	This is lost in conversion
Margins	These are modified. To control the layout of your page use a table
Newspaper columns	This will be lost. If you want a multi-column effect, use tables
Page borders	This is lost in conversion because there isn't an HTML equivalent for a page border. If you wish to make your page/s more attractive add a background (Format – background).
Page numbering	Page numbering is removed
Tables	Tables are mostly converted, although some settings that aren't supported in the Web page authoring environment are lost. It is better to use the Draw Table tools (click on View, Toolbars, Tables and Borders to get started) when you design a table. This is because there are some differences in how borders are applied and cells formatted by this method, and it is more compatible as a layout tool on Web pages
Tabs	Tabs usually appear as spaces in Web browsers so you might want to use indents or a table instead

you have the time it is. Go ahead and try it out; very often converting a file, or even just sending a word-processed questionnaire over the Internet has very little effect on its layout.

▶ Designing a Web page questionnaire

Before designing your own Web questionnaire, it is helpful to get clear in your own mind the background to what you are doing. The WWW publishes information in pages and these Web pages can include text, graphics, animations, videos, sounds, as well as links to other Web pages. You can move from Web page to Web page by clicking links that have been inserted within the individual page design.

Your Web page image
There are many opinions about the best way to structure and design Web pages and what makes a good Web site. The design of your questionnaire is bound to please some people but not others; but providing it is clear, can be followed readily and completed easily you will have achieved your goal. Designing a simple questionnaire within the bounds of small-scale research is not where you should include the gizmos such as video links or animation as these would only detract from your main purpose, which is to gather data. Also, downloading Web pages that contain lots of animations or sounds and so on takes longer and costs more, so your proposed respondent will probably not wish to pay extra in order to see your special effects, even if you think they're great. Keep things simple.

Restrictions in Web page design
Because of the unique nature of HTML, there are certain restrictions that you should bear in mind before you begin designing your questionnaire. Most of these have been outlined in Table 6.4, so it would be sensible to read these through again before proceeding further. HTML is much more powerful than .doc when used expertly.

Learn from other Web site designs
At this point in your research you should have a rough draft of the order and content of your questions, together with an approximate idea of your proposed layout. Before you begin to design your own Web questionnaire, you should visit several other Web sites to see what other people have designed.

If you search the Internet using keywords such as Questionnaire,

Questionnaire design, Research and so on, you will be surprised by the wealth of information available. You will also notice many companies and individuals that will design Web pages and questionnaires for you – at a price.

Software specifically written for online questionnaire work

As you surf the Internet looking at the layout of other people's online questionnaires, you will notice articles and advertisements for specific questionnaire software. There is even questionnaire software that runs on a palmtop computer that enables the respondent to select or write answers with a special pen directly onto the hand-held screen. This could be useful for forms that need to be filled in on the move, during home visits, or perhaps for a salesman at a trade fair, who has to deal with half a dozen people at once. Although lots of the software will not be relevant to a small-scale one-off research project, it will give you some idea of how big a market this is, and, if you ever decide to go into a career in marketing, you will know exactly the scope of what is available.

Web page basic design training

If you have time, it would help if you looked at one or two specialist books or perhaps joined an evening class so that you are armed with some background and hands-on experience that will raise your confidence. There are many short, inexpensive courses on offer at local schools, colleges and universities, sometimes Web page design is offered as a short one-day Saturday course. This is all you would need to get you started. Microsoft FrontPage is a popular beginners' software and you can find free tutorials and details online at http://wsabstract.com/frontpage.htm. Once you have mastered the overall concept of Web pages, you are ready to create your own.

▶ Creating your own online Web questionnaire

The biggest advantage of creating your questionnaire as a Web page is that its layout can look very professional and when returned to you the answers will be clearly indicated – you cannot mistake where the tick is, as sometimes happens with manually filled in questionnaires.

You will quite easily be able to insert small check boxes or option buttons that enable your respondent to click where they wish to indicate an affirmative or negative reply and an automatic tick will appear in that box. Or you can insert a box where your respondent can choose from the pre-prepared drop-down list of optional replies just by clicking on a downward arrow beside the question. You could add a scroll bar to enable quick access around your document, or a background texture, pattern effect or colour wash that if chosen carefully is pleasing to the eye.

One of its important features is that you can protect your questionnaire (Protect Form) so those users can only enter information where you indicate. They are then unable to move text around or mistakenly insert spaces or other unwanted formats, which is something that could happen with a word-processed questionnaire sent over the Internet.

You can combine various features when creating your Web questionnaire, using tables alongside text alignment or borders to designate areas to be filled in, and shadings to highlight headings, together with other special elements that can make your form easier to fill out.

If you are using Microsoft software, you could have a practice run simply by trying out the Wizard sample Web pages available (Click **File** – **New** – **Web Pages** – and then choose the Wizard you fancy by double clicking on it). When you have played enough, have a go at creating your own Web page from scratch, this time choose '**Blank Page**' but check that you have the 'Forms' toolbar on (**View** – **Toolbars**). Remember that if you wish to use a table it is better to use the **Draw Table** tools (click on **View**, **Toolbars**, **Tables** and **Borders** to get started) when you design the table.

When you have finished your online questionnaire, you need to give your respondent a return email address, and a brief thank you at the end is polite.

Before you embark on actually sending out a trial questionnaire to a friend, do read the next section as you do not want to end up having to cancel your email account and choking up your server.

If you do not feel ready or able to produce your own Web page question-naire just yet but feel comfortable with word-processing software, perhaps this is the road that you should go down initially. Put Web page design on the back burner until you have the time to devote to its creation, which will prob-ably be after your research has finished.

▶ A touch of caution before you begin

It has been known for email communications to grow so large that they become unwieldy. Several newspaper reports have highlighted the problems involved when one recipient of email passes copies of the email on to several of their friends. Sometimes this is at the encouragement or explicit instruc-tion of the originator of the email. We have all heard the horror stories of people passing on supposed computer viruses, or chain letters that get out of hand, which at best can waste people's time, but even well-intentioned communications sometimes go awry.

The proliferation of these kinds of message puts a strain on email systems. As messages are forwarded, gathering more names in the header as they go, they get bigger and take up more bandwidth in the system. This wastes time and resources and slows down legitimate email traffic. If anyone is in doubt about how far and fast an email communication can spread then read on.

According to the TechNews pages at the Canadian online news agency 'Canoe', officials pulled the plug on an Internet project started by a 5th grade class at a school in Nova Scotia, Canada. The class teacher decided to enrich her pupil's geographical and computer knowledge by asking her 17 pupils to email the following message to one friend.

> We are in grade 5 at school [They gave details of their school at this point]. We have 7 girls and 10 boys in our class. We have decided to map an email project. We are curious to see where in the world our email will travel by Internet between the period of 8 April–7 June. We would like your help. If you receive this message, we ask that you:
>
> 1. email back and tell us your location so we can plot it on our world map, and
> 2. send our class email on to more people. Thank you for any help you can give.
>
> Our e-mail address is . . .

According to Canoe, the class project started on a Wednesday and on the Thursday morning there were 208 responses. The volume kept increasing and when the email account was closed down they were getting approximately 150 responses *per hour*. Responses came from as far afield as Riyadh, Saudi Arabia, Sarajevo, Bosnia-Hercegovina, Los Angeles and a research vessel several hundred miles off the coast of Brazil. The class teacher said that they had started by putting coloured pins on a wall in the classroom each time a new location came in, but they ran out of coloured drawing pins pretty quickly.

Cancelling the email account seemed to be the only solution, but according to Wired News even that was not enough:

> after their server choked and they cancelled their email account the phone calls started coming. Faxes too. Messages even arrived via that quaint mode of communication, the post office. (Wired News 11 June 1999)

This is not an isolated case of well-intentioned emails eventually becoming unmanageable. It is for this reason that you are advised to seek out a distinct group of people to email as has already been discussed in Finding your inter-view audience online, pp. 116–17.

It would also be wise to include a short sentence at the beginning of your email to the effect that after a given date it is too late for the data to be included. Don't give your recipients too long to reply, most emails are answered within a day or so of receipt, so a week (or two at the outside) can be ample time. Also let your recipient know that you do not want them to pass on a copy of your questionnaire to a friend because you do not have the resources or time to collate and evaluate a large questionnaire return. It is very important that you put these instructions at the very beginning of the questionnaire, as the deed may have been done before they read to the end.

7 Analysing the Data

PART A

A chaotic mass of paper strewn over the desk is not the trap you want to fall into when you begin to analyse the data that you have collected. In a small-scale research study it is important that you plan how you propose to analyse your data at the same time as you plan how you are going to gather it. Data should be recorded in a format that facilitates the easiest possible analysis, so the decisions you made earlier in your research process will have a crucial impact on how long or short, easy or frustrating the analysis is.

At the outset you must ensure that your analysis is as true and accurate a picture of the data gathered as possible. All your data will need scrutinising, and, if your data gathering focus was originally well designed, you should now be in a position to produce a meaningful, non-biased interpretation.

You do not need to be a mathematical genius or a statistical specialist in order to follow the methods of analysis that follow. Many people despair at the very mention of the word 'maths' but, rather than going down that path, think of this stage in your research as an exciting one – you are about to test your hypothesis and find out whether your gut feelings about your research topic have been supported by the views of others.

▶ Qualititative observation research

Let's say that your research remit was to look into the use made of a company's canteen facilities. The management would like to know why more staff do not make use of the facility. Your initial feelings had been that the layout of the canteen was wrong, there wasn't enough sitting space and customers felt that prices were too high.

You divided your research into two distinct parts, the first was a question-naire completed by a cross section of staff who were not necessarily canteen users. The second part was field work carried out by you, in which you sat at regular intervals and at different times of the day in a corner of the canteen recording what was taking place. You have now ended up with 25 pages of handwritten A4 notes plus several tick lists where you recorded, for example, each time a customer purchased just a hot or cold drink, whether customers were male or female, or how many people were in a queue at given times.

Where do you begin? Well, during the time you sat in the canteen there would have been particular incidents that featured regularly. Perhaps the cutlery box ran out of clean spoons at regular intervals, or a would-be customer walked in the door, saw a long queue of people and walked away. These happenings would be recorded in your notes with, hopefully, a note of the time that they had taken place. What you need to do now is extract that information into separate categories.

Start by writing general headings at the top of A4 paper or large cards; you might find it useful to use the paper landscape (longer width). In the above case, some of the headings might be:

Queues
Customers
Staff
Cleanliness
Cutlery/crockery

From the main headings you need to break the information down further by drawing columns down the page. The heading Customers might now look as follows:

Customers						
Time	**Gender**	**Location**	**Problem**	**Outcome**	**Staff Involvment?**	**Comments**

With hindsight it is easy to say that this type of form would have helped had it been prepared in advance, but in many cases you have no idea what is likely to happen, that is the nature of research. However, you could 'second guess' possible situations and create some sort of form (with plenty of space for the unexpected) to take with you when you start your research initially.

Work systematically through your handwritten notes and, as you transfer the information to the various headed sheets, cross it through in the notes. A personal coding added to the above will ensure that the minimum writing takes place, so, for example, if everything is fine insert a ✓. As you transfer more and more information, your form might begin to look as follows:

Customers						
Time	**Gender**	**Location**	**Problem**	**Outcome**	**Staff Involvment?**	**Comments**
am 8.30 X 8.35 X 8.37 X 8.40 X 8.44 X 8.50	F F × 2 M M × 3 F & M M × 2	At table	No sugar	Taken from another table	N	No sugar on ¾ of tables
8.40	F	At counter	Waited – no staff to take money	Shouted to staff in the kitchens	Y	Waited two mins before calling (had hot food)
8.55	M	At table	Upset coffee	Went to counter (& returned cloth to counter)	Yes – gave cloth	Customer wiped table & left floor wet
9.00	F Staff member	Canteen	Filled sugar bowls placed on all tables. Ignored wet floor.			

Key: ✓ = everything fine; X = identical incident; Y = Yes; N = No; F = Female; M = Male

From the small amount of information given, it is already easy to see a picture building up. It looks as though some staff buy early morning coffee before starting work, so why don't canteen staff arrive earlier to fill up the sugar bowls, or prepare them the night before? If there is a surge of people between 8.30 and 9.00, perhaps canteen staff time needs to be investigated; there may need to be someone on duty at the till throughout that period. Perhaps the food available needs to be considered, hot buttered toast or cereals offered at this time might sell well if not already on the menu.

When the researcher looks at the results of these findings and compares them with the findings of the staff questionnaire that was also used, it may be that a clear picture emerges as to why staff do not use the canteen.

Depending on how many times an incident occurs, you might wish to further break your data down into a number format, for example:

Between 12.00 and 13.00 hours:
  12 staff could not find a table
  11 staff looked in the canteen and immediately walked away
  4 staff had to search for a full salt pot
  2 staff hit their ankles on trays balanced on floor by the 'return tray' pile

Staff numbers using canteen:
  8.30–9 am = 49
  9–10 am   = 10
  10–11 am = 41
  11–12   =   2
  12–1 pm   = 155
  1–2 pm   = 109
  2–3 pm   = 15
  3–4 pm   = 35
  4–4.30 pm =   6
  . . . and so on. You could break this down further into gender or age if this had a bearing on your research.

It is worth considering the presentation of the analysed results of most of this kind of data in a diagram or chart, which has more impact and is easier to see at a glance the findings when compared with pages of written description. However, some overall concepts or individual points will merit an individual mention when you are writing up your findings.

▶ Audio/video data

Audio or video data is likely to be either original data that you have generated yourself or archive data produced by someone else that you wish to view. To analyse this kind of material the researcher needs to have some idea of what they are looking for or hoping to extract from the 'snapshot' presented. The advantages and disadvantages of using this method for collecting data have been covered in Chapter 3 (see Observation, pp. 40–2) but, whether you are analysing original or archive data, the successful extract of useful data still depends on one thing – preparation on the part of the researcher.

An audio or video recording may have been used in order to observe behaviour, but there are many situations where behaviour is so complex that it is not possible to isolate clearly what is happening. One of the biggest problems with observational studies is that it is extremely time consuming to make sense of the data and much evidence can be missed because the researcher is not focused. To overcome this problem, categories need to be drawn up in advance and decisions made on the types of behaviour to be recorded. Definitions of what constitutes 'correct' behaviour, or 'incorrect' behaviour, what is 'normal' or 'acceptable' must be devised so that the researcher has clear criteria before they begin to view or listen to the evidence.

For example, let us imagine that the focus of the research is to discover the initial impression that visitors have of a company. As well as using questionnaires with customers and reception staff, a video was made of the reception area on a busy morning. The videotape will enable the researcher to view the sequences of personal interaction, which include the totality of each person's verbal, gestural and postural communication. The researcher may decide to concentrate on the actions and gestures of the reception staff alongside the administrative procedures in place. The checklist that is drawn up might look something like the list on the following page.

Before viewing the video the researcher would have drawn up a checklist of what constitutes open or closed body language on the part of the receptionist and would be able to check against this if necessary as the video is played. Bales (1950) devised an example of drawing up checklists for observational studies when studying group discussions. For example he arrived at the following major categories of behaviour:

- Emotionally positive responses, for example agrees
- Problem-solving responses, for example answers giving opinion
- Problem-solving responses, for example answers asking opinion
- Emotionally negative responses, for example disagrees

The advantage of preparing categories in advance is that the observer knows what to look for and it is a simple matter just to tick a column rather than endeavour to write down details of what is happening.

Having decided on the behaviour(s) that is to be observed and drawn up the necessary checklist(s), the researcher is ready to view the video and tick the

Customer M = male F = female	Length of time before greeted	Did receptionist smile at customer immediately?		Receptionist's body language?		Was receptionist able to deal with customer's requirements personally?		Did customer need to wait?		If so, was a seat offered?		Total time of wait	Notes
		Y	N	OPEN	CLOSED	Y	N	Y	N	Y	N		
2 M	15 secs	✓		✓				✓		✓		5 mins	* only three chairs, parcels piled on one
M	25 secs	✓		✓			✓		✓				
F + child	20 secs	✓			✓		✓	✓			✓	6 mins	No chairs free *

appropriate columns. The advantage of using a recorded medium is that it can be rewound and reviewed at any point should the action become 'very busy' or 'confusing'. At this stage it is often useful to carry out a trial run first to discover any glaring errors in the checklists or techniques.

To establish the reliability of the observation the researcher might enlist the help of one or two colleagues who would be willing to watch and score the same video using the checklists.

The above advice is equally relevant for video or audio recordings, although many of the visual signals will be missing when there is only voice. However, it is still possible to pick up on certain cues through the inflection of tone, or pauses that might signal embarrassment or personal feelings and so on. In some research situations it is necessary to transcribe word for word what has been said before analysing the material and this is a very time-consuming task, especially if the researcher has to write out in longhand the transcript.

▶ Coding data

Where the research has involved a lot of open-ended questions, the analysis can sometimes be problematic and needs to be carefully handled.

Simple coding

If the respondent was given a limited space within a questionnaire format to fill in personal comments, it is somewhat easier because they will be answering within the framework of a topic. It might be useful to draw up a simple coding frame once you have gathered in the questionnaires and have had time to glance through the individual responses.

The questionnaire that accompanied the canteen research in the previous section might have had a question that gave the respondent an opportunity to express a personal opinion as to how they feel that the canteen could be improved. Answers are likely to fall into predictable categories, such as lower prices, improve service, modernise premises and so on. You could code these categories, lower prices becoming 01, improve service 02, modernise premises 03 and so on. On each occasion that the reply falls within a pre-coded category all you have to do is write the number beside it. When you eventually analyse the questionnaire in detail, your coded categories are ready.

Individual topic coding numbers

There will always be an answer that falls outside a coded area and then it is up the researcher to decide whether it is important enough to mention in the write-up. It might be that the comment is very important, had not been thought about before and the researcher wishes to follow it up, if there is time.

If the open-ended answers are individual and perhaps in more depth than a simple sentence answer, it is likely that the researcher will wish to include those comments or opinions as an integral part of the write-up, in some cases perhaps quoting certain observations word for word. Some researchers organise this type of information by transferring whole paragraphs of relevant information to subject sheets. If, for example, the research was about school-aged teenagers in the new millennium and the researcher had interviewed ten teenagers in one-to-one in-depth interviews, it is likely that these interviews will have generated a substantial amount of written notes, all of which will now need to be analysed.

Analysis could be tackled by giving the young people individual coding numbers which will help a little to reduce the amount of writing that will need to be undertaking. Relevant topic headings could then be written at the top of sheets of A4 paper (for example Home experiences, Friends, Family, Drugs, School and so on) and each time a teenager discussed a particular subject that comes under a topic heading then reference can be made to it on the appropriate page. This can be done in several ways:

1. If the researcher's notes are easy to read, single-sided photocopies could be made using a different colour paper for each child's interview notes. Then each time that child talks about a subject that comes under a topic heading it is an easy matter to cut and paste the information onto the relevant heading sheet. The colour of the paper gives instant information about the identity of the child, which will save coding numbers.
2. Once all the relevant information has been extracted from the notes the original versions should not be needed again, but they should not be thrown away until the research is completed, just in case verification should be needed. The disadvantage of this method is that original notes are sometimes very wordy and ramble on before getting to the important section, which could involve the researcher in rereading unimportant ramblings more than once.
3. The researcher could extract the important information and transfer a much shorter version of the important points to the appropriate topic sheet. A coding number for the teenager and the page from which the summary was made would need to be added in case it was necessary to refer back to the original at some point.
4. Lastly a combination of method 2 above where the researcher is

summarising information plus the recording of the exact wording of any pertinent sentences that a teenager might utter or important issues that the teenager raises. This has the advantage that when the final writing is made the researcher has immediately to hand the individual insights and comments which they might wish to include in the final documentation.

By grouping the information under subject headings the researcher can easily see the frequency with which a subject is raised and will be in a position to draw out from the research similarities that exist between the respondents as well as any patterns that emerge. It might be that the female teenagers in the study seem to report that they have fewer friends than the males who seem to have a wide range of friends with whom they enjoy going out socially.

On closer inspection it might be that, although the girls have only one or two friends, these friendships are quite intense, with both members of the friendship supporting the other, sharing secrets and generally behaving in a closer alliance. On discovering this pattern, the researcher might wish to look at existing research to see whether this pattern is the norm within this age group. The findings could lead to a whole new avenue of research or at least highlight an area that had not been considered before.

▶ Coding questionnaires using summary sheets

Once all the questionnaires have been collected, the researcher needs to draw from them the necessary information, and, although this may seem to be a purely mechanical and straightforward task, it can be fraught with difficulties, especially if a number of open-ended questions have been used.

A sheet needs to be written on which various ticks can be recorded as the researcher works through the completed questionnaires. Ideally this sheet should be designed at the draft stage of preparing the actual questionnaire sheet and used at the pilot questionnaire stage. Preparation in advance will save an immense amount of time at the analysis stage, as it is easier to iron out any 'bugs' before the actual questionnaire is sent out.

A summary sheet (Figure 7.1) has been drawn up for part of the Youth Club Survey (Figure 6.8) used earlier. Look especially at the way that the open-ended questions have been dealt with. It may not be as easy to record open-ended questions, as shown in Figure 7.2. Sometimes the answers are 'wordy' or more complicated, and, if this is the case, it may be better to record the responses on a separate summary sheet. The questionnaire number can still be used so that it is possible to refer back to the original if necessary.

Transferring the information from questionnaires to summary sheets can

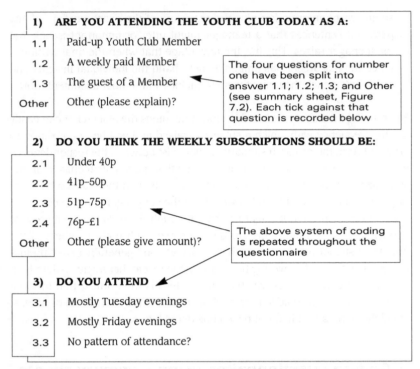

1)   ARE YOU ATTENDING THE YOUTH CLUB TODAY AS A:

1.1	Paid-up Youth Club Member
1.2	A weekly paid Member
1.3	The guest of a Member
Other	Other (please explain)?

The four questions for number one have been split into answer 1.1; 1.2; 1.3; and Other (see summary sheet, Figure 7.2). Each tick against that question is recorded below

2)   DO YOU THINK THE WEEKLY SUBSCRIPTIONS SHOULD BE:

2.1	Under 40p
2.2	41p–50p
2.3	51p–75p
2.4	76p–£1
Other	Other (please give amount)?

The above system of coding is repeated throughout the questionnaire

3)   DO YOU ATTEND

3.1	Mostly Tuesday evenings
3.2	Mostly Friday evenings
3.3	No pattern of attendance?

Figure 7.1 Example of coding a questionnaire

No.	Question 1				Question 2					Question 3		
	1.1	1.2	1.3	Other	2.1	2.2	2.3	2.4	Other	31.	3.2	3.3
1	✓				✓						✓	
2		✓				✓					✓	
3		✓							35p			✓
4			✓		✓							✓
5	✓					✓				✓		
6				gate-crashed					free			✓
7		✓					✓				✓	

The No. refers to the number of the questionnaire. If you number all the questionnaires in the top right-hand corner, you can easily refer back to the original if necessary. The open-ended questions in this questionnaire are not too problematic as the answers are likely to be limited. In the case of question 2 the answer can only be an amount of money, therefore it is fairly straightforward to look at the summary sheet when it is finished and see whether any regular pattern has emerged.

Figure 7.2 Example of a summary sheet

be boring, and, if the questionnaires were not well written or the summary sheets not prepared at the time the questionnaires were originally conceived, it can also be problematic. However, it is something that has to be done as part of the research process and it is better to lay aside several large chunks of time in order to complete it quickly. If you let the operation drag on over a number of weeks, you will be utterly fed up with the whole process. Remember to keep all original questionnaires until the research is completely finished just in case they are needed.

▶ Tabulation

In most research, the data, once collected, coded and analysed, is presented in some kind of tabulated form. There is nothing particularly complex about this; it is simply a matter of counting different data findings into different classes. A simple example of this can be seen in Table 7.1.

However, by displaying information in its simplest form, useful specific detail may be lost. For example, in Table 7.1 the reader might like to have been able to see at a glance a breakdown of the different gender opinions, or details of the exam subjects being undertaken – questions might arise as to whether those students undertaking political studies tended to have different opinions compared to other members of the group. It might be that parental opinions or voting tendencies had a bearing on the students' opinions. Unless you plan to gather this specific information in advance you will obviously be unable to present this kind of detailed information at analysis.

TABLE 7.1

Party political preferences of 6th form students

Party	Number of students
Conservative	29
Labour	35
All other parties	14
None	12

It is helpful to form some idea in the planning stage of research of what tabulations might be required, as this can help to clarify the research objectives and act as a check that relevant information is being sought during the research itself. It is not possible, however, to draw up exact tabulation plans at the planning stage, as many tabulations cannot be decided until initial analysis of results take place.

▶ Cross tabulation

Quantitative social science results are frequently presented in a cross tabulated analytical table. When you want to show how respondents answered on two or more questions at the same time, the results can be displayed clearly in a cross tabulation table.

Tables should always have a simple self-explanatory title and for maximum impact they should show *only* the relevant points that you wish the table to illustrate. Some indication of the number of cases on which the statistics are based, whether presented as a subheading or a note placed immediately underneath the table itself, is also very useful.

Had the research been about the amount of time that young teenagers spent in front of the television, the cross tabulated results might look something like Table 7.2 below. Note the self-explanatory title.

TABLE 7.2

Percentage of younger teenagers who watch television for more than four hours every day [table of results one]			
Gender	Age 13	Age 14	Age 15	Age 16
Female	49%	58%	87%	65%
Male	32%	60%	89%	55%

200 teenagers between the age of 13 and 16 were interviewed in this survey.
The ratio was 50% male/female.

It is possible to see at a glance in this tabulation the percentage of males compared with females in various age categories who watch TV for more than four hours each day. Notice that information on the number of cases on which the statistics are based has been given in the note underneath the table. This cross tabulation presentation obviously gives the reader much more information than the simple tabulation presented in Table 7.1.

Formulating a cross tabulation

In order to draw up cross tabulated results you must first determine which is your independent variable (traditionally a column heading) and which your dependent variable (usually found in the row). Cross tabulation is a way of representing how categories of one variable (independent variable) are distributed across the categories of another variable (dependent variable). This puts researchers in the position of being able to see whether there are any patterns of association.

In the case of Table 7.2, it might be that other collected data indicated possible reasons for the findings. For example, perhaps the parents were more likely to control the viewing times of 13/14-year olds or maybe the extra freedom normally given to 16-year-olds enabled them to choose to go out with friends rather than stay at home. The research might highlight the fact that the females watched the 'soaps' regularly, whereas the males showed less interest, or that the males preferred to spend their time playing computer games. A more complex cross tabulation presentation would be one way of presenting these kinds of pattern.

Complex cross tabulation tables (sometimes known as contingency tables) describe and analyse the data between several variables in the data set; usually the rows and columns all have their own totals. In such multifaceted data tables it can be difficult to show the reader the nature of the causal relationship to be found among the variables, that is if the researcher can determine them in the first place.

Reading a cross tabulation matrix

The figure that is contained in each cell is known as the raw frequency. The tabulation below (Table 7.3) shows adults' satisfaction with their daily newspapers. As part of the research, data has also been collected on each respondent's final educational attainment.

Independent variables explain or predict an outcome or response, which is the dependent variable under study. In Table 7.3 the independent variable of 'very satisfied indeed' shows a dependent variable of 10% in respect of those respondents with advanced university degrees being very satisfied with their daily newspaper. Unless the variables being studied are demographic, the independent variable is determined by the study's objectives. For instance, if the objective is to determine whether the level of satisfaction with the newspaper is influenced by educational attainment, the level of satisfaction is our independent variable and the educational attainment the dependent one.

TABLE 7.3 OVERALL SATISFACTION WITH DAILY NEWSPAPER

Satisfaction rating					Highest level of educational attainment % within each 'satisfaction rating' group				
Very satisfied indeed	Satisfied	Not very satisfied	No regular daily paper bought	Other*	No formal examinations	At least one – five GCSE passes	At least one A or A/S level pass	University degree	Advanced university degree
✓					36	18	20	16	10
	✓				30	14	14	32	20
		✓			10	32	21	10	27
			✓		10	25	18	19	28
				✓	24	11	27	23	15
Totals					100	100	100	100	100

Results of questionnaire completed by 160 men and 150 women

Calculating tabulation tables

It is possible to calculate tabulation tables using an ordinary calculator and then present the information in a table format. If the data to be analysed is quite small, this might be the simplest way to proceed. However, if you have gathered quite a lot of data or if you are beginning to enjoy letting the computer do all the work for you, then read the information on computer packages that will do everything for you. See Popular specialist software packages – SPSS, Ethnograph and NUD*IST, pp. 179–81. The very least you should do is let the computer draw up the table for you using a word-processing or spreadsheet package. See Using a computer to lay out a questionnaire on p. 141 if you'd like to know how to do this.

▶ Different data measurement scales

There are many methods of measuring research findings and it is usually at this point in a small-scale research project that researchers feel inadequate in their ability to correlate the data. The approach taken for turning the collected material into meaningful data will depend on the research design and methods of investigations chosen but there is usually a distinction between quantitative and qualitative data analysis. Hitchcock and Hughes succinctly contrast these two styles of analysis:

> Quantitative analysis principally involves the measurement of the amount, extent, incidence, or patterning of particular events so as to draw some general findings. In contrast, qualitative analysis, under-pinned as it is by a commitment to the situation, focuses primarily on identifying the meanings of social situations and the organisation of the activities in question. (Hitchcock and Hughes 1992:73)

It might not be possible to draw general findings from a small-scale research project because of its very size. It is impossible to generalise if you have only interviewed a small number of people, but small-scale research findings can be enlightening and informative and an instrument in bringing about change within a company or educational setting.

There are four main scales of data measurement which small-scale researchers need to be aware of and these are now explained.

Nominal scales

A nominal scale is a classification of measurement that has distinct differences; it is neither scaled nor measured in any way. An example of nominal scales would be

    male/female
    yes/no
    user/non-user

Nominal scales tend to be the simplest measurement scale. Data is generally classified as nominal if no order exists between the categories (for example eye colour).

Ordinal scales

These are nominal scales that order the data in some way, often by ranking it into order of magnitude. If a list reflected that person A was better at tennis than person B but it did not indicate 'better by how much', that could be thought of as an ordinal scale.

School reports are often given in the form of ordinal scales; the parent can read that their child came third in a maths test, but is not told the difference between the various positions of the children. Perhaps the child that came first obtained 85% correct answers and the child that came third achieved only 30% correct answers, but, to the parent, coming 'third' implies a good achievement mark.

In a questionnaire this might have been reflected in a question that asked the respondent to tick from an appropriate list similar to the one that follows:

I agree wholeheartedly	☐
I agree somewhat	☐
I do not have an opinion	☐
I disagree	☐
I disagree strongly	☐

Measuring the exact difference in agreement or disagreement to the question is not possible, it can only be ordered into a scale.

Measurements with ordinal scales are ordered in the sense that higher numbers represent higher values, however, the intervals between numbers are not necessarily equal. There is no 'true' zero point for ordinal scales since the zero point is chosen arbitrarily.

Data is classified as ordinal if an order exists, for example socio-economic status, exam results.

Interval scales

These are similar to ordinal scales, but they have intervals between points to show relative amounts, so that the statistics have more meaning. One of the most common examples of an interval measurement is the Fahrenheit temperature scale. The difference between 45° and 55° is the same as the difference between 65° and 75°. Equal distances measure equal amounts.

An interval scale does not have a 'true' zero point and therefore it is not possible to make statements about how many times higher one score is than another. For example, if you were measuring anxiety ratings, it would not be possible to say that a person with a score of 30 was twice as anxious as a person with a score of 15.

If an interval scale was applied to IQ scores, there would the same difference in intelligence between two people with IQs of 110 and 90 respectively as there was between two people with IQs of 70 and 90. It is very dubious that this is borne out in practice and it would be better to treat this data as ordinal level data.

Ratio scale

A ratio is used to compare amounts. For example, a friend is mixing cement to make a patio and uses four shovels of sand and gravel and one shovel of cement. The ratio in that case would be 4:1 (the sign : is used to compare). Ratios are like fractions in that whatever you do to one number, you do to the other. So, if the above ratio was doubled and your friend used eight shovels of sand and two of cement, you would express it as 4:1 = 8:2 (4 × 2 = 8 and 1 × 2 = 2). The numbers are never changed around and it is not necessary to have the smallest number first.

It is easy to calculate the ratio providing you have certain basic information. In the example of the canteen research discussed at the beginning of this chapter, you could work out a ratio of various drinks sold. For example:

8 cups of coffee/4 cups of tea/4 glasses of soft drinks
The ratio of coffee to tea and soft drink is 8:4:4

You can make numbers smaller in a similar way to that used with fractions by dividing each number by the same; therefore you could express the above figures as 2:1:1 (that is, divide each number by 4).

If these figures were magnified to reflect the higher and more likely figure of the real world and the canteen sold 800 cups of coffee, 400 cups of tea and 400 soft drinks daily on a regular basis and your research remit was to find painless ways to make the canteen pay for itself as its operation costs were soaring, the ratio is still the same 2:1:1 even with the higher figures. If you increased the cost of coffee by 5p a cup but reduced the tea by 5p a cup to 'sweeten the blow of increased prices' and left the soft drink price static, you will still recoup more money since the coffee:tea ratio is 2:1. Therefore you will have made an extra £40 (800 × 5p) on the coffee, while only losing £20 on the tea (400 × 5p). This scenario would need to be considered in much more depth and all prices and sales considered alongside other factors involved, but it should give you a basic understanding of the use of ratio scales.

A ratio scale is like an interval scale in that equal differences represent equal amounts, the difference being that, in a ratio scale, an absolute measurement is valid.

▶ Other types of variable

In statistics the word variable generally means an item of data collected on each sampling unit. There are two broad types of variables – qualitative and quantitative (or numeric). These can be broken down further into subtypes if required, qualitative data that can be ordinal or nominal, and numeric data can be discrete.

Qualitative data

Data is said to be *qualitative* if the observations belonging to it are separate and distinct. For example, the number of employees in a department, number of students in a class group, the number of females, males and so on.

All qualitative data is inherently *discrete*, in that there are a finite number of possible categories into which observations may fall. Data can be further classified as *nominal* if there is no natural order between the classifications or categories, for example eye colour, or *ordinal* if some kind of ordering exists, for example age 20–30, 31–40, 41–50 and so on.

Quantitative data

When quantitative observation data is numerical, the data is said to be *discrete*, that is, the data *must be able to be counted*, for example the number of cups of coffee sold in one day, or the number of schoolchildren who smoke cigarettes daily.

The data is also said to be *continuous* if the measurements take on value often within the same range, for example the number of schoolchildren *aged 14* who smoke cigarettes daily.

Quantities such as age, gender and so on are called *variables* simply because they vary from one observation to another.

▶ Averages

It is better to avoid the word 'average' when you come to write up the results of your findings. Average is often taken to refer to the arithmetic mean (see below), but it can also signify the median, the mode, the geometric mean and so on. To avoid confusion and be more precise in your presentation use the correct term to sum up how you arrived at your figures. The main terms are summarised below.

The arithmetic mean

The word arithmetic is often written before mean in statistical data because there are other things in maths that are called mean. A mean figure is the result obtained by adding together the numbers or quantities in a set and dividing the answer by the total members in that set. So, if you wanted to find out the average cost of three articles for which you paid £3, £5 and £4, you add together 3 + 5 + 4 = 12, and divide the total by 3 because there are three articles, that is, 12 ÷ 3 = 4. In this case you would say that the average cost was £4.

When to use the mean average. In small-scale research the mean average could be used when the data gathered included lists of numbers that need to be divided by total numbers in order to highlight demand or lack of demand, pressures on staff and so on. If your research involved the number of telephone calls that workers received when sat at their desk within a given period of time, it would be a simple task to count the number of calls and divide by the number of workers.

Ways to present findings. Bar charts, column charts, histograms, or as written data.

The mode

For lists, the mode is the most common (frequent) occurring value. To discover whether your data has a mode value you need to look at reoccurring figures. If, for example, you notice when you calculate and assimilate the given salaries of staff that one band of figures stands out as being the band within which most people are paid, then that is the mode average (see Table 7.4 below).

When to use the mode average. When it is clear that there is a frequent re-occurring value or values, you can have more than one mode in a list.

Ways to present findings. Histograms, bar charts, column charts, scatter charts, pie charts, or as written data.

TABLE 7.4

Yearly salary band	Number of full-time staff ticked within this band
Under £10,000	21
£10,001–£15,000	40
£15,001–£20,000	189
£20,001–£25,000	56
£25,001–£30,000	9
Above £30,001	4

This figure is the mode

The Median

The middle value of a list is called the median average. If you sorted your data from the smallest to the largest and they fell into categories as below:

$$1,1,2,2,2,3,3,3,3,4\,|\,4,4,4,4,5,5,5,6,6,6 *$$

there is an even number of values, so the middle (or median) is between the first and second 4. Because they are the same we can easily say that the median is 4, but what if they were different? Had your middle values been between a 4 and a 5, then the median is equal to the sum of the two middle values divided by 2, that is, $4 + 5 = 9 \div 2 = 4.5$.

Ways to use median average. A median can only be used for data which can be put in order, so if the figures above* were the ages of children in a hospital ward, you could say that the median was 4 years of age.

Ways to present findings. Line charts, scatter charts.

Mean, median or mode, which is better?

It is up to the researcher to decide which is the best way to calculate and present their statistical data, but the important thing is to be clear and explain the system you use. Unfortunately too many inexperienced researchers call mean, median or mode by the same name – the average.

The method you choose will have a bearing on the statistical evidence that you present. If you were presenting statistics about the salaries of executive staff within a large company that has ten directors earning £40,000, a chairman earning £150,000 and vice-chairman earning £100,000 a year and you use *mode* (the most frequently reoccurring value) you would present the figure of £40,000.

If, however, you wanted to put a different emphasis on your statistics, let's say that you are the company's human resources officer and you want to present an impression of high salaries for most executive staff, you would probably use *mean* to calculate your figures.

$$(£40,000 \times 10) + \quad £100,000 + \quad £150,000 \quad = £650,000 \div 12 \quad = £54,000$$

| The sum of ten directors earning £40,000 | added to the salary of the vice-chairman | added to the salary of the chairman | the total of all salaries divided by the total number of staff | the mean average earned by executives |

Perhaps Disraeli had something when he said, 'There are three kinds of lies . . . lies, damned lies and statistics!' (also attributed to Mark Twain, *Autobiography*).

▶ Data presentation

The presentation of your data is important. Often a diagram or chart is easier for the reader to understand instantly the point that you are trying to make when compared with a written explanation of the same information. Compare Figure 7.3 and 7.4 below; both are saying the same thing but one is presented in written form and one as a column chart. Which presentation would interest you more?

There are many ways of presenting data in a graphical or pictorial form. It is generally accepted that pictures, graphs and diagrams are a favourable way of presenting data of a statistical nature; just look at your newspaper or television coverage of this kind of information.

However, it is very easy to misrepresent data either inadvertently or purposely when using diagrams, charts or graphs, and you need to evaluate your work discriminatingly and be as fair as you possibly can when presenting your findings in this way. Hoyle emphasis this point emphatically:

> Deliberate distortion aside, enthusiastic individuals with a point of view to express which they believe to be in the public interest may unwittingly bring biased, incorrectly presented data forward in the genuine belief that it is correct. You should appraise all you own work critically, and also the presentations put before you by others, to detect shortcomings. (Hoyle 1988:291)

Asking a colleague to verify your findings is one way to minimise the bias

The school absence records for the past 12 months were scrutinised. Of the 100 12–14-year-old pupils, a large number had been absent from school at some time during the year. The aggregated amount of time varied from one-day to six weeks. There seemed to be little difference in the total amount of absence between male and female pupils, although girls did seem to have more single-day or short-term absences up to one week when compared with boys. Boys tended to be absent from school for longer periods of time than girls. Neither gender was absent for more than six weeks.

Figure 7.3 Example of written data

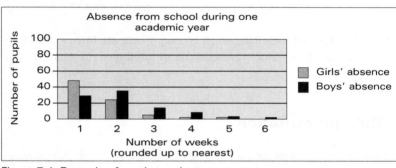

Figure 7.4 Example of a column chart

that might unwittingly creep into your statistical findings, especially if you choose a colleague who, although interested, has no particular 'axe to grind' over the subject area.

Unless you are using a computer to work out your graphs and diagrams they will take time to construct. Part B of this chapter explains how to achieve the charts listed below by simply letting the computer do all the work.

However, it is possible to use traditional methods and brief mathematical explanations follow each figure below on achieving the graphical representation shown. If you need a more in-depth mathematical coverage of the actual calculations, you will need to consult specific books on producing graphs and charts (see the Bibliography at the back of this book or consult your local librarian or bookseller).

Listed below are the most common forms of presentation used.

Pie charts

One of the simplest methods of presenting the way in which whole statistical data breaks down into various parts is to use a pie chart (Figure 7.5).

The data is presented as though slices of a pie with the complete circle representing the whole set of data. The various parts of the pie which show the subdivision of data can be labelled separately with the topic and percent-

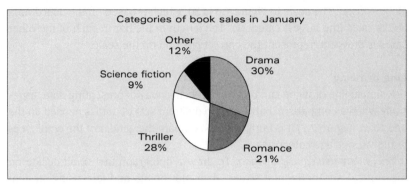

Figure 7.5 Example of a pie chart

age or a legend can be added explaining that various coloured shades or patterned slices represent specific data figures.

Brief mathematical explanation. The whole pie represents 100 per cent, which is the 360° degrees of the circle. Each segment or slice of the pie is constructed by using a protractor and measuring from the twelve o'clock position.

Bar or column charts

A bar or column chart uses rectangles of equal width with heights or lengths proportional to the varying quantities of data (Figure 7.6). It displays the information so that the reader is able to compare one category against another. Look again at the column chart in Figure 7.4 that compared the absences of boys and girls; at a glance it was easy to see the differences between the two.

Brief mathematical explanation. To construct a bar chart a scale must first of

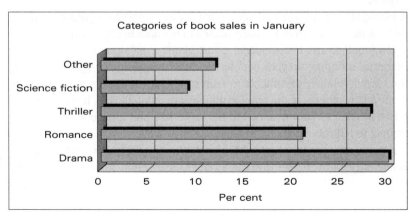

Figure 7.6 Example of a bar/column chart

all be chosen. The scale in Figure 7.6 is 30, which is based on the 30% drama books sales (the largest category). The length of the bar in each of the other cases is drawn to represent the correct position on the scale.

Line drawing

A simple line drawing can be a very effective way of presenting data, especially when a comparison between two different sets of data is needed. In the line chart (Figure 7.7) it is fairly easy to compare the gender of the employees in the various age categories.

Brief mathematical explanation. To draw a line graph first of all decide on the vertical and horizontal scales, then plot points and join using straight lines.

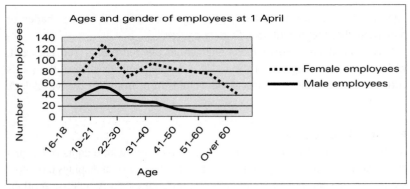

Figure 7.7 Example of a line chart

Pictograms
Type A

A pictogram is a frequency diagram that uses a symbol to represent so many units of data. The symbol usually relates to the data being shown.

Brief mathematical explanation. Constructing a pictogram is a fairly easy matter of rounding up your data to the nearest meaningful figure and using the correct number of symbols to represent items. It is always necessary to show a key, otherwise the representations are unintelligible. It is also important that each symbol is drawn to the same size and if necessary use half a symbol to indicate smaller amounts.

A pictogram can be an interesting and attractive way of presenting data, it is also easy for the reader to see at a glance the essential findings of the material.

Number of people who bought local newspapers during the first week of August	
Monday	🧍 𝑗
Tuesday	🧍 🧍 🧍
Wednesday	🧍 🧍
Thursday	🧍 🧍 𝑗
Friday	🧍 🧍 🧍 🧍 🧍
Saturday	🧍 🧍 🧍 🧍 🧍 🧍
Sunday	🧍 🧍
KEY 🧍 = to the nearest 1,000 𝑗 = to the nearest 500	

Figure 7.8 Example of a pictogram

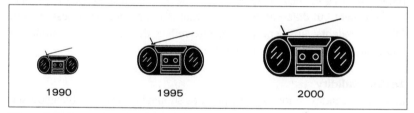

Figure 7.9 Example of a pictogram

Type B

The second type of pictogram uses one symbol of different sizes, but if this is used the reader must be made aware of exactly what is being compared. For example, in Figure 7.9, is it the size of the radios being compared – or what?

If you are using this type of pictogram ensure that the reader can interpret and understand what it is that is being represented, and include the summary of the actual data if necessary.

▶ Methods of testing reliability and validity

Testing reliability

Test-retest reliability

Respondents answer the questions twice and if the test is reliable the two scores will be comparable. There should be a period of time between the two tests so that the respondent will not recall what was said the first time. The period of time between the tests should not be too great (no more than a month), otherwise the respondents may have changed in some way which will have a bearing on their answers.

Split half

This is often used when it is not possible to use the test-retest method. After the questionnaires are finished the answers are split into two, perhaps all the odd number questions composing one half and all the even number questions the other half. The findings are then correlated, which allows the relationship between the two separate findings to be compared.

Equivalent or alternative forms

In this case the researcher composes two questionnaires that are sufficiently dissimilar so that the respondent does not find himself repeating information, but the questions are addressing the same issues. Writing such questionnaires takes a great deal of thought and time because it is not easy to produce an equivalent but different version of what is in essence one questionnaire. The respondents' answers in each test reflect the reliability, assuming of course that the two questionnaires are equivalent.

Testing validity

Measuring validity is not easy and perhaps should be viewed as being outside the scope of small-scale research projects. However, some of the main methods are outlined very briefly below.

Predictive validity

This is sometimes called criterion-related validity. The results of research are sometimes used to predict what will happen in the future and the predictive validity of the results is investigated by correlating the prediction made at the time with what actually happens later on. For example, the validity of the written theory test for car drivers and motorcyclists is checked, in this understanding, by the relationship between the scores people get in the written test and how well they drive in the practical driving test. The driving ability is the criteria.

Content or face validity

If independent experts in a subject area agree that the research test looks as though it does what it is supposed to do, you could say that it has content or face validity. Other methods of validity should be used alongside this method if possible as it is generally thought of as being a very unrefined way of validating tests.

Concurrent validity

If you were researching the spelling ability of six-year-olds and compared the results of your findings with their teacher's estimate on their spelling ability, you would have obtained concurrent validity of your research. Concurrent validity is the comparison of independent data.

Construct validity

Comparing the research results with what would be expected as a result of common sense or academic theory is known as construct validity.

Evidence of reliability and validity is normally published with the results of any new research of any significance, and as you can see there are a number of ways to check reliability and validity using correlational techniques. However, given that you are undertaking small-scale research, it may not be considered necessary for you to go to these checking lengths. Nevertheless you would be wise to ask and then you will be able to mention in your final written document whether you used correlational techniques (comparing the relationship between two separate findings) with your new data and if not you will be able to clarify the reasons why it was not thought to be necessary.

The main methods have been briefly outlined and should be sufficient for small-scale research, but if you wish to pursue the topic further and learn more about reliability or validity there are many excellent books devoted just to this topic. I suggest that you consult the Bibliography at the back of this book or consult your librarian or local bookshop for more in-depth information.

Analysis – getting confused?

If, in the middle of analysing all your gathered data, you find your head in a complete spin, don't despair. Try to keep sight of your original hypothesis or objectives. That 'gut feeling' that you had about something at the start of your research is about to be tested – it's exciting. You are about to find out whether you were right.

If you feel that you are surrounded by a web of interlocking statistics and findings that you cannot interrelate, don't worry, it will all come together when you get down to the writing up your research. The important thing is to remain focused on what it was that you were originally trying to find out, if you do that, everything will fall into place at the next stage.

PART B

The purpose of this chapter is to describe methods of converting research data into a form in which the computer can help you with its analysis. Computers have been used in social research for well over 100 years, but they did not bear any resemblance to the ones that we use today. Punched cards that could be read by machines were the earliest forms of help and these were developed to a sophisticated level for the USA Census of 1890, when Herman Hollerith adapted the punch card system and invented a tabulating machine that could read the card. The entire population of America was counted within six weeks – ten years previously it had taken nine years to gather identical information without the help of machines. Incidentally, Hollerith's company went on to merge with other pioneering firms and was eventually renamed IBM (International Business Machines Corporation).

▶ Decide method of analysing data before it is needed

It is very important that you consider the eventual method by which you will analyse your data at the design stage of your questionnaire. This cannot be stressed enough. Unless you design your questions with a thought to how you intend to break down into parts the given answers, the analysis stage of your research will be a nightmare. For example, with a simple question such as needing to know the respondent's age, you give yourself far more work if you ask the question 'Please give your age', compared with a tick box where the respondent can indicate their age within an age band. Do you really need to know that they are 31? Would the information that they are in the age range 25–34 not be sufficient for your research needs? It is far easier to count the number of people in age bands than work out that you had 6 × 20-year-olds, 3 × 21-year-olds, 2 × 22-year-olds and so on. If you don't need the specific information, don't ask it, and often specific information such as age can be sensitive to some people.

▶ Specialist software analysis programs

Today's computers are sophisticated tools and can carry out quite basic functions such as sorting and counting as well as being able to calculate complex statistics at an incredible speed. Specialist software packages enable the computer to read pre-coded data and analyse it as required. Do note, however, that the computer can only produce the goods if the data has been coded, it is not able to read masses of text and understand responses or pull out statistics unless the individual paragraphs, tick boxes and so on have been pre-coded.

Computer Assisted Qualitative Data Analysis Systems (CAQDAS) have been around for some time now and have met the needs of paid researchers working under the pressure of time constraints. However, some researchers believe that using these computer analysis programs weakens the competence and craft of well-established research traditions. Others are concerned that the researcher is merely following a set of mechanical procedures and that the software could contain program assumptions that might bring bias into the research results.

There are many specialist software packages available that can analyse your data but, as you are only carrying out small-scale research, why not ask your educational establishment or company whether they have any in-house software and ask permission to utilise their facilities. Unless you are going to use the software over and over again, it seems a waste of money to buy a specific analysis software package. Not all educational establishments provide analysis software for student use, but, when you measure the number of students who could make use of this facility, it is easy to see that it could be very popular and an asset to the campus. Perhaps this might be a matter to write to the dean or principal about, or at least galvanise the student union into action.

Popular specialist software packages – SPSS, Ethnograph, NUD*IST and so on

During the past few years a number of specialised computer programs have been developed to support the analysis of qualitative data. Most of these programs, with names such as Ethnograph and NUD*IST, were developed by qualitative researchers to support their own work. These early versions were sometimes informally shared with colleagues interested in doing the same types of research. Then, as the programs matured and interest in them increased, commercial programmers began to develop their potential and they can now be purchased by anyone.

SPSS (Statistical Package for the Social Sciences) is one of the most widely used data analysis packages. It has the advantage of appearing on the screen looking like most other Windows programs. Even the menu options that appear across the top of the screen will look familiar to a Windows user:

File Edit View Data Transform Analyze Graphs Utilities Window Help.

Two windows are initially available: the data input and data output window. When SPSS first comes up, it is ready to accept new data. It is particularly easy to use and can cope with most kinds of data, however, it is not quite as versatile in very complex analyses as some other packages. For this reason, professional researchers, government departments and so on do not find SPSS suitable for their requirements. The home page of SPSS is http://www.spss.com if you want to use the Web to learn more.

Tablee 7.5 gives a brief description of the more popular analysis software around at present.

TABLE 7.5 POPULAR SOFTWARE ANALYSIS PACKAGES

SPSS	A popular and widely used package which is useful and easy to use. Copes with most kinds of data.
BMDP	A general purpose statistical program, similar to SPSS.
MINITAB	Very easy to use, but its scope is limited. It is rather like an extremely advanced calculator.
SAS	More flexible than SPSS but not very easy to use, especially for a beginner to statistical packages.
SNAP	Offers simple analysis including tabulations, but few statistical tests. It can handle a survey all the way through – from designing a questionnaire, coding and so on to automatically analysing subsequent data.

Whether you wish to take the time to learn how to use a specialist analysis program if you do not anticipate carrying out future research is a matter for your consideration; perhaps talking to your education or in-house IT staff would help you in your decision. It is as well to remember that the decision to use these types of software should be largely related to the number of people interviewed and the complexity of the information sought, together with the amount of time you have to devote to learning a new software. If you only have a small amount of data from 75 respondents, utilising normal PC software is probably quite sufficient.

If you think you would like to get involved with specialist analysis programs, you need to find out about the needs of the software *before* you design your questionnaires. If you are aware of the coding needs of the particular software at the start, the eventual analysis of the collected data will be far easier.

For up-to-date online information look at the following Web pages:

http://employees.csbsju.edu/rwielk/psy347/spssinst.htm
reliabilityanalysis
http://www.scolari.com/
http://www.atlasi.de/
http://qsr.latrobe.edu.au/
http://www.ualberta.ca/~jrnorris/qda.html
http://www.soc.surrey.ac.uk/caqdas/
http://www.oit.pdx.edu/~kerlinb/qualresearch/

▶ Utilising everyday software

Although not dedicated to research analysis, the everyday software that is available for PCs can be extremely useful in helping you to analyse your research data. Computer programs can take much of the drudgery out of analysis and help to reduce the menial and sometimes boring part of the job. The computer has the capacity to locate and retrieve, cross-reference and search for data, which is remarkable by human standards. Anyone who has obtained research data utilising their computer's help will immediately support the value of this facility.

There are many different software packages available on the market today and therefore it is not possible to be especially software specific in the paragraphs that follow. However, the principles outlined apply to all software. PC and Mac computers seem to dominate the market and the Windows software is available everywhere, therefore, where specific instructions are given, they are written for Microsoft Windows software.

▶ Folders (directories) and files

Being tidy and logical is an immense help in smoothing the sorting out of research data. In Chapter 3 you were advised to make directories or folders (pp. 49–51). If you haven't already done so, it is vital that you do so now to help your analysis.

If you can keep similar topics together, it will help you in the long run when you want to analyse what has been said. Opening folders or directories and saving 'or filing' your documents logically is the way to do this.

▶ **Analysis of open-ended interview data using a word processor**

If you look back at this topic on pp. 157–9, you will read of the necessity to code this information, summarise it, or, in the case of complicated answers, photocopy, cut out relevant parts and paste onto headed sheets. All this is made easier if you are using the computer.

If, as soon as each interview is finished, you key in the information into a document file, save it with a relevant name and file it in an appropriate folder, when it comes to the eventual analyse of the data you are ready to go. By saving it as you go along, you are saving time at the analysis stage, and by saving directly into the relevant folder it will not get 'lost' somewhere in your computer memory, necessitating wasted time wondering what you called it, and where on earth you saved it.

There are many ways that a word processor can help you to pull out relevant data. If your interview was a one-to-one in-depth discussion about the relationship between mothers and daughters and you had saved seven pages of text from one interview with a 14-year-old girl, you could now use your computer to extract specific information. Let us say that you want to know whether and in what way she talked about the love between parent and child, or the rules in her home for grounding, you could instruct the computer to 'Search' for specific words, in this case 'love' or 'grounding'. If these words are contained in the document, the computer will find them by searching through and stopping on each and every occasion that they occur. You could then, if you wished, highlight the specific information, copy it and paste it to a separate file headed perhaps Child–parent love or grounding. If you gave this teenager's file a reference, such as No.1, this should also be added so that you can refer back if necessary.

If you searched other saved interview documents, you could repeat the same search, and transfer that data to the Child–parent love file. Repetition of this process would soon lead you to aggregate the information from all the interviews about that particular topic.

Often the contents of an individual topic file can be used within the final research document without the need for retyping, apart from the odd tidying up. This is another bonus gained from using the computer to analyse data. Again, if you are using the ever-popular Microsoft, the following instructions will help you to achieve the above.

Search for specific word (or hold down the control key and tap f)	Click on Edit → Find Key-in the word to be found . . . → Click on 'Find Next' → If you wish to transfer this information to another file, click outside the Find dialog box on screen and follow through the instructions below:
Highlight	Click, hold the mouse button down, and drag the cursor on screen across the text you wish to copy.
Copy	With the relevant text highlighted, click on the copy icon (or control c).
Paste	Open the relevant topic file and place the cursor where you wish the highlighted text to appear. Click on the paste icon on the Standard toolbar (or control v).

When you return to your original file you can reactivate the Search dialog box by clicking on Find Next

▷ Analysis of questionnaire data using a database

Unless a very small amount of data has been collected, it will be much quicker to analyse the information from the questionnaires using a database package rather attempting the same task manually.

A database is a collection of information that shares a common theme, for example a company might set up a database with the names and addresses of all its employees. Added to this might be their current job, qualifications and date of birth, which would be needed by the human resources department. The health and safety manager might also need their car registration number, driving licence and car insurance details. The finance department would wish to add their current salary details, and so on. You can see how filing all these details in one place saves the duplication of various departments keeping their own bits of information but also enables all those with authority to access the information and pull out the parts relevant to them.

By saving the information on a database it is also easy to find the answers to specific questions. Using the above fictitious database it would simply be a matter of pressing a few computer keys in order to find out the names and addresses of all the employees over 40 years of age. All staff under 25 years of age with a car and relevant insurance could be found, or the finance department could sort all the staff into order of salary. The possibilities are endless.

The first step would be to set up the database. You would need to choose headings (called labels or field headings) for the various parts of the information that you wish to record. Let us imagine that your research had been connected with 6th form pupils on work experience and as part of the questionnaire completed by 150 teenagers you asked the following questions.

1		Tick the appropriate box →	Yes	No	Unsure
(a)	Did you enjoy your work experience?				
(b)	Was the Work Experience Induction Day held at school beforehand useful?				
(c)	If you answered no to (b) above, please say briefly how the Induction Day could be improved.				

To decide on the relevant field headings in the above case you would need to ask yourself into what categories the answers might fall. If the answer is that the only possible answer can be a 'yes'; 'no'; or 'unsure', those will be the field headings for each question.

You could gain more detailed information from these three questions by devising a code for certain answers (see box below).

Question 1(a)	A separate field heading for	Yes	No	Unsure
Question 1(b)	A separate field heading for	Yes	No	Unsure

Question 1(c) The answers given to this question will not neatly fall into a yes, no, unsure format and may not be possible to record all answers given because they may not fall neatly into categories. But the answers given may fall into a pattern, for example 25% the pupils may say that it should have been longer, or 15% say that they would have liked a written reminder to take away afterwards. If this is the case, a code will need to be devised (for example longer = L; or written reminder = R) so that as you work through the completed questionnaires you can fill in this field. Those that do not fall into a code will need to be recorded separately.

As you work through the completed questionnaires the answers given are transferred to the database. Whether you use Y for yes, N for no or U for unsure is your decision, you could if you preferred simply insert a tick as relevant throughout. You would need to draw up a key to answers given to question 1c. In the case below (Figure 7.10) it was decided that L = needs to be longer, B = boring; H = health and safety too long, but there could be many other options. The headings given to each column are known as fields. Notice

Ques No	1a Enjoy? Yes	1a No	1a Unsure	1b Induc Day? Yes	1b No	1b Unsure	1c Improve Suggestions
1	Y			Y			
2		N		Y			L
3	Y				N		
4	Y					U	
5		N		Y			
6	Y				N		B
7	Y			Y			
8			U		N		B
9	Y			Y			H
10	Y			Y			H

Figure 7.10

that a column has been added for the questionnaire paper number, this is always sensible as you may wish to refer back.

When you have saved a completed database, it is possible to search for specific combinations, for example had the gender of the questionnaire respondent been recorded with the above database it would be easy to find out how many girls found work experience enjoyable and how many boys. Or you could interrogate the database to find out whether more girls found the Induction Day boring compared with boys.

Sometimes the answers to questionnaires would produce a large single database and it may be easier to save your work in manageable chunks. This would enable you to have several collections of information and tie them together in ways that suited you. This is known as relational databases and you will need to define the relationship between new database tables and any existing tables as you proceed.

Learning to set up and use databases is not difficult but it does need a little practise before you launch into attempting to analyse your questionnaire returns. There are hundreds of books dedicated to the various database software available, why not look when you are next in your local bookshop or library. Alternatively, short courses are often available through your local college or university. A couple of hours spent in learning databases could save you an immense amount of time in analysis.

Using spreadsheets

The most commonly used program next to a word-processing package is a spreadsheet package. A spreadsheet can be used to create financial calculations, list and total expenditure, keep a track of finances and so on. In fact if you think of it as an extremely advanced calculator you won't be far wrong.

The advantage of using a spreadsheet for the small-scale researcher is that

Computer Support

	A	B	C	D
1	COST OF DRINKS IN THE STAFF CANTEEN			
2				
3		COST PER	NO OF ITEMS	DAILY
4		ITEM (pence)	SOLD PER DAY	INCOME
5	Tea	40	210	£ 64.00
6	Coffee	70	410	£ 287.00
7	Hot chocolate	70	90	£ 63.00
8	All soft drinks	50	40	£ 20.00
9	Fizzy drinks	75	190	£ 142.50
10	TOTAL			£ 596.50

Figure 7.11

any numerical data that you have gathered can be input and interrogated to find various answers. If your gathered questionnaire data highlighted that staff were not buying food in the staff canteen because they believed that it was too expensive, you could use a spreadsheet to work out various options.

Formulae (mathematical equations) are frequently used in spreadsheets in order to quickly work out the answers to mathematical questions. If maths has never been your favourite subject, do not be put off by my talk of equations, remember the computer is going to do all the work for you, all you have to do is learn how to make it carry out the tasks or functions that you require.

Figure 7.11 shows the number of drinks sold, their prices and the daily income; the subsequent illustrations show the simplicity by which information can be obtained and changed using a spreadsheet for calculations.

The Daily Income in column D and the total has been obtained by inputting a formula in the cell D5, copying this formula to the other drinks cells, and then adding a different formula in cell D10 that will total the whole column (Figure 7.12).

The advantage of keying your data onto a spreadsheet can be easily illustrated in Figure 7.13. Using the same spreadsheet, the cost of the drinks has been reduced in order to see what effect this would have on the daily income. Without changing any other cells except the Cost Per Item cells you can see instantly the reductions in income.

Given the ease with which these type of calculations can be carried out, it could be useful in certain research situations to predict the various consequences of acting on research data. In the case of our fictitious staff canteen situation, the management might decide that it could afford to reduce certain prices in order to encourage staff to use the facilities. Depending on the questions asked by the researcher it might be that people have indicated that they would use the canteen more if prices were cheaper. This too could be built

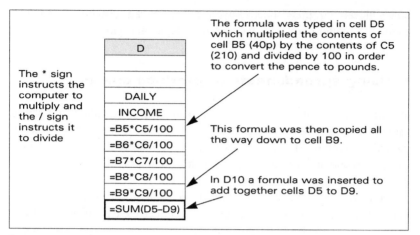

Figure 7.12

into the spreadsheet so that the projected rise in income could be computed using lower prices but more sales to give another option to the research recommendations.

Learning to use spreadsheets is not difficult, in fact most people find it easier to learn spreadsheet software compared with database software. However, neither is that complex and a few hours spent mastering the software before you analyse your data will be time well spent. The added

All drinks have been reduced by 10p

	A	B	C	D
1	COST OF DRINKS IN THE STAFF CANTEEN			
2				
3		COST PER	NO OF ITEMS	DAILY
4		ITEM (pence)	SOLD PER DAY	INCOME
5	Tea	30	210	£ 63.00
6	Coffee	60	410	£ 246.00
7	Hot chocolate	60	90	£ 54.00
8	All soft drinks	40	40	£ 16.00
9	Fizzy drinks	65	190	£ 123.50
10	TOTAL			£ 502.50

Instantly the drink prices are reduced a new daily income and total is automatically calculated by the computer

Figure 7.13

bonus in learning spreadsheet software is that you can subsequently produce charts in a matter of minutes without any additional keying in of data.

▶ Using spreadsheets to produce charts

In Part A of this chapter you learned about data presentation and saw a sample of various basic chart presentations. Producing these charts without the aid of a computer demands more from the researcher in mathematical calculation and drawing ability, not forgetting that it takes longer to produce these by hand.

If you input data straight into a spreadsheet, you only have to highlight the relevant areas and instruct the computer to produce the type of chart that you require. There are no mathematical calculations on your part, no messy drawing of bars or curves, neither do you have to plot the points. The computer does everything for you.

Taking the spreadsheet just used (Figure 7.13), if you decided that a pie chart would be the best way to illustrate income, all you would have to do would be to highlight the appropriate area (that is, the data that you wish to work with) and tell the computer that you want a pie chart. If you are using Microsoft software, once started it is just a case of a set of on-screen prompts, some of which are reproduced in Figure 7.14 below.

1. Highlight the items to be included in the pie chart (these are shown white against a black background here).

	A	B	C	D
1	COST OF DRINKS IN THE STAFF CANTEEN			
2				
3		COST PER	NO OF ITEMS	DAILY
4		ITEM (pence)		INCOME
5	Tea	30	210	£ 63.00
6	Coffee	60	410	£ 246.00
7	Hot chocolate	60	90	£ 54.00
8	All soft drinks	40	40	£ 16.00
9	Fizzy drinks	65	190	£ 123.50
10	TOTAL			£ 502.50

2. Choose the chart icon and then the chart type (that is, pie) and type of illustration you prefer. Notice all the other types of chart that you could choose.

3. Click on Next to move on to the next screen.
4. You will be presented with a screen similar to the one below; it confirms the data range you have chosen. Click on Next once again to move to the next screen.

5. On the next screen decide whether you would like to change the title, label the pie chart, etc. To do this, simply click in the appropriate box and follow the screen prompts. Click on Next to move to the next screen

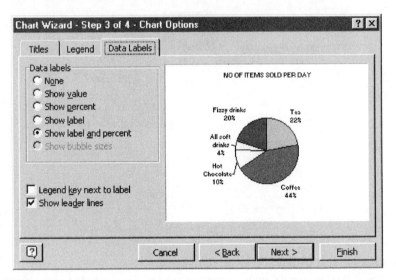

6. The completed pie chart is now ready to insert into your research work, where you will be able to enlarge or reduce its size as you require. If you don't like what you see, it is now a case of starting all over again and choosing different options as you proceed.

The whole process only takes a few minutes, which is far less than the time you would spend drawing by hand.

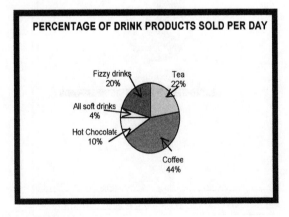

Figure 7.14

Computer Support

You could have chosen various different options and produced your information in one of many different layouts. You can see from the four examples below that the identical data looks completely different when presented in a different form.

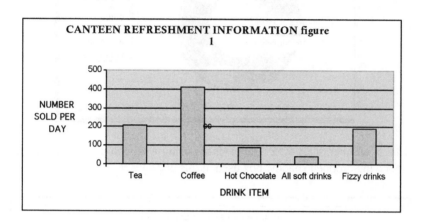

This is a column chart. Notice the use of various fonts and sizes used in this layout.

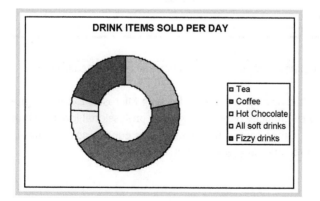

This is a doughnut chart with legend. A grey line and surround box has been added for effective display. Doughnut charts are especially good when printed in colour.

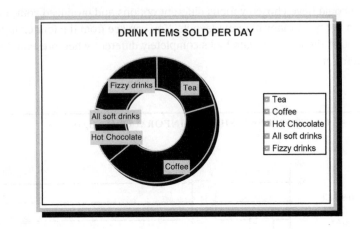

This is another style of doughnut chart, using a legend plus named rings. Notice the dropped shadow box used in this display.

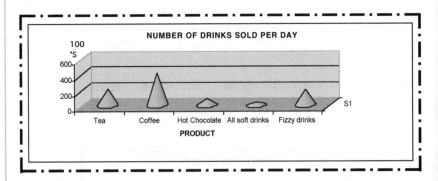

The last example is of a cylinder chart, using a dotted border.

The above charts have been made using Microsoft Excel and give you some idea of the simplicity of producing quite professional looking charts using the computer. Other spreadsheet software is equally easy to master providing you spend a little time practising it.

8 Getting Down to Writing

PART A

Once you have reached this point you are well on the way in your research and should feel justifiably proud of what you've achieved so far. Just think of the abundance of work you have undertaken and what you have already accomplished from those tentative beginnings. You have:

- identified your research area
- decided on aims or possibly a hypothesis to test
- looked at various research styles and methodological approaches
- read around your topic
- kept records
- carried out original data collection through interviews and/or questionnaires,
- analysed the findings.

Now you have to bring all the above elements together, but where do you start? You will find that different books will give you divergent advice on how to go about writing up and presenting your findings, but there really is no single correct way of 'getting it all right'.

Certain examining boards, academic departments or workplace supervisors may have clear expectations about some of the essential features that they require, but there is often a degree of flexibility about its format. The contents of your research document is the most important part of the research, it is where you are going to communicate your findings with others and your ability to write a clear and accurate picture of what has taken place is the more important feature. Heyes et al. succinctly sum this up:

> Do however bear in mind the following yardstick: your report should be sufficiently detailed to permit someone else to replicate your study without them having to contact you to ask questions about it. (Heyes et al. 1990:104)

If you bear this advice in mind, your finished report should give the reader all the information needed.

▶ Before writing the first draft

You will be very tempted at this stage to rush into writing by immediately committing your thoughts to paper. In the long term this could be costly on your time when you realise the need to emphasise some areas, write to a set number of words, change the order and redraft. It is far better to spend a little time initially sorting out exactly what you want to say. Clarify your ideas, possibly talk about them with your tutor or supervisor, and then jot down a plan of what comes where, possible chapter headings and some idea of how much emphasis you want to place on various areas.

As you sift through the mass of data that you have gathered, try to be clear in your mind who you are writing for and what you are trying to achieve. Without this goal your writing could become diffused and undisciplined.

Length of the report

You may have been told that your report must be of a certain length, and, if this is the case, you need to make some rough allocation of words or pages to each section of your report. This of course will be revised as you write, but unless you discipline yourself at the outset by giving more space for the important areas, you might find that you have written 3,000 words on describing exactly how you decided what to research but only 400 words on the findings, in which case your emphasis would be wrong.

Timing available

Writing up a research report is a very time-consuming business and you need to allocate a regular amount of time for the purpose. It is no use spending three whole days writing and then doing nothing for three weeks, as you are likely to have forgotten what you have already written and will have to reread the whole lot or fall into the trap of repeating information again. Also your work is more likely to appear disjointed if you divide your writing periods with long gaps of inactivity and the rhythm of your writing will be lost.

Many people work better if they regularly allocate a certain time of day or day/s of the week to writing and then regard this time as sacrosanct. So if someone invites them out to the pub, or they're asked to baby-sit for a friend, they must discipline themselves to answer no, for this is their allocated writing time. Friends and family will often encourage and help people when they know that certain periods of time are out of bounds for interruption.

It might spur you on if you reward yourself with small treats when you have written a certain number of words; choose something you'd like to do, for example a short break with a cup of coffee and a bar of your favourite chocolate. Completion of a whole chapter or research area could call for a trip to the cinema, or the local pub, or whatever treat you decide. Cheer yourself up with the thought that it is only for a limited period and the quicker you complete the work the easier it will be for you.

Set deadlines
You have been working to certain deadlines throughout your research and now is not the time to stop. Armed with your possible draft chapter headings, set yourself a deadline by which certain sections will be finished or better still ask your supervisor or tutor to set you a deadline.

Aim to write a minimum number of words at each session. Even if you believe that you have got 'writer's block' before you sit down to write, you will surprise yourself how the words will come if only you will make a start.

Writing by hand?
If you are in the unfortunate position of handwriting or typewriting every-thing, remember to leave plenty of space between lines for eventual correc-tion or rewording. If you write paragraphs on separate pages, at least you can move their positions around if you wish, however this can get very messy with lots of separate pieces of paper and crossed out page numbering details. Writing on one side of the paper only can be helpful, because at least you can then physically cut out a paragraph with scissors and staple it where better suited.

Most universities now demand that reports be word processed, so do check this. If you are unable to word process it yourself, do book the work in with a word processor and check how much it is going to cost. It is normally worked out on the total number of words keyed in. You will find adverts offering this service in telephone directories and pinned on notice boards within the educational establishment, but do book a typist well in advance. Some word-processing companies and typists stop accepting dissertation or research work in the summer when student demand is at its peak.

In the workplace you can hardly present your work to your boss in a hand-written format, and now is the time to speak nicely to someone within the workplace who can do the job for you. It is worth remembering that they are doing you a favour, so you should be prepared to reward them with a suitable present.

▶ What to write

You don't have to write the report in the order in which it will eventually be read, in fact some sections are better left until the end. For example, the abstract or outline of the research undertaken, which usually appears at the beginning, is far better written when the main body of the work has been completed. This enables you to reflect on what has been written and pull together more accurately a picture of the research.

Be structured and logical

Imagine that you are going to read a research report written by someone else. I am sure you would appreciate it if it were organised in such a way that it presented you with a structured view of what had taken place. You would find it more interesting if the researcher painted a picture for you of why it was undertaken in the first place, what it was hoped would be gained from the research, how they went about doing it and what their results and conclusions were.

Not all researchers agree on the order or structure to be used for writing up research findings, and if you have not been told exactly how your research is to be formulated, look at the following suggested outline (Table 8.1). If you feel that you can work within this framework, check with your tutor or supervisor that this is acceptable and work along these lines.

Note that throughout the report you will be addressing other people's views, and possibly bringing in direct quotations (see Writing the record, pp. 53–4).

TABLE 8.1

Suggested chapter structure	Brief description
1. Abstract or outline of the research	The *why*, *how* and *what*. This is meant to be a sound bite of why you researched, how you researched and what you found. It is usually a very short summary of the research aims, the methodological avenues explored and the results.
2. Setting the scene and setting out the aims	A more in-depth explanation of how and why you came to choose your research topic, which would include definitions and explanation of the research aims and the setting of a hypothesis if applicable.
3. Review of other similar work	Any historical background, current happenings, different approaches, or reviews of previous research would be included in this section. Your background readings and literature searches will prove beneficial now.

4. Methodology of the research	Outlines of the various research methods that could have been used and the evaluation paths that they would have entailed in your research. Reasons why you chose particular methodological approaches. Any limitations or problems encountered, and what you did about them.
5. Your unique procedures	How you went about doing the actual research. Reports on the procedures used (that is, interviews, questionnaires, videos and so on). Detailed description of the when and where. The problems encountered, the rethinks, and any measurements or tests used.
6. The research findings	Analysis of the data gathered and the procedures adopted for that analysis. This is a very important area of the research, which should highlight significant findings.
7. Discussions on research and findings	What went right, what went wrong. Any deficiencies in the research design, whether you would do it all in the same way again. Did your research findings test the aims or the hypotheses (if applicable)? What does your evidence suggest? It is also important that you relate your findings to other research in this topic area here.
8. Conclusion and summary	This should not be a long section but should summarise succinctly and clearly what conclusions have been drawn from the evidence.

▶ The practical details

If you haven't been given definite details of exactly what is required in the layout of your research report, the following guidelines will give you some idea of what will be required.

A Title Page
This should give the following information:

- The title of your research report
- Your name

- If an academic award, then its title
- The year

The title should succinctly explain what your report is all about, but don't be afraid to use a subtitle if necessary.

Thanks and acknowledgements (optional)

It is nice to be able to thank people who have given you their time and help and if you would like to do this a separate page inserted after the title page is the place for thanks and acknowledgements. However, you do not have to do this, it is your choice.

Assessment criteria (arbitrary)

Some academic bodies require that you insert a list of the assessment criteria to which you have been required to work. Check with your tutor whether this is necessary in your case.

CONTENTS

Figure 8.1 Contents page

Contents

This is a list of the chapter headings, the paragraph subheadings (which may or may not be numbered) together with the appropriate page number (see Figure 8.1).

The contents list is an aid to the person reading your report. It enables them to turn quickly to an area of interest and also to see the substance of your work in a summarised format. The list is usually one of the last things to do because it is likely that the page numbers and subheadings for the various topics will change as the report evolves. Don't forget to add a list of any appendices to the contents.

The main body of your work

It is at this point that your chapters will be placed. See Table 8.1 if unsure of the structure of your work.

Appendices

You should include a blank copy of any research documents used, such as interview questions and questionnaires, together with schedule lists, tables of results and so on and each individual document should be clearly referenced (for example Appendix A) and included in the contents.

Bibliography

A list of the books and articles that you have read which are relevant to the research is essential at the end of your report. Also relevant Web sites visited need to be listed. The bibliography *should not* include items that you ought to have read but haven't. The layout of the bibliography has been covered in detail in Citing references and writing the bibliography, pp. 59–65.

▶ Writing clearly

It is not profound to be obscure. Aim to write your report as clearly and simply (don't confuse with simplistically) as possible, as the purpose of your report is not to impress by using masses of technical jargon, it is to make sure that the reader can understand what you have said.

Structure your writing into ordered paragraphs that deal with a single topic area or a string of related topic areas and keep them in systematic order. If you dot your thoughts or findings about all over the place and do not bring your work together in a logical and coherent manner, the reader will be lost and so will the impact of your report.

In academic circles reports have traditionally been written impersonally, avoiding the use of personal pronouns such as 'we' or 'I'. This practise has diminished in some educational establishments, and if you are writing for a school, college or university, it would be wise to check what they want before you start writing. However, it is still relevant to avoid using slang in a research document and witticisms or throwaway comments are not usually well received.

In the workplace the aim of your research paper is usually to inform and, providing this is done in a businesslike manner with a well-documented and informative paper, whether you use personal pronouns is usually a matter for your decision. However, you would be wise to check with your supervisor just in case a different approach is needed.

▶ Writing the conclusion

Inexperienced researchers often find it difficult to write the conclusion to their study. They will work their way through the structure of the research (see Table 8.1) without too many difficulties, but bringing it all together in a conclusion is sometimes problematic. Bouma and Atkinson (1995:240) acknowledge this problem and advise researchers that a useful way to organise a conclusion is to begin by referring back to the beginning where the problem and hypothesis was stated.

When the research produces a negative or inconclusive result, the problem of writing a conclusion is made worse. All researchers feel sure that their hypothesis is right, but if the research results point clearly against this being the case, they must say so; and if their results are inconclusive (not pointing decisively in one direction or the other), it would be wrong to write a biased conclusion that tilted towards the researcher's own feelings. It is difficult to achieve this impartiality because most inexperienced researchers become emotionally attached to their topic and find it difficult to be open minded when the research ends.

However, it is useful to future researchers in the area to read the truthful results of your research, since there will be lessons to be learned, perhaps regarding the design, methodology or scale. Addressing questions such as those below will add to the findings of the research:

• How efficient was the design of the research method?
• How far did the achieved sample of respondents differ from that intended initially?
• What weaknesses occurred during the research process?

What to do about new ideas at a late stage

Sometimes in qualitative research the actual results and the discussion about them get intertwined because the very nature of this type of research leads you to start by asking about one issue which then leads you to ask about it in a slightly different way. You will have the results from both enquiries, which may very well have led you to think differently again and target your research in another way and so on. This can often happen quite late in the research process.

If that's what has happened in your research, summarise it all in a logical way, explaining what happened. Always remember that the main objective of your research is to explain it in an honest and effective way, not to try to fit it into some preset mould of what ought to have happened.

What is the purpose of the conclusion?

The purpose of a conclusion is to provide a thoughtful and attentive end to a piece of writing; it is *not* just a summary of what has happened. A good conclusion will:

1. Summarise what was learnt and point out the direction for future research.
2. Evaluate the benefits, rewards, actions, applications and so on of the research.
3. Discuss the weaknesses and assess how these could affect the findings.

There are several general points that a researcher should bear in mind to help them to write a good conclusion:

1. Never introduce a new idea in the conclusion.
2. Do not focus on a minor point in the research.
3. Never try to cover up incomplete work but be honest.
4. Do not apologise for your view by saying things such as 'at least this is what I believe' – you are dealing with the facts of your research.
5. Do not repeat yourself.

A reader should be able to pick up your research report, and grasp the significance of it by reading only the Abstract and the Conclusion, both of which should be very short sections.

Common problems in writing conclusions

Not keeping in mind the research objectives. Sometimes your research objectives will change during the research itself; there is nothing wrong with this. It is an indication of an interesting and a 'live' piece of research.

However, if you change the line of your research you should look again at your original objectives at the same time. Your conclusion should address the objectives that you addressed throughout the actual research, not the objectives that you initially decided to accomplish but later discarded in favour of others. Address all of this very briefly in the conclusion.

Failure to focus on the significant issues. The mass of your research work has been *specific,* the conclusion should begin to move back to the *general.* Relate your research to its effect in the area in which it is placed, in other words put it in context.

Too much unnecessary detail. This is the wrong place for bringing in detailed information about your analysed results or methodology. Summarise concisely what you learnt from your research (this might only take one quite brief paragraph) and emphasise the implications and evaluations.

Failure to reveal incomplete or negative findings. Do not ignore those parts of your research that in your opinion did not arrive at a satisfactory conclusion.

Too long. A conclusion should be short – one or two A4 pages at the most.

Your research should aim to give leads to other researchers and suggest what part of the field would benefit from further work being carried out, perhaps from a different angle or on a bigger/smaller scale. The accuracy of your observations would not only minimise the risk of fruitless duplication but would give a appropriate starting point to others.

▶ Dictionaries and thesauruses can help

Do check your report for spelling errors once it is finished. Some people find it disruptive to check for spelling errors when they are in process of composing the substance of their writing, but that shouldn't mean that no spelling check is ever made. If you are unsure about a word, look it up in a good dictionary.

Another invaluable tool is a thesaurus, which is very useful for finding an alternative expression or the right word to fit a thought. Sometimes it is difficult to express a point without using the same word over and over again and by looking up that particular word in a thesaurus you will be offered a long list of alternatives.

For example, I looked up the word *research* and was offered 4 areas to pursue – be curious; enquiry; experiment; or study. I chose enquiry and was presented with another 14 areas of possible use. If I followed the offered word *search*, I was presented with a list of 30 words with a similar meaning to that of search, for example probe, investigate, enquiry and so on. This could be invaluable to eliminate endless repetition of the same word.

More help is given if you read the corresponding computer information in this chapter on Computer dictionaries (spellcheckers) and grammar checkers (pp. 209–14).

▶ Grammar, correct words and abbreviations

We are often unaware of why we write in a certain way, we often do not know the rules of grammar but we know when something sounds wrong. 'The examiners *is* happy' would jump out of the page, screaming at you that *is* should be replaced with *are*. The rule behind this knowledge is probably long forgotten.

One or two of the more common areas for grammatical error may be worth checking when you proofread your finished report, and these together with other points worth watching are listed below.

Double negatives that produce a positive statement are worth looking out for. 'The answer was not lacking' means the same as 'there was an answer'. The first statement is not as easy to understand as the second, and it also makes the writing rather more boring and stuffy. It is not uncommon nowadays to read sentences that have been constructed in a similar manner to the one that you are reading at this moment. If you find yourself writing 'It is not uncommon', ask yourself whether what you are saying could be better expressed by writing 'It is common'.

Adjectives. Avoid an adjective that qualifies and weakens the meaning, for example 'it was *rather* difficult'. Ask yourself whether the word *rather* does anything to emphasise the word difficult. It might perhaps be better to leave the adjective out altogether or choose one with a better explanation, such as '*very* difficult'.

Ambiguity. Are you saying what you mean? If you had written 'The secretary and treasurer agreed to talk to me', do you mean there is one official holding a double position, or did you speak to two separate officials?

Long sentences. If you try to say too many things at once, the result is likely to be a confusing mess, especially if you have tried to impress the reader with your knowledge. Wordiness, padding and needless technical jargon, together with sentences overloaded with unfamiliar words, make for difficult reading. A leading authority in the education field wrote the following:

The possibility of conflict between the quasi-autonomous centres of immediate decision making and the 'mutual orientations' of the groups participating at the national level is overcome through the inertia of the system which remains in equilibrium because no one group of interest can predominate in all spheres of educational activity (although it should be said that [name withheld] does recognise that there is a wieldy determinant authority and great power and that makes him uneasy about the concept of partnership, as he feels that it implies equality between the partners, whereas the model of the 'senior partner' is more appropriate).

This 100-word sentence contains only two commas and one full stop. It makes such interesting reading, doesn't it?

Sexist language. It does not make for easy reading if, in an effort to avoid sexist language, you randomly alternate the use of 'he' and 'she' in your writing. It is confusing and rather clumsy, although it can work if used very sparingly indeed. Linguistic mutants such as 's/he' are distracting when used in text, as in some cases the eye picks out the mutant instead of concentrating on the meaning of the written words. Moreover, it is difficult to pronounce – how on earth do you read it aloud?

Plural pronouns offer a solution, and this method has been used frequently throughout this book. For example, 'Researchers often choose two methods of gathering data' or 'People said that they would prefer to pay less'.

Use the correct word and avoid abbreviations. Some words are fine in everyday speech or in the right context but are misused when applied in a serious or business report. Colloquial abbreviations, such as *hasn't*, *can't*, *don't*, are inappropriate in official research papers (although they are becoming more acceptable), and using 'America' where you mean 'United States', or 'England' when you mean 'United Kingdom' doesn't help to clarify the substance of your topic.

Conventions on what is acceptable in report writing are changing, due in part to the influence of the Internet. My own style tends to be less formal than that of some of my academic colleagues and you will read textbooks that advocate a far more formal approach than I have outlined. It is best to be guided by the educational or work establishment in which you are carrying out your research.

▶ Full stops, commas and colons

The use of punctuation marks is an area that is often misunderstood and consequently they are misused. When we speak we help to indicate the relationship between one idea and another by changes of tone, gestures, facial expression and pauses in speech. In writing we do not have these aids and their place is taken by the symbols we know as punctuation marks.

The rules of punctuation are not rigid and a skilful writer will use punctuation in order to express a subtle hint of meaning. Nevertheless there are practices that are commonly followed and when punctuation is used carefully it will assist clear writing.

The full stop *(.)* is used after a complete statement and is the strongest break that can be used between ideas. If you are in doubt, always put a full stop and start a new sentence.

The comma *(,)* marks a shorter break than the full stop and indicates a pause in sense. The comma can be used to show a slight change of direction, as in the following sentence:

> The university football team ended the season well by winning the Kingsway cup, although earlier in the year this seemed unlikely.

It can also be used to prevent the reader misunderstanding what has been written or where its omission might completely alter the meaning of a sentence. Consider the following sentences, each of which implies a different meaning:

> The external research paper, I found was relevant to my needs.
> The external research paper I found, was relevant to my needs.
> The external research paper I found was relevant to my needs.

Semicolons *(;)* are used when a comma does not seem to offer enough of a break but when a full stop makes the break too divided. It is often a matter of personal preference whether a comma or semicolon is used and there are no rigid right and wrong rules in most cases.

Observe the following example where a comma could quite easily replace the semicolon:

> I started the research in January. The work took up most of my weekends; and I would not wish to have to go through it all over again.

The extra pause given by the semicolon gives the reader time to appreciate the first part of the sentence.

The colon *(:)* is often used for introducing lists of words or quotations. For example a list of adverbs follows:

> Loudly

Slowly

Quickly

It is also used to amplify something that has been said in the preceding part of the sentence. For example:

> The research department started in the 1960s with only 3 members of staff: now it has more than 200 employees.

▶ Layout intricacies

Individual institutions have different ideas of what constitutes good layout detail in exactly the same way as individual people have. You may have been given a list of what layouts are required or you may have been left to your own devices.

If you are unsure exactly what layout to adopt, read through the following suggestions and adopt those parts that you like. There is more advice on how to achieve these layouts using the computer in Part B of this chapter.

Line spacing. It goes without saying that you will have no choice when it comes to the line spacing of your document as it will almost certainly need to be printed in double line spacing rather than single (see the difference in the following boxed examples). However, longer quotations are normally displayed in single line spacing.

Single-sided paper. It is usually a requisite of research reports that they be printed on one side of the paper.

Page numbering. This is essential and needed for the contents page.

Margins. The left margin, which may have to be bound or clipped into a plastic binder, should be larger than the right. A left margin of 3.17 cm and a right margin of 2.5 cm is usually sufficient. Margin measurement is one of the items that is usually specified by educational establishments.

Display of headings. Normally more prominence should be given to main headings than to the subheadings. The body of the text should be displayed in a slightly smaller font size than headings or subheadings. Consistency is the key for a professional look.

Quotations. If you are quoting only a short sentence or a few words, indicate the quotation by inserting double quote marks (inverted commas) in the main text, with the source in brackets. Occasionally some educational establishments will request that you use single quotes, so you would be wise to check this before you start.

An example of single line spacing

This is an example of single line spacing. You will notice that there is not enough space between the lines to write any comments or advice. It does not use as many pages to present identical amounts of text when compared with text presented in a double line spacing format.

An example of double line spacing

This is an example of double line spacing. Double line spacing is used in education to offer examiners and lecturers a space between the lines of text in which they could write comments or advice. It is also used in business for the same reason.

Also notice the extra space between the heading and the text that follows and between the two paragraphs. It is considered to be the clearest and easiest line spacing presentation available.

If the quotation is longer, it will need a paragraph to itself. This is normally in single line spacing and indented by approximately 1.27 cm.

There is a lot more information on quotations and referencing which you can find in Citing references and writing the bibliography, pp. 59–65.

The presentation of your word-processed work goes hand in hand with accuracy, one without the other produces poor work. If you produce accurate text but do not adopt good presentation skills, the finished document will fall well short of what could be achieved. One of the secrets of success is to be consistent in whatever spacing style you adopt.

▶ First, second, third draft?

There is no golden rule about how many rewrites are needed to produce an acceptable research paper. The more you apply the advice given so far in this book the less likely you are to need to redraft your work.

When you have finally completed your first draft, it is a good idea to put it to one side for a week or so. Try to forget all about it if you can and give your brain a rest from the constant thoughts of research that have been with you over the past months. Don't leave it for longer than two or three weeks, however, or you will no longer be able to pick up the threads of ideas and judge whether what you have written is a true indication of what happened.

Now reread it and produce your second draft. Almost certainly you will wish to amend some areas, scrap certain paragraphs and insert new ones as you re-evaluate what you have written. Check that the spelling and grammar is acceptable and that the paragraphs link coherently. Ask someone if they would help you by reading through your draft for any remaining errors, and if they can give you some indication whether the substance of your work is clear and the sentence construction easy to understand, so much the better. They do not necessarily have to be an expert in the field of your research to be able to do this.

If you are carrying out small-scale research in an educational establishment, your tutor is likely to ask to see your first draft a couple of times during its formative period. They like to check that you are working along the right lines and this can be of immense help to the first-time researcher. If your research is outside education, you might find it supportive to ask your supervisor to glance over your early work to see whether you are working along the right lines. It is comforting to know that you are doing it right, and the advice that they may give could help you to use your time to the best advantage.

It may be that your rewrites run to a third, fourth or, if you haven't planned it, even a fifth attempt, but the more you have used your computer to produce your research paper the easier this will be.

When you are finally sure that you have got everything right, it is time to check final page numbering, write the contents page, check your bibliography is complete and hand in your research paper – hopefully within the allotted time.

PART B

You alone are responsible for seeing that your work is well written and properly presented. As well as addressing the issues of your research, your research paper should look professional, be clean and neat, and the golden rule that will help you to achieve the professional look is to be consistent in your layout details.

If you can allow yourself time at this stage to check all the last minutiae of detail, you will be well rewarded with a proficient and well-presented report. Unfortunately this part of the process is very often viewed by researchers as being tedious when compared with the intellectually exciting or interesting areas that have gone before. It can be tedious, especially if the researcher has not come to grips with using the computer because then all the work has to be done manually. However, if a researcher is able to manipulate a few keys and make the computer do the tedious work, this stage does not take long.

The actual writing of the research paper is also not so onerous if a computer has been used throughout the research process. Now the researcher is in the envious position of having quite a chunk of the work already keyed in and saved on computer, it will just need bringing into the appropriate section and adjusting a little for clarity and continuity in writing.

▶ Using the word processor

If you have not yet used the word processor in your research process, now really is the crucial time when typing your final document and saving it into a computer will save you so much time. Even if you haven't mastered using the word processor at this late stage, a day away from your research writing just to master the basics will be hugely rewarding, even now. It is unlikely that the first draft will be the finished version and you are going to have to rewrite several sections more than once.

If you are approaching this with the idea that you can use an old-fashioned typewriter, please think again. Once committed to paper via a typewriter, any alterations will mean typing whole pages of text, whereas if the same alterations have to be made on a word processor, you need only alter the particular paragraph in question. There is no need to retype or rejig the position of the surrounding paragraphs; the computer will see to that automatically for you.

Similarly, if you have in mind handwriting your paper, you are making life very difficult for yourself. It is probably still worth taking a quick crash course in using a keyboard and set about saving the work to computer even now, in what is almost the last stages of your research process.

If you were one of those wise people who began to use a computer before you even decided for sure on your research topic, you are now in the very strong position of being able to let technology do the hard work for you.

▶ Computer dictionaries (spellcheckers) and grammar checkers

It is possible to instruct your computer to check your documents for grammar and spelling errors either as you proceed or at the end of keying in your work.

However, allowing the computer to check your work *is no substitute for doing the job yourself by proofreading it*. The computer does a marvellous job but it is not able to differentiate between the meanings of words, for example it does not know the difference between *there*, *their* or *they're* or *weather* and *whether*, and so on. The same is true of grammatical errors; it doesn't alert you to all errors, so use these very helpful aids in addition to proofreading, not as a replacement for checking things personally.

If you are using Microsoft software you may notice a red or green squiggly line under some words as you type. This is Word alerting you to a possible error. The red colour indicates a spelling mistake, while the green alerts you to a possible grammar error. You have the choice when this happens of either

1. ignoring it until you have finished the whole document and then checking all the spelling and grammar errors in one go, or
2. looking at each error as it is flagged up.

Most softwares have very similar checking systems and if you consult your on-screen help facility using the words 'spellchecker' and/or 'grammar checker' you should be presented with detailed instructions on operating that particular system. To use the Microsoft spelling and grammar checkers follow the instructions below.

Spellchecking your document as you proceed
When a word is underlined in a red squiggly line indicating a spelling error, you have several choices, the main ones being:

* Delete the word and retype immediately if you know the correct spelling
* Click the *right* mouse button on the incorrect word, and choose the correct word by clicking on it (*left* mouse button) from the list presented (if the correct word is shown).

The incorrectly typed word is then immediately replaced. If the word is not shown in the list, then try typing it with a slightly different spelling – even if your second attempt is not correct, it might be recognised by the computer which will then offer you the correct spelling.

- Ignore the suggested spelling. The computer will highlight as a misspelling any word that is not in its dictionary, however sometimes you know that the word you have typed is correct and you have no wish to change it, for example the name of a person such as Mr Brause. When this is the case, you can either ignore the red squiggly lines, or if you find that they irritate you, right click on the word in question and then instruct the computer to *ignore* this word or *add* it to the dictionary by clicking as appropriate.

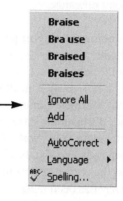

Autocorrect spellchecking function

If you frequently mistype a particular word, perhaps always typing 'reassearch' instead of 'research', you can instruct the computer to automatically change the incorrect word to the correct spelling each and every time that you key it in.

To do this click the right mouse button on the incorrect word and then click on AutoCorrect. Next choose the correct spelling from the list by clicking on it once with the left mouse button. From now on, whenever you type this

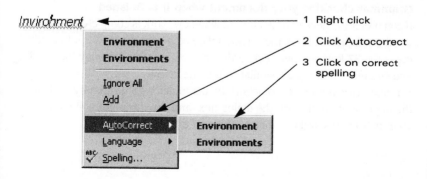

Computer Support

incorrect version of the word, it will automatically be corrected.

Spellchecking your document when it is finished

Some people find that it interrupts their flow of thought if they stop frequently to correct errors, and they prefer to leave this task until the end of their work or at least until the end of the particular working day. It is easy to do this by simply clicking on the spelling icon 🔤 on the standard toolbar, and answering the screen prompts as appropriate. The computer will check the document from the cursor point onwards.

Grammar checking your document as you proceed

The computer will highlight with a green squiggly line the word, phrase or sentences that it believes to be incorrect. Unfortunately the grammar mistakes that are flagged aren't always mistakes and sometimes the computer will overlook really obvious grammar errors. Nevertheless, it's worth skimming through your document in case an error is highlighted that you might miss when proofreading your work. To do this, click the right mouse button on the green squiggly line and the computer will display grammatical suggestions. Click on the correct replacement if it is offered and you consider a grammar error really has been made.

Alternatively you can instruct the computer to ignore the offending word/s by clicking on **Ignore Sentence** or if you want further information on any error click on **Grammar** . . . and follow the screen information.

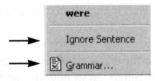

Grammar checking your document when it is finished

If you prefer to check your document when the work is completed click on the word **Tools** at the top of the screen, followed by **Grammar** . . . (alternatively press the F7 key on your keyboard). The computer will display the Spelling and Grammar dialog box, similar to the one below.

Decide whether or not to action the computer's suggestion by clicking on the appropriate button on the dialog box, and the computer will then act on your instructions and move on to the next error that it finds.

Spelling and Grammar: English (U.K.)   ? ✕

Subject-Verb Agreement:

This list is only a minute glimpse at what is obtainable; there is a huge range of CD-ROMS that cover almost any area that you can think of.	**Ignore**
	Ignore Rule
	Next Sentence

Suggestions:

a huge range of CD-ROMS that covers	**Change**
——————OR——————	
huge range of CD-ROMS that cover	

Dictionary language: English (U.K.)

☑ Check grammar

[?]   Options...   Undo   Close

If your spelling/grammar feature does not work

Word software will underline an incorrect word with a red squiggly line, if this does not happen on your machine it is probably because the feature has been turned off. To turn it on, click on the word **Tools** (top of the screen), followed by **Options**.

File Edit View Insert Format Tools Table Window Help

Body Text Sect ▾ Arial   ▾ 12 ▾   **B** *I* U ≡ ≡ ≡ ≡ □ ▾ 🖉 ▾ A ▾

Check that the **Spelling and Grammar** tab (see the following illustration) is on top by clicking on it. There should be a tick in the **Check spelling as you type** box, plus one in the **Check grammar as you type** box if you wish possible spelling and grammar errors to be pointed out. To insert a tick simply click in the empty box. Finally click on **OK**.

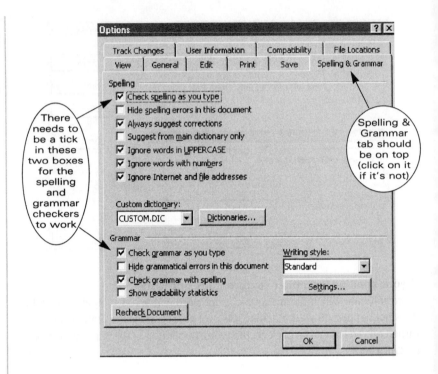

► Bringing together previously saved files

If the advice given in previous chapters has been heeded, then, at this point of writing up, the researcher is in the lucky position of being able to bring together into one document the various bits of already keyed in and saved work. There should be separate files saved with various bits of research information, hopefully the files are in relevant folders and saved with logical names. Perhaps there are files of interview information, questionnaire results, a bar chart, a pie chart and a write-up of the analysis results, together with Internet material.

Some people now like to print a hard copy of their various documents, making sure that they have indicated the file name and where it can be found on the computer as they do so. Incidentally most computer software will add and print automatic file names for you at the top or foot of the printout if you request it. (If you are using Microsoft Word click on **View – Header/footer – insert AutoText – File name and path**.) Then, when they are clarifying their ideas prior to the actual writing (see Before writing the first draft, pp. 194), they insert their printouts in the relevant parts of the draft layout, ready to be inserted when they reach the writing up of that area.

Researchers who have saved parts of the work as they proceed save themselves an immense amount of time at this stage.

▶ How the computer can assist your writing up

There are many ways in which the computer can help you smooth the way when you are writing your research paper. A few of the most useful ones are listed in Table 8.2, but this is not an exhaustive list; it would fill an entire book to list everything that would aid your research writing.

If brief instructions are given they are for Microsoft Word software because it is the most popular software in use at present, but many of these functions are available in other software packages, so do consult your online help facility or buy an instruction manual for your particular software package.

TABLE 8.2

Function	Description
Double or single line spacing	Line spacing is one of the essentials of display in a research paper and both spacing styles are needed. The document as a whole is normally in double line spacing and a lengthy quotation must be presented not only in its own paragraph but also in single line spacing. To put work in double line spacing: • Highlight paragraph/s that need to be in double • Hold down the control key on the keyboard and tap the number 2 (for double) at the top of the keyboard If you want single repeat above but tap the number 1.
Emphasising text	Italicising, emboldening, or underlining any words that merit important emphasis is simple to do and effective in presentation. • Highlight the relevant words • Click on the screen icon for bold, italic or underline **B** *I* <u>U</u> It is not good display to use all of these at the same time – it looks much more professional if you keep it simple.

TABLE 8.2 CONTINUED

Function	Description
Enumeration (numbered items)	You can add numbers to the left side of your work quite simply. This is useful for lists or numbered paragraph work, etc.

- Highlight area you wish to enumerate
- Click on Format
- Click on Bullets and Numbering
- Click on Numbering tab (if not on top)
- Choose the display you prefer, ie
  1 2 3
  1.1 1.2 1.3
  A B C or
  (1) (2) (3) etc, by clicking on it
- Click OK.

You can do this more simply by highlighting and clicking on the Numbering icon ▦ , but then you will have to take whatever display is given

| File reference | This is useful if you have saved a lot of documents in various directories and would like a printout on the bottom of hard copies of exactly where this document can be located in the computer: |

- Click on View
- Click on Header and Footer
- Insert Autotext
- File name and path
- Click on Close

| Headers and footers | If you wish to print the main heading at the top of every page: |

- Click on View
- Click on Header and Footer
- Key in appropriate information
- Click on Close

| Insetting paragraphs | This is essential for quotation work, when any quote of length must be keyed in its own paragraph and indented from the left: |

- Highlight the text to be indented
- Click on the Increase Indent icon ▦

| Move paragraphs | When you read through your first draft you may decide that a certain paragraph or section would have more impact or be more appropriate if placed elsewhere. This is easy to achieve. |

- Highlight paragraph to be moved
- Click on Edit – Cut (or click on the scissors icon ✄)

- Put the cursor where you wish paragraph to appear

• Click on Edit – Paste (or click on the paste icon 📋)

Move quickly to another area of your work

As well as using Page Up/Page Down keys and the scrolling bar on the right side of the screen, you can instruct the computer to move swiftly to a certain page. This is very useful when you have a lot of pages of text in the document:

• Click on Edit
• Click on Go To
• Type in page number required
• Click on Go To
• You will see that you have a wealth of choices of areas on the left side of the dialogue box (Go to what?), so you could just as easily go to a heading or a comment as a page number
• Click on Close when finished

Outline numbering

The numbering in detail of headings, subheadings and so on can be added automatically as you key in by using outline numbering. (See Figure 8.1 as an example of this use in a contents page.) To achieve this:

• Click on Format
• Click on Bullets and Numbering
• Click on Outline Numbered and choose display required by clicking on it
• Click OK

(Note some people prefer to use 'tables' to achieve this)

Page numbering

Automatic page numbering is brilliant in that if you insert an extra page or a few extra paragraphs at any point, then the computer automatically moves text around and changes the page numbering correctly to match:

• Click on Insert
• Click on Page numbering – choose position (bottom or top of page) and alignment (left, right or centre)
• Click OK

Remove a paragraph

On second reading you may decide that you've written rubbish and want to get rid of it before anyone else sees it:

• Highlight the 'rubbish'
• Click on Edit – Cut (or click on the scissors icon)

Search for a particular word

If you wish to find out where you have mentioned a particular word before, it is easy to request the computer to search for any given number of words for you. This is particularly useful if you have a long document and you cannot remember what, if anything, you have said about a topic or person before:

• Click on Edit
• Click on Find
• Key in the required word/s
• Click on Find Next
• Click on Cancel when finished

TABLE 8.2 CONTINUED

Function	Description
Search for a particular word and replace in with another	Perhaps you have mistakenly spelt someone's name wrong or keyed in an incorrect word throughout the document. This enables you to change all the entries of the word/s in one go, or to view each occasion that it occurs and decide in each individual case:

- Click on Edit
- Click on Replace – Key in word/s to be found
- Key in word/s you wish to appear in their place
- Either click on 'Replace All' (which will search the entire document and replace throughout) or click on 'Find Next' (which gives you the option of deciding whether to replace on each occasion)

Function	Description
Sort into alphabetical order	This is especially useful in the bibliography section when you want to display your list of authors in alphabetical order – these few keystrokes will save you hours of working out. *Be careful with this, however, because once sorted you can't undo it.*

Highlight the text you wish to be sorted into alphabetical order. (remember *not* to include any headings if you are working in a table):

- Click on Table
- Click on Sort – key in which column to sort on (if you have more than one)
- Click on appropriate format (ie text, numbers, etc)
- Choose either ascending or descending order (ie A to Z or Z to A)
- Click OK

Function	Description
Styles	When you are typing a long document over a number of weeks it is easy to forget what font sizes you have chosen in previous sections – essential if you wish to be consistent and your work is to have a professional look.

You can automatically set up styles for your document which is very useful if you would like your computer to automatically choose the same font in the same size, perhaps emboldened, for all main headings; and automatically choose a slightly smaller font, perhaps emboldened for all subheadings. At the same time it will produce the main body of text in a slightly smaller, not emboldened font. You choose the styles and the computer will do the rest:

- With your document on screen (and saved) click on Format
- Click on Theme
- Click on Style Gallery
- Choose a style by clicking on one of the names in the left column – the style of your document will change accordingly in the Preview Window. You can preview different styles by clicking on other names in the list

- If you want to change the style of your document click OK when the Preview Window shows you a preferred layout style. Your document will immediately change style
  or
- Click Cancel if you prefer the original document style

Word count | The ability to count pages, sections or the whole document. This is extremely useful when you have been set a maximum/ minimum number of words to work to:

- Click on Tools
- Click on Word Count
- Highlight beforehand the area you wish to count if it is not to be the whole document

▶ Merging files together

Word-processed files

As you write your research paper you will reach various points where you wish to insert a document or an area of work that you have composed or calculated previously and have saved under a different file name. It is a relatively straightforward matter to insert previously saved documents into an existing new document on screen.

In the first instance let us suppose that you have an older previously saved word-processed document that you wish to insert into the current on-screen document. To do this you need to leave the current document open on screen and also open the older previously saved document, then follow through the steps outlined below:

1. When both documents are open, highlight the text you require from the older previously saved document and copy it (in Microsoft Word just click on the **copy** icon on the toolbar).

2. Now bring the current document to the front so that it is on top. There are several ways of doing this but one way would be just to close down the older previously saved document (Click on **File** and then **Close**).

3. Place the cursor where you want the text to appear, and paste the highlighted text. (In Microsoft Word you do this by simply clicking on the **paste** icon on the toolbar.)

The text from the older document will now appear in the current document, but no doubt you will need to tidy it up and check that it reads well and uses the same tense and so on.

Files from non-word-processing software

If you are bringing a document that has been saved in different software into your current research document, such as a graph or pie chart, then you need to ensure that you have the 'handles' on screen. Handles have the same function as the 'highlighting' in a word-processed document – it marks out the area that you wish to move or act upon in some way (see Figure 8.3 below).

Note the handles in the four corners halfway along each line. You can obtain the handles just by clicking once in the centre of the chart with the left-hand mouse button. Once you have the handles you can follow the numbered advice given in the previous section, Word-processed files.

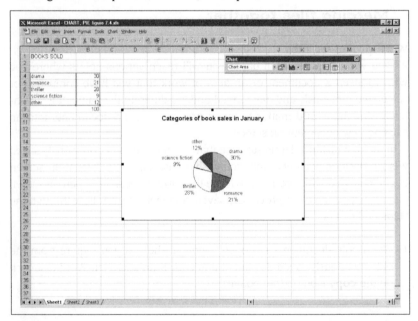

Figure 8.3

Internet files

Inserting information that you have saved from the Internet is handled in a very similar way to the above. The problem with Internet files is that they are likely to have various illustrations and the diversity of fonts, text sizes, colours and special effects that have been used will be very different to the style that you have adopted for your research paper.

Some pages can also be problematical because of the links and effects that have been used. If you wish to use information obtained from the Internet you must obtain the permission of the person, university or company who owns it. If you are intending to read the information and quote a part of it, you need to make it clear that the words are not your own. You do this in just the same way that you would if it you were quoting from a book or an article – you would cite its source.

Look at the sample Internet page (Figure 8.4, below) which has been downloaded without alteration. It was put on the Web by Palgrave Publishers and saved as an HTML file. You can see the wide range of fonts and styles used in just this starter page.

As has been mentioned elsewhere in this book (Folders (or directories), pp. 49–50 and How to make folders on the computer, pp. 50–1), it is better to save Internet files to a specific Internet folder to read later, rather than try to read, cut and paste or save edited parts when online. You can continue browsing when online and then read at your leisure later.

Don't forget to bookmark the addresses of saved files, then you will be able to find them again without difficulty. You will also have the information ready should you need to cite that source. See Bookmarking useful Internet sites, pp. 78–9 for more detailed instructions.

Should you wish to incorporate some of Internet text into your own document once offline, then you could highlight it and cut and paste in the usual way. See Table 8.2 if you need help to do this.

To remove a picture or graph from an Internet page it is usually better to point at it from the left and click the left mouse button once – the picture will then highlight and you can press the keyboard delete button. If you try to click in the centre of the picture then your computer might try to take you back online if it has an Internet connection.

Figure 8.4 Web page produced with the kind permission of Palgrave Publishers Ltd

9 Powerful Presentations

PART A

Standing up in front of a group of people is not everyone's idea of having a good time. Apprehension and sheer terror are just two of the words that spring to mind when considering this thought.

As a research student you may well be asked to explain your research project to your colleagues, and as an employee your line manager might request that you attend a meeting of senior staff and explain what you have been doing and what the results are of your research work. If terror and anxiety set your heart racing at the very thought of being required to do this, don't worry. You are not alone. You will often hear actors and actresses say that they experience a rush of nerves before a performance and the same is true of lecturers and teachers, especially when a new term starts and they are faced with the 'unknown' of new pupils.

There is no one, correct way of producing a good presentation. The interaction between the speaker and the audience cannot be guaranteed and the same presentation can be perceived differently by two different audiences, thus producing different outcomes. However, this chapter sets out to offer a set of guidelines and suggestions to help the inexperienced speaker to develop strategies to cope with what can be a nerve-racking ordeal.

▶ How do you listen?

We all have our own ideas about what makes a good speaker. As people come out of a meeting, comments always abound, and you can hear the murmuring as you leave. 'Wasn't that interesting', 'what a good speaker', 'that was so boring!' or 'what a waste of time!' If you would like people to receive your presentation well, think first of all about what it is that a successful speaker does, and what makes an audience listen.

When you are listening to a colleague speak in a one-to-one situation it is doubtful whether you concentrate on *every* word they say. At times your mind will go off at a tangent and you will find yourself thinking about something totally different; perhaps you have an urgent task you want to finish, or you'll suddenly remember that you haven't any food in the fridge, or your colleague may suggest a course of action you're not sure about and you immediately start to work out an alternative solution. So listeners are often distracted by their own thoughts. Stuart explains this as the 'Route 350' system.

> The human mind processes words at a rate of approximately 500 a minute but we speak at about 150 words a minute, so the difference between the two is 350. When listeners 'switch off' the chances are they are on Route 350 . . . Most listeners are not like dry sponges ready to absorb everything the speaker gives them. They are continually assessing, digesting, rejecting or accepting what they hear. (Stuart 1988:2)

So the trick is to use devices to capture, by other means, the 350-word void; or at least not fall into the trap of encouraging the listener to think about other things.

▶ Helping your audience to listen

People stop listening or only half listen for a number of reasons, and some of these are outside your control. If the listener has overwhelming personal problems, these are going to encroach in all other areas of their life, and you have little chance of retaining their attention for long. However, not all of your audience is going to fall into this category and in the points that follow you are in a position to do something positive.

Practical issues
- The room is too hot/too cold
- The chairs are uncomfortable
- Some people can't see the speaker easily
- It is noisy outside or inside

Personal issues
- The speaker's voice is too quiet or they shout all the time
- Their annoying habits distract people (shuffling papers, rocking to and fro on the spot and so on)
- The appearance of the speaker is off-putting
- Some speakers use fillers annoyingly (for example umm, hahs, I mean, in fact, you know and so on)
- There is no eye contact with the audience

- The script is virtually read word for word from pre-written text
- There is no expressive body language
- The speech is delivered in a monotonous or dull voice

Subject issues
- The issues addressed are too complex or too simple
- The presentation is boring
- The audience anticipates what is about to be said, as everything is so predictable
- The presentation is muddled
- The speaker lacks credibility
- The presentation is full of jargon

The practical issues outlined above could be checked once you know which room you will be using to make your presentation.

The personal issues are difficult for the person giving the presentation to judge. Once the talk is prepared, you need to practise it on a sympathetic colleague or two, whom, you must insist, tell you the truth – there is nothing like constructive criticism to put you on the right track, but you must be prepared to take on board well-meant advice.

The speaker can address the subject issues in the first instance by reading through the proposed presentation, and at the same time considering whether any of these traps have been fallen into. Sometimes, however, the subject matter is so interwoven with the researcher's every waking minute that they are not the best person to judge whether they have fallen into these traps. Once again a trusty colleague could come to the rescue and give you helpful feedback.

▶ Preparing the presentation

Ask yourself what you want to accomplish from the talk, what reaction you want from your audience, and how this talk will benefit you. Don't be negative and say that this is not relevant for you because you are only giving this talk because you have been told to. Even if that is the case, you and your audience might as well gain something along the way, and if you prepare properly the very least you will gain is a feeling of confidence.

Ask yourself whether you want the talk to persuade, inform, warn, amuse, convince, teach or perhaps even inspire your audience. You might want it to do all of these, but if you can decide on just one or two clear objectives it will help you to prepare the presentation.

Write down your objective, making it distinct, detailed and achievable. There is absolutely no point is saying that your objective is to change the way in which managers communicate with their staff if there are no managers in the audience. You have the wrong target audience. If your research has been about changing practice within an organisation and your audience is to be your tutor and the rest of your cohort, perhaps your objective might be to inform the audience about your research and its outcomes. Persuading that audience on your theories on change would be pointless, as they are not in a position of being able to bring about that change.

▶ Pitching the level

Knowing your audience is part of giving a successful presentation. Ask yourself how much they already know about the topic or how much they need to know. It can be very irritating and boring to listen to a detailed account about something that you are completely familiar with. If you are addressing your tutor and class, detailed explanations about the various methodological issues involved in the research would be pointless. They have all had to research around them for their own research paper. However, you might touch briefly on why you chose certain methods and the problems or successes that you encountered.

▶ Building a logical structure

By building a logical structure into your presentation and letting your listeners know what that structure is, you are helping their minds not to wander. By summarising at the end of each part of the structure you will help them back into listening mode if they have wandered off. Put yourself in your listeners' position, if your concentration had lapsed and you had missed five minutes of a talk, would you be able to pick it up again easily? Summarising at the end of each section will help to bring the wanderers back into the fold.

There are several types of structure that you could use and they are outlined in the following paragraphs.

Natural time structure, which is sometimes called chronological structure. This is rather like telling it in the order in which it happened. Audiences quite enjoy listening to a talk structured in this way, as it is similar to 'telling a story'. It lends itself as a logical structure tool if you are using your talk as a training tool, building the blocks of knowledge one on top of the other. The disadvantage is that the most important part of the topic can sometimes get lost in the middle of the structure somewhere, so special attention has to be drawn to important areas by emphasis and summarising pertinent points.

Qualitative structure. If you choose this method you list the points of your presentation in order of importance beginning with the most significant. This is useful if you want to make an impact at the beginning (when most people are listening) but not a good method if you are trying to build up blocks of knowledge. Providing you keep the rest of your structure interesting and relevant, you will, hopefully, retain their attention.

The practice and the theory. This structure compares the one with the other and works better if the audience is familiar with the theory and/or the practice in the first place. This might be ideal in the case of a student addressing his tutor and class in an area known to them all, such as 'student participation in university affairs'.

Solutions to problems. If your presentation is about an identified problem and through your research you think that you have identified the answer, this might be a suitable structure to use. If you are seeking to impress the boss and are sure that your solution could work, this is definitely the method for your presentation. By setting out the problem initially, addressing it with solutions that have already been tried but have proved unsatisfactory in some way and finally outlining your suggested solution, emphasising all the advantages, you can only put yourself in a good position.

Tell your audience your chosen structure

Whatever structure you decide is right for your talk, let your listeners know the format you have chosen. Tell them the pattern of your presentation without being too wordy. For example, if your presentation was about 'The use of computers in administration work' you might choose to preface your talk like this:

> Today, we are going to look at the use of computers in administration work, and I have split my talk into three main areas. First of all we'll look at present practice and what is happening right now; then we'll look together at how the computer could help improve present practice and finally we'll look at the possible advantages and disadvantages and what I see as being the way forward. At the end of each section I'll stop so that you can ask questions and we can discuss what has just been said.

Your audience knows immediately the pattern for the next half an hour and they know when they're expected to ask questions, which hopefully will eliminate questions thrown at you at any time (as an inexperienced speaker this could be difficult to cope with). By summarising what has been said at the end of each section, you not only bring back into the fold those whose attention has wandered, you also encourage people to ask questions and discuss matters by reminding them of what has been said.

▶ Your opening words

You only get one chance at a good beginning, blow it and you will lose the attention and goodwill of some of your audience immediately. You need to capture your listeners' attention in the first few minutes which is when you will be feeling your most nervous, but this is not the time for a dry mouth and racing heart. You must concentrate all your energy on your audience, and try to put yourself in their position. Be well prepared for these opening few minutes. Good preparation is the key to overcoming those nerves.

The first impression a speaker makes will set the tone for the next 15 minutes. Bell sees this initial communication with listeners as a duty:

> Effective communication is an intimate relationship with other folk, not something that one does alone. . . Your first duty is to stimulate this state of affairs. . . The audience must immediately be made confident that the speaker knows what he is doing. They must find his very first thoughts intensely interesting. This, of course, rules out the usual dreary openings, where, for instance, the speaker talks about himself and his worries as a speaker. (Bell 1987:19)

You need to persuade your listeners quickly that you are worth listening to. Don't make the mistake of immediately launching into your topic in the first 30 seconds. Woo your audience by telling them what they'll gain by listening to you, try to relate it to a personal level. For example, some opening lines might be:

- Have you ever considered how you would manage if a fire broke out in a building and you were visually impaired and unable to see?
- Did you know that our canteen serves 300 cooked lunches every day and they've only had one complaint this year?
- What would you do if your child came home crying because they said they were bullied at school?
- Are you an only child or a first-born child? Did you know that you are considered to be one of the more intelligent of us mere mortals? And those

of you born in the middle somewhere, did you know that you are among the more relaxed of the race. And what of those born last? Well, listen and I'll tell you more.

▶ Keeping their attention

You have immediately captured their attention, but now you need to convince them that they are going to gain something by listening to you. Think about what the wants and needs of your audience might be. If you are in the workplace and addressing managers, they might want to know how methods could be improved or profits maximised, and in this situation you might continue along the following lines:

• I'm going to describe a new communication method that is so good that you'll never have a member of staff complain that 'nobody told them about it' again.
• If you decide to take on board the recommendations I am about to make today as a result of my research, our staff canteen will make 5% more profit and the staff will benefit from a better and, incidentally, cheaper menu.

Of course you are not going to claim something that is not true, but if you are undertaking small-scale workplace research there is bound to be some positive area that you can focus on initially. You can coat the bitter pill later on in your talk. With both of the above statements your audience of managers may only half believe you anyway, but if you make the talk interesting at least they will listen and remember your presentation skills in the future.

If your audience is within the educational establishment, you need to convince them that you are worth listening to in a different way. Your tutor wants to know that you have understood the research process and effectively researched your chosen topic; your fellow students hope that you will be interesting and lively. You need to take them into your confidence and provide them with a deeper outline of the scope of what you are about to say. Tell them that you have no intention of wasting their time labouring over areas of the research process that they have probably been studying in detail themselves for the past six months and are likely to be totally fed up with by now. Let them know the areas that you intend to concentrate on within your topic, and define the exact areas you hope to share with them.

▶ Remembering what you're going to say

So, how will you remember everything you want to say? How will you be sure to deliver it in the right order? Are you proposing to write out your speech word for word? You could do that if it gave you more confidence but please don't then read it out verbatim. A bowed head reading out a speech can be very boring for the audience and you will never have any eye contact with your listeners, and therefore not much interaction. What if you miss your place and become flustered? Perhaps you should think again.

You might find it comforting to write out in detail the beginning and end of the speech; first it will get you over those initial two or three minutes when you will be at your most nervous. Second, as you near the end of your presentation, you are likely to forget an important point (such as to say thank you very much for listening) as a feeling of relief kicks in when you realise the end is in sight.

Writing out the whole speech word for word is fine, albeit time consuming, if you then look through what you have written and make a list of the important points, which could become the main topic areas about which you intend to talk. You can then use this list to prompt your memory into not only covering certain points but also introducing them in a logical order.

If your list could be written as one-liners on small individual cards labelled in numerical order then so much the better. Cards are easier to manoeuvre and turn over than sheets of paper, and they also have the advantage of not waving about much should your hands be a little shaky at the start. It's also a reassuring aid to know that you have mapped out in front of you the main points of your presentation.

Some people also advocate little side remarks written on certain cards (perhaps in a different colour pen), such as smile, look around at the audience, give out handout now and so on. If you think that this will help you, then do it. Some people also punch holes in cards and thread them in order on a treasury tag just in case they drop them: once again if you think this is helpful then copy the idea.

If you are going to talk to an audience for the first time, I really do recommend that you use some kind of card or note system – it will make your talk more logical and interesting and having the notes in front of you will help you to relax.

▶ Timing

Because of nerves, inexperienced speakers will sometimes rush through their presentations at breakneck speed without realising that they are talking far too quickly. Be aware that this happens and try to slow down if you feel that you might be falling into this trap; attempt to pause when you are moving from one point to another, or pause to emphasise certain points. For example, the following sentence is far better with pauses.

> I know that each and everyone of you in this room today has been studying the methodology of research until you are sick to death of it. (*pause, look around and smile*). And you now know absolutely everything there is to know (*big grin, pause and nod head in affirmation statement*). Yes? (*slight pause*). So, if I now proceed in great detail with my views on methodological approaches, then (*very slight pause*), no doubt, you'll get out those rotten tomatoes and start to throw them at me!

Practise your presentation all the way through with a stopwatch. You could write the time taken for various sections in pencil on your cards to give you some idea of where you seem to be taking the most or least time. I say in pencil because you will probably refine the time when you rehearse for a second time and you don't want your cards with crossings out or becoming difficult to read. When you are fairly happy with the timings you could then put a permanent note on each card with an estimated time you've allowed for that topic.

▶ Rehearsing your presentations

It is easy to find excuses not to rehearse aloud your presentation. You will have spent a lot of time deciding what topic areas you will address, putting together the actual presentation and preparing aids which will visually engage your audience and provide variation to your talk. You may even have rehearsed parts of the presentation in order to give yourself some idea of timing, but unless you pull the whole thing together *before the actual event* you are unlikely to do yourself justice and your listeners will get an adequate rather than memorable presentation.

Rehearsing at home

Most people rehearse in the privacy of their home the first time they practise their presentation, and this is a good start. Some people find it helpful to video or record themselves – don't dismiss this immediately! It might help you to see whether you have any annoying habits, what your body language is like and whether you smile at your pretend audience and have eye contact. Listening to your voice is also useful. Check whether you are varying the pitch and volume, using silent pauses and above all rushing through everything at breakneck speed in an effort to get it over as quickly as possible.

Rehearsing to others

The second stage of your rehearsal should involve other people. Although you will probably find this embarrassing, it will help you if you enlist the help of friends or family. Explain to them what you are doing, how important it is to you and just how much practising your talk will help you. Let them know that this is a serious undertaking and you really do want constructive criticism and feedback.

You and they might find it less disrupting if they note points for discussion after the talk rather than during it. If they stop you to offer advice as you proceed, you will probably lose the flow of your talk. During the talk encourage them to ask relevant questions as this will help to prepare you for the kind of questions that your real audience will ask.

You might wish to give them a list of points to look out for, such as body language, eye contact, smiling, voice pitch, topic interest, visual aid/s and so on. When you receive their feedback, accept it graciously and learn from their comments. If you find it too painful to take adverse comments on board immediately after the event, make a note of what is said and put it to one side for another day. You will feel stronger to consider disagreeable comments the next day. Be honest with yourself and try to evaluate the comments dispassionately and remember that they are only trying to help you.

It is a good idea to use a stopwatch for this second rehearsal because rehearsing with an audience will give you a more realistic timing compared with rehearsing to yourself.

A final dress rehearsal

If you are lucky enough to be able to rehearse finally in the room in which you are to give your presentation, so much the better. You will be able to view the size of the room, see whether it is suitable for the type of visual aid/s you have chosen (for example ideally you need blinds if you going to show a video clip), and decide the important issues of where to place the chairs, overhead projector and so on.

It would be helpful if you could familiarise yourself in situ with any equipment that you propose to use; it will be a little late to rectify any minor problems that are discovered as you are about to start your presentation.

However, it is not always possible to see the room in which your presentation will take place, let alone be given time to rehearse in it. Sometimes you will only gain access to the room half an hour or so before your talk and in these circumstances it is not possible for you to check out any physical details in advance. Thirty minutes is better than nothing though, so do quickly check the position of plugs for your equipment and set it up, before anyone else arrives. You might even be able to enlist the help of the first person to arrive in arranging the chairs to your best advantage and so on.

However, not being able to rehearse in the room beforehand does not mean that you shouldn't have a final rehearsal of your speech. You have now, hopefully, amended your presentation to take into account the comments of your friends. At this point you should run through your amended presentation, using all your visual aids, either to (a) a small group of friends, (b) a video camera or tape recorder, or (c) if all else fails, simply to the cat. By doing so your confidence will be boosted and you will be armed with a new timing schedule.

▶ Visual aids – why use them?

Using a visual aid can help to make your presentation come alive, bring a change of scene into the proceedings and, if used well, reinforce certain ideas and points. A computer can produce wonderful visual aids and help you in the actual presentation, but this is dealt with in full in Part B of this chapter.

A visual aid should not use too many words, so summarise in short sentences but do not write masses of text. Compare Figures 9.1 and 9.2. If you were in the audience and the speaker projected the first one onto a large screen, would you bother to read it? Far too many speakers will present a slide such as this, and then proceed to read out every word – very boring for the audience. A visual aid should succinctly explain or clarify a relevant area of your talk or explain a difficult concept.

In Figure 9.1 it would have been far better to have simply listed topic areas, and then the speaker could have used the visual aid as a memory aid to expand each topic area, while the audience would have had something different to look at. Visual aids such as these are even better if a small illustration or picture is incorporated into the slide.

All visual aids should be a support, and focus the listeners' attention to a pertinent area of your topic, and should link easily into the flow of your talk, not stick out like a sore thumb and be a distraction.

Seeing is easier to understand than hearing. Statistics and mathematical concepts are far easier to comprehend when presented in a visual form and comparisons can be highlighted very easily, whereas to explain the same information would demand that your audience concentrate intently in order to understand what is being described.

Considering what type of visual aid to use will depend not only on what

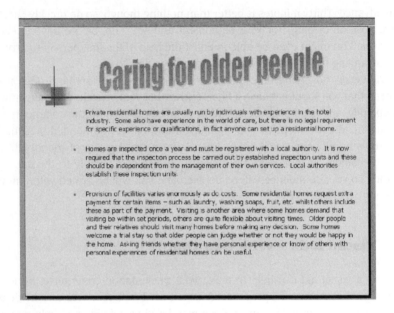

Figure 9.1

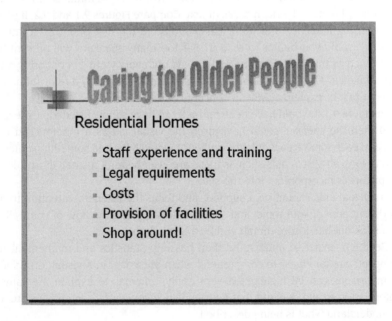

Figure 9.2

type of material you are planning to present visually, but also on the room in which you are going to give the presentation. Ideally it would be helpful if you could see the room beforehand, and then you would be in a better position to judge suitable aids. For example, a flip chart would be of little use in a long narrow room, or a big room, because those members of the audience seated halfway back will not be able to see it clearly. In fact, if you have a large audience, a flip chart would not be your ideal choice in any case.

▷ Types of visual aids

The types of non-computer visual aids you might consider are listed below, together with a brief list of their advantages and disadvantages and potential audience size.

Black- or whiteboards

Everyone is familiar with the old-fashioned blackboard where the teacher wrote in white chalk, although many colours were and still are available. The whiteboard is the update of this; the surface is a smooth white sheet and special thick dry marking pens in a wide range of colours are used. You must have the correct pens, otherwise it is extremely difficult to wipe off what has been written.

One of the commonest faults in using the black- or whiteboard is talking *to it as you write*. If you do this, your audience will only see your back and hear a mumble and even if you do have a booming voice, they will be reading what you write on the board rather than listening to what you say. Many people also obscure what they write as they write it. It takes quite a bit of practise to be able to stand to the left of the board if you are right handed (and vice versa if you are left handed) and write so that you do not obscure the view of the audience. Even then, some boards are so wide that you cannot help but obscure the view if you write all the way across.

They are useful for noting down audience ideas (brainstorming), or for summarising essential points from your talk, and it does help if you write words in a fairly large, clear hand and can manage to keep the line straight as you write.

If the boards are old, you will not have a clear base on which to write and this can make it difficult for your audience to read or if they are mounted too high on the wall, you will be standing on tiptoe in an effort to reach, and it is almost impossible to write in a straight line on a board when standing on tiptoe!

Advantages
- Easy to use
- No training necessary
- Different colours can be easily used to emphasise different points

Disadvantages
- Old boards cannot be adequately cleaned and chalk can be messy
- Special marking pens must be used
- Handwriting needs to be large and clear in order to be seen
- If spelling is a weakness and you do not have the aplomb to enlist help from the audience, its use could be demoralising
- You need to remember to turn to face the audience when you speak and try not to obscure what you are writing

The overhead projector

An overhead projector is a box-shaped piece of equipment with a transparent top. There is a bulb in the box and a lens and mirror system mounted above the box. By placing a translucent (acetate) piece of material on the transparent top of the box, an image is projected onto a wall or screen.

You can prepare material in advance or draw new material onto the translucent A4 size acetate sheets and project it as your presentation proceeds. It can be used in the same way as the flip chart but it has the advantage that you can build up acetate on top of acetate to unfold a complete picture. Special marking pens are used and these are available in many colours.

The size and clarity of the image portrayed on the wall or screen is adjusted by moving a knob on the vertical column, moving the machine itself backwards or forwards or adjusting the light brightness switch. It is easy to operate but it is better to spend five minutes trying it out before the actual presentation. You will also need to set it up in advance in the correct position in the actual room before your presentation. A good tip is to portray one of your own prepared acetate sheets and view it from different parts of the room – is it clear from all angles?

When using the projector there are several points to bear in mind:

1. When you first display an acetate give your audience time to absorb it initially, before launching into explanations, and then leave it in view for a little time when you have finished your descriptions – remember, you may be familiar with its contents, but your audience isn't.
2. Point at the acetate on the projector not the screen; your pointing image is

clearer if you use this method. Also you may not be able easily to reach the image on the screen.

3. When you first display an acetate look at the screen just to check it's not upside down and so on and from then on look at your audience as much as possible; keep eye contact with your audience, and glance at the projector if you need to remind yourself of what's displayed.

4. If you place a pre-prepared acetate on the projector, you could cover up part of it with a piece of plain paper, and reveal it section by section as relevant (if you place the plain paper under rather than over the acetate it is less likely to slip off). This is useful if you have bullet points that you want to talk about individually. It introduces an element of surprise to the listeners who wonder what might be revealed next, it also stops them reading the whole acetate as you try to address the first point. However, don't use this as a ploy throughout your entire presentation – it becomes rather boring and irritating if used more than once.

5. Switch off the projector when it is no longer needed, as the fan that keeps everything cool within the projector can be quite noisy, especially to listeners nearby.

It is possible to use continuous rolls of acetate if you have a lot that you wish to write during the presentation, but in my experience these are not so easy to obtain as the single A4 sheets. If you do use a continuous roll, support both ends, as it can become wieldy and difficult to manoeuvre if unsupported.

Advantages
- Easy to use
- No real training necessary, only familiarisation before use
- Work can be prepared in advance if required
- Portable (some machines more so than others)
- Displays pictures, charts or text equally well
- Use of colour can enhance
- Material can be photocopied onto an acetate for subsequent display
- Can be seen clearly in a well-lit room

Disadvantages
- Need to check focus and set-up immediately before presentation
- Bulbs do wear out and suddenly fail. Check there is a spare bulb (often clipped inside the box) because you do not wish to be unable to use the projector in the middle of your presentation
- Needs special acetates and pens

A projector is useful for small or large groups of listeners because the size of the image on the screen can be varied according to need.

Flip charts

A flip chart is an easel onto which standardised pre-cut paper is attached. After the speaker has used one piece of paper it can be flipped over to reveal the next clean sheet. The standard flip chart white paper size is approximately 810 mm × 510 mm (although it is possible to buy non-standard sizes), and thick marker pens are used to write on the paper.

Most easels are adjustable. This is important especially if you are not very tall, as it can be difficult to 'flip' large sheets of paper over. If you are short, you could enlist the help of someone taller to flip the paper over – this could produce a well-meaning wise crack, all of which lightens and livens the proceedings. So don't rule out using a flip chart solely on height!

Flip charts are useful for noting down audience ideas (brainstorming), or for summarising essential points from your talk. In some cases you could write them beforehand and use them as a link, flipping over the paper when you reach the pertinent part of your talk.

Advantages
- Easy to use
- No training necessary
- Work can be prepared in advance if required
- Portable easel

Disadvantages
- Quality of paper varies – if too thin, pen marks leak through to sheets underneath
- Handwriting needs to be large and clear in order to be seen
- If spelling is a weakness and you do not have the aplomb to enlist help from the audience, its use could be demoralising

A flip chart is useful for small groups of listeners (maximum of approximately 30) and is best used in small rooms.

Slides

Slides are an effective way of presenting certain material. Perhaps your research involved taking pictures of various buildings or people, then using slides would be the second best way after the computer of presenting this material. Taking pictures and having them developed as slides is inexpensive, and if you intend to use them many times over, it is probably worth paying a little extra and having them mounted professionally in order to prolong their life.

Once developed the individual slides are placed in a carousel or rack and loaded into a slide projector. The projector then displays an image of each individual slide on a screen (or white wall) each time you press a button (hopefully on a romote control). The disadvantage is that the room usually has to be darkened for the image to be clear. So, perhaps you would arrange to show your slides at a certain point during the presentation, when dimming the lights and showing colourful images with your background description would make a nice break from the other methods of presentation that you have adopted. Do be aware of overkill however; you shouldn't only use this method of presentation as it can become very boring.

Advantages
- Fairly easy to use
- Provides a colourful interlude in the presentation
- Portable
- Once made slides can be used over and over again

Disadvantages
- Quality and content of slides are only as good as the photographer
- Loading slides into a carousel needs rehearsing – it is very easy to get them upside down or back to front
- The order in which slides are loaded into the carousel cannot be changed easily at the last minute, should if you wish to change the running order
- Presenter needs to learn when not to talk. Sometimes an audience needs time to look at a particularly interesting slide
- Low lights means that the audience cannot make notes
- Eye contact with the audience is not always possible because of low light or the lack of a remote control means the speaker is unable to stand at the front

These 35 mm slides can be used for all sizes of groups and in most rooms, but it is advantageous if the room has blinds or curtains to block out daylight if necessary.

Video or audio clips
Never underestimate the power of moving pictures or audio sounds, they can inform the listener or move the emotions like nothing else. If you think it would enhance your presentation to bring in a few minutes from a video, CD

or tape, be sure that it will support what you are talking about. It is no use using an amusing clip from a video when it only has a very remote connection with your topic and music that needs its connection explained loses any impact or amusement it might have had.

If you plan to use material that you have *not* made personally, ask yourself whether it is ethical to do so. Perhaps it would be better to ask the permission of the people involved before showing it to others.

Using these tools carefully can enhance a presentation, especially if the audience is primed beforehand on what to look or listen for during its playing. The speaker needs to be in control of starting and stopping the machine at the precise times and rounding up the visual or audio interlude as well as tying it neatly into the next part of the presentation.

Advantages
- Provides a distinctive interlude in the presentation
- Fairly easy to use
- Can make an impact on the listener
- Pertinent parts can be played a second time
- Presenter can use lead-in/out time effectively if well planned

Disadvantages
- Quality and content of home-made materials only as good as the expertise of the researcher
- Familiarity with equipment needs to be explored
- Organisation of the running time needs rehearsing
- Low lights means that the audience cannot make notes
- Permission may need to be sought from people involved

Video or audio clips can be used for all sizes of groups and in most rooms, but it is advantageous if the room has blinds or curtains to block out daylight if playing a video.

Physical objects

Showing an audience a physical object is useful when it would be difficult to describe, or it would help the listener to understand better if they could actually see what you were talking about.

Perhaps your presentation might be about a health and safety matter within an engineering company. You may have researched minor accidents that have occurred and decided that if a second safety guard could be attached to a certain piece of machinery it would eliminate human error completely and thereby cut out the minor accidents. It would be unrealistic to plan to bring in heavy or awkwardly shaped machinery; but you could show an illustration of the actual machinery on an overhead projector, and bring an actual or a prototype mock-up of the proposed safety guard. It would add interest to your presentation and save a lot of unnecessary description.

It is not wise to bring in something new if you decide to circulate the object, as you will only have the attention of some of the audience. Deciding how much time to allow an audience to handle an object can be difficult, as you may find that somebody will take ages scrutinising every minor detail of it, and in so doing will hold up the proceedings. It is a good idea to tell your audience precisely what to look for before you circulate the object, and if you find it is moving slowly, circulate as well and control the speed of circulation by pointing out individual attributes and moving the object on yourself. If you leave a visual illustration on the overhead projector at the same time, the remainder of your audience has something else to look at. Of course circulating an object is only possible if you have a very small audience.

Advantages
- Can save a lot of unnecessary description
- Provides a pleasant change in the presentation
- Portable
- Objects and props are often easily available
- People remember handling an object (good learning ploy)

Disadvantages
- It can be time consuming to pass around an object
- Can only be used with small groups
- Simply holding up an object is not suitable (most people won't be able to see the detail)
- If you have to prepare a special model it can be time consuming

Circulating an object is only useful for small audiences because of the time taken to pass it around. Holding up an object is not suitable because most people will not be able to see the detail.

▶ Nerves under control?

Before leaving the subject of making a presentation a word or two should be said about nerves. Everyone who has ever had to make a speech, especially for the first time, is nervous and frightened of being made to look foolish. But, in fact we all need a controlled amount of anxiety if we are to put vitality into our speech.

Nerves are quite normal and some people advise that deep breathing helps relaxation and therefore controls nervousness. I have found that if I fix my mind firmly on the purpose of the presentation and the key ideas that I want the audience to take away with them, it helps me to forget myself and therefore minimises initial nervousness.

The secret of not letting ones nerves dominate and ruin what could be a good speech is to try to learn to control them. Three things could help to overcome nerves.

1. *Plan the speech*, not by jotting a few headings on the back of an envelope, but really considering what you want to say and what visual aids will make the information more interesting to the audience.
2. *Rehearse the speech*. Ask yourself: Have I got the timing right? Am I talking too much without illustrating my main topic areas? Am I involving the audience and giving them a chance to ask questions?
3. *Confront your nerves*. Imagine it is the day of your presentation. What is the very worst thing that could go wrong for you? Imagine it vividly – is it that you will dry up, lose your voice, or forget what to say? Whatever your worst fear, concentrate on it. Let it run its course in your head.

Let us work through confronting your nerves in more detail. If your worst fear is that you will dry up, imagine it happening. There you are in front of your audience and you've forgotten what to say. You've dropped your carefully prepared cue cards and they've scattered all over the floor; you panic; you can't remember whether you've shown your video already and you feel that your audience is judging you as a total incompetent. What a dreadful position to be in! Take it one step further. What will you do next? Rush from the room in embarrassment? Cry? Shout at the audience? Become flushed and very hot? Let your imagination play the scene through.

Now, when it is all over, put it into context and think to yourself: I'm still alive, the place where I live hasn't caught fire, the people close to me haven't suddenly said they no longer want me around. In fact, all the really important things in my life haven't changed.

Try to put this presentation into perspective. This is just a short period in your life, when you are required to tell other people something about your research, so look at things positively. You are now going to be given an opportunity to share with others what you have found. During the research process you have learned a lot and you will have found out some very interesting facts along the way. Your research analysis may have a bearing on what happens next in a work situation, at the very least you will have fulfilled your aim to test a hunch, and now you know the outcome, you can share it with others.

Think of your worst nightmare again, only think of it with a positive ending. Tell yourself that if you drop your cue cards, so what, you had numbered them, hadn't you? You'll just have to smile and apologise to the audience and ask them to wait a minute while you sort them out. Treat it lightly, joke about your incompetence, what are they going to do, shoot you? Actually, they will probably be feeling very sympathetic towards you, and respond with empathy.

By facing your worst nightmare and letting it run its course, you can then try to turn it towards the positive. You can also try to ensure that it doesn't happen by eliminating its possibility. In the above example, it would be difficult to lose one's place had the pre-prepared cue cards not only been numbered but attached to each other with a treasury tag. A second insurance would be ticking off each card or folding over a corner when it had been used. Dropping the pile of cards then would be nothing more than a ten-second inconvenience, and all you would need would be a quick 'sorry about that' to your audience, if anything.

To summarise what has been said:

- You are not the only one to be nervous
- Planning and rehearsing your speech is essential
- You can control your nerves by confronting them
- Imagine the worst thing that can happen
- The really important things in your life will not change, whatever happens in your presentation
- Think positively – imagine your nightmare again with a better ending
- Eliminate the risk of your nightmare ever happening or decide on contingency plans if it is not possible to eliminate it altogether
- Tell yourself that your presentation is going to be successful. It will.

PART B

You need to read through the beginning of this chapter in order to polish your personal presentation skills, but your computer could help you to produce a professional presentation. In fact a computer with screen projection can carry out most of the functions of the equipment outlined under the Visual aids heading – except of course with the passing around of a physical object. Having said that, however, the computer would be able to show a picture of an object in three-dimensional form, or from whatever angle you choose so that your audience would be able to see clearly the object that you were talking about. Alternatively you could take video pictures of the object being handled by someone, if you wanted to give dimensions of size to it, and project the images through your computer.

▶ Presentation software

There are many ranges of software available on the market that can help you to create a simple or sophisticated presentation, and they are not difficult to learn, neither are they wildly expensive. They allow you to create various different types of slides that can have a wide range of special effects; you could use moving video pictures or scan in your own images; you could download information (and moving images) from the Internet or show pictures taken with a digital camera, or bring in a sequence from a CD-ROM.

PowerPoint software

One of the more popular software packages available in colleges and universities (and business) is called PowerPoint and is part of the Microsoft family. It is very easy to learn and you will be amazed at what you can produce in just a couple of hours.

You can create bullet points or brief text sentences that you can flash on screen one at a time simply by clicking the mouse button. You have the option of introducing your text and graphics in varying and novel ways, for example the words could slowly slide in one by one from the left or right of the screen (you control the speed), or drop down quickly from the top of the screen. You can use special fonts which appear in a curve or half-circle. You can use various patterns and colours for the background area, add sound effects, in fact the possibilities are endless. Once you have tried computer presentations you will become addicted to this method – it is so easy and effective. Even the most inexperienced person can produce a very professional looking presentation.

The argument against PowerPoint-type presentations

There is one big drawback against electronic presentations in the hands of the beginner and that is *if it is badly used it can divert from the presenter's message*. Most people go over the top when they first discover the ease with which they can churn out colourful, moving slides. It can free them from the worry of fumbling with note cards, or 'building' an overhead transparency by holding a piece of cardboard over various parts, it's goodbye to flip charts and squeaky pen marks. Everything is at your fingertips and so you may be tempted to use 'everything'!

Remember that a visual aid is meant to enhance, explain or clarify your presentation, it is not meant to take it over. It shouldn't be a Disney film in the making. Bill Wheless, an executive trainer and coach in Greenville, USA, says that the use of PowerPoint is 'like alcohol in the hands of a drunk'. Not that he has anything against presentation software, but, because PowerPoint is so easy to learn and use, it needs to be used in moderation. He explains:

> I think that PowerPoint itself is fabulous – it does everything that it is designed to do well in the hands of an accomplished presenter. But when an inexperienced person starts using it as a crutch, watch out: PowerPoint is very user-friendly, but it wants you to sit down and create the whole presentation on PowerPoint. Instead, presenters should choose visuals only after they have a firm idea of what they're going to say. http://www.presentations.com/techno/soft/20000/02/29_f2_ppl.html

A good presentation will have the presenter as its prime focus. The words they use, the inflection of the voice, the eye contact they make will all become part of a memorable presentation. The visual elements will, of course, support the presentation, but should not be the pivotal point driving the presentation.

Slides are not handouts

The PowerPoint slides that you prepare should not then be printed and used as handouts. A handout should be an extensive background compared to the slide. Your slide should be brief and to the point, your spectators should get it in a single glance. A handout, on the other hand, should tell them more, give them the background and expand the one-liners used on the slide. It is likely that a handout printed from a slide will be meaningless in a few days – if you were given a handout with the word 'cataclasis' bulleted with an illustration of a rock, would you remember the minute detail and explanations about rocks made in a presentation?

▶ Professional company presentations

There are many companies who would be willing to put together your computer presentation – at a price. I am not advocating that you use them for presentation preparation because putting together your own simple computer presentation is fairly easy and something that you will get a great deal of fun out of doing for yourself. However, you should be aware of their existence.

The quickest way to find out who offers what is to use the Internet and search on certain words, such as computer presentations, data projectors, business presentations and so on. You will be offered a choice of sites to view, some of which will offer you everything including a full-service graphic design, where everything is done for you from using graphics and files to output of professional slides, colour overheads or prints and large format wall displays. Alternatively some sites simply offer to produce a template for you on which you can then base your own work.

If you bring in the professionals, you will have to pay, and you need to consider whether this outlay is justified if your presentation is a one-off. If the presentation of your research is to take place in the workplace then you may have an in-house marketing or IT department that can help you put together an effective presentation using in-house computer software and equipment.

▶ What does the equipment do?

In educational establishments there is very likely to be a central pool of computer presentation resources, such as LCD projectors, interactive white-boards, video and camera equipment, that you will be able to book out on a temporary basis. Sometimes you are required to take out a short-term insurance policy in case of theft or damage if you are going to use the equipment off the premises. The very least you will have to sign is an undertaking that you will pay the replacement costs of the equipment should it be lost or damaged.

However, before you book out any equipment it is helpful if you know what it can do for you. While what follows is not meant to be an exhaustive list of what is available, it does give you an idea of the basic presentation resources around nowadays. If you would like more information consult the product information of the well-known companies involved in this field, for example Sony, Olympus, Toshiba and so on. You can usually find this information by simply typing in their name and searching online. Alternatively try typing in the product itself, for example digital camera, scanner, and then search online.

For those of you who get really interested in this, there is a multitude of specialist magazines that are normally printed regularly and available at your local newsagent. Also most technicians in this field, if they have the time, are only too happy to discuss the merits (or otherwise) of equipment and they can be very helpful in helping you to solve any problems that might arise.

Cameras (still)

A digital camera can be filmless and the amount and type of memory in a digital camera affects your ability to store and deliver a presentation. Some cameras have only removable digital filmcards or disks, some have permanent digital memory and some have a mixture.

The pictures that you take with a camera that only has permanent digital memory are transferred from the camera to the computer via a serial cable connection. Removable digital filmcards can be transferred to the computer in the same way, but there are special floppy adapters that allow you to put the film into a special floppy disk and read it. This can be more convenient than using cables.

There are cameras available that just need a normal high-density $3\frac{1}{2}"$ computer disk and these are extremely simple to use. Instead of inserting a film as you would with a conventional camera you insert a computer disk. As you take your pictures the disk gradually fills up (you can take, on average, about 24 pictures per disk). When one disk is full, you simply insert another and providing the camera battery has enough charge you are ready to shoot again. The camera battery is charged from the mains.

Most cameras save images in industry-standard JPEG format so that they are compatible with computer image editors, word processors or desktop publishing applications. You can then touch up your photos (or remove any unwanted wrinkles from your picture!).

Some cameras allow you to view the image you have captured on a small LCD (liquid crystal display – see LCD projectors below) screen which is part of the camera before committing it to memory or disk, and depending on the sophistication of the model you can really go to town with features such as shooting in quick succession a dozen or so automatic photos at half-second intervals (useful at the races!) or built-in telephoto lens for really good close-ups.

Digital camcorder

Most people are familiar with the conventional camcorders of yesteryear, the sort that Mum and Dad used to take embarrassing moving images of their offspring's first sneeze, walk, bath and so on. The quality of product, size, weight and technological advance of modern camcorders bares scant relation to the earlier models. You can record (often in nightshot mode with very little light) superb moving images that you transfer to the computer through an interface link. You can then edit, cut, paste, swop round scenes, add special effects or sounds – the possibilities are almost endless.

Digital media remote controls

If a piece of equipment does not come with its own remote control, there are on the market remotes that operate computers, CDs, DVDs and many other digital media players and presentation programs such as PowerPoint. Usually a receiver unit connects to a computer port and operates a infrared remote keypad.

Digital video system

There are several systems available on the market and they usually plug into the PC's port for fast and easy installation. Video systems enable you to create good quality videos for multimedia presentations. You can edit photos, cut and paste, use best shots, rearrange the order of shooting and then add titles, music narration and special effects.

Interactive flip chart

An interactive flip chart is based on the traditional paper flip chart that uses marking pens, but in this case the board has a special surface and you use special pens. Its advantage is that you can save to computer the information you write on the flip chart. You are able to electronically erase or highlight text and print the flip chart pages or distribute the saved files to other computers at any time.

Once again this is very useful if you have used audience participation to brainstorm ideas for subsequent expansion, or in any presentation where you would like your audience to have a paper copy of what has been written on the flip chart.

Interactive presentation manager

IPM is a digital electronic board that connects to a computer and an LCD projector creating a large interactive projection screen. By touching the board surface with a special electronic pen the presenter controls the computer environment. All program functions are transferred to the pen, which enables the presenter to stay in front of the audience and maintain that all-important eye and voice contact throughout the presentation.

It is possible to use video, animation, graphics, audio, in fact anything that the computer can handle can be portrayed through the pen. Annotations can also be made directly onto projected images and saved for printing if this enhances or helps to clarify the presentation.

Interactive whiteboard

Most people have probably seen the whiteboards that teachers use in class-rooms, when they use coloured marking pens to illustrate or write notes on the board. An interactive whiteboard is often similar in size and initial appearance but it is a much more powerful tool. It is connected to a personal computer and displays on screen whatever you portray through the computer. This might be an active writing area, it might be a picture that you took earlier with your camera, it could be a moving video image or a compli-cated illustration that you have scanned to disk. You can reveal the entire image at once or reveal it step by step.

Interactive whiteboards have the advantage of being able to print work during or after the presentation and, especially useful in a business, to export all or part of the presentation via email or fax. Notations written on the spot can also be instantly saved to computer disk for printing, so presentations that, for example, involve brainstorming with the audience and producing an ideas list could be followed up immediately by handing out a printed hard-copy of the list at the end of the presentation.

Laser pointer

This can be useful if you wish to point out certain items being portrayed on a large screen and it cuts out the need to stand right next to the screen. Also, if you are not tall, you no longer need to use a ruler or stick to reach the rele-vant part of the data or image you wish to draw to the attention of your audi-ence. You can stand up to about 300 yards away from the screen and by simply pointing the laser pen at the area it will highlight. This also eliminates the possibility of obscuring parts of a projected image by standing in front of the screen.

LCD and DLP digital multimedia projectors

The two different projection systems of LCD (liquid crystal display) and DLP (digital light processing) do the same job, but if your presentation is to include video, the DLP system usually gives you a crisper image. DLP is the newer technology and it works by using thousands of tiny mirrors to produce the picture. LCD uses light split and channelled through panels made up of pixel currents (liquid crystal dots) to do the same job.

The projector, once connected to a computer, gives you the freedom to portray almost anything, from presentation slides, video, data and so on, with the added advantage of adding the sound/s of your choosing and controlling everything from a remote handset. Projectors are normally positioned in the middle or back of a room and projected forward onto a screen, but if you are lucky enough to have the choice of using a rear projector then do so. A rear projector is placed behind the screen and has the advantage of allowing you to stand next to the screen and point out relevant details without obscuring the projected image, also other people cannot walk between the screen and projector and block out the image. Rear screen projectors are frequently set up permanently in a boardroom or lecture theatre, so if you can book the room for your presentation it will save you the fuss of setting everything up.

The room does not have to be dark to portray good images, especially with the latest projectors, so you can still maintain eye contact and your audience can see any handout you might wish to use.

Remote transparency scroll system for OHP

When using the standard overhead projector you often only want to reveal parts of the screen at a given time, and this usually involves covering some areas with paper and slowly moving the paper down the screen in order to reveal, bit by bit, the whole transparency. Sometimes this can be a bit of a fiddle.

However, a remote transparency scroll system fits any standard OHP and saves the fuss involved in the manual system. It is easily used by placing it on the transparency and using a remote control to scroll down the screen and reveal what you wish, when you wish. It is quite a small piece of equipment and can be carried in a briefcase.

10 Finding a Voice – Sharing your Research Findings

PART A

Having spent a long time researching your topic area, you are likely to be in one of two states. Either you will feel that you need a break from the whole research business and are adamant that you never again want to get involved in the area that you have been researching. 'Never' is a long time, however, and if the area was one of your choosing in the first place and therefore one that you are likely to have an interest in, then in a few months time your interest is likely to be rekindled.

On the other hand you may feel weary but still raring to go. Perhaps your research has brought some new ideas to light, it may be that you feel that you've only just looked at the surface of your topic area and want to know more. Some people become very involved in their research area and wish to share what they have discovered with others and hopefully gain a further insight into problems and matters that have arisen in their own work. If you want to share your work with others and give them a chance to respond, you have somehow to let people know what you have been doing.

The quickest way to do this outside using the Internet is to publish your findings in a relevant professional journal or magazine, however, if you want to produce something more in depth and substantial than this, perhaps writing a book would be the best way. Books take far longer to be published, so if you'd prefer quicker feedback perhaps magazine publishing would be your better option.

▶ Books

The writing publication requirements of the commercial market are very different to those writing skills that you have cultivated so efficiently while you have been writing up your research findings. It is likely that you will need to do a great deal of rewriting, in order to remove the 'academic' inclination of the work. There are many writers' handbooks available that can guide you in the right direction and give you a list of possible research publishers to approach.

It is worth contacting several publishers at the same time. Different publishers are looking for different criteria at any given time, and while one publisher might have enough material in your particular research area, another might be looking for new work. It is extremely unlikely that everyone you write to will be interested in your work, in reality you will be lucky if one publisher is interested.

Synopsis

The best method is to prepare a synopsis of what your book is about. Turner describes well what you should concentrate on when beginning your synopsis:

> A few lines of justification will start the ball rolling. What is the book about? Why does it cry out to be written? Who are the likely purchasers? This last question deserves particular attention . . . every author likes to think that he is reaching out to the mass audience but in reality each book has a core appeal on which the sales potential will be judged. (Turner 1994:89)

Unless the publishers consider that your proposed book is financially viable they will not consider publishing it.

Your synopsis should be word processed, well presented in double line spacing and you should give guidelines on whether you intend to use illustrations and if you are going to do them. Commissioning drawings adds to the cost of the book. The publisher will also require some estimation of the length of your book; normally you tell them this by estimating approximately how many words will be used – another important bearing on cost.

The synopsis should also state the date you would be able to deliver the completed manuscript. Because it will be some months before any agreements are made and contracts signed, you could say something like 'six months from the commission of the manuscript'. It is usually up to you to suggest how long you need, but once you have agreed on a date, the publisher will expect you to deliver the goods on time, so don't underestimate how long it will take.

Sample chapters

Along with your book synopsis you need to send one or two sample chapters of your intended work. You might like to take the beginning of your research and look at it again with a critical eye. Bear in mind that this time your intended audience is much wider than your tutor, cohort group, or boss and work colleagues; you will need to paint a clearer picture for a fresh audience who will know nothing of the background. You cannot assume a prior knowledge and will need to alter your manuscript accordingly. Your chapter/s should be word processed in double line spacing, with no errors or handwritten amendments.

Covering letter

It is wise to telephone the publisher before you post your manuscript and obtain the name of the relevant person to whom you should address your letter. Some publishers like an author to include a CV that highlights any previous publishing experience and the relevant specialist knowledge that they have, particularly in the case of a first-time author, so do ask whether your CV is required.

Your letter should be polite and fairly formal. Explain that you are enclosing the synopsis and sample chapter/s of your proposed book and you hope that they will consider your manuscript for possible publication. If you want a reply and your manuscript returned, publishers would expect you to enclose a stamped addressed envelope.

Don't be impatient if a reply has not arrived on your doormat within a week or two. Some publishers can take up to two months to reply. If you haven't heard anything after a month, make a polite phone call to make sure that the manuscript was actually received.

Success?

If a publisher is interested you may be asked to supply more information or a meeting will be suggested. Either way it is a positive and encouraging sign. Now you really do need to firm up your ideas for your proposed book. Seek out statistics or newspaper reports to support any claims you are making. Search for 'rival' books offering similar information and prepare reasons why your proposed publication is better. You need to be well prepared before the next stage.

Rejection?

Publishing is a competitive business and thousands of would-be authors receive 'sorry, no thank you' letters every day, so do not take it too personally if you receive a rejection letter. It is rare that you will receive any in-depth reason why your work was not suitable, rejection usually comes in the form of a standardised letter that doesn't really tell you why they are not considering your submission.

Money, money, money

Overnight success bringing vast amounts of cash is as likely as winning the lottery. It is extremely unlikely that you will be able to live solely on the money you earn from publishing, even if you go on to produce many books, so don't give up the day job just yet.

Usually, if your manuscript is commissioned, you will be given a small advance, normally paid in two or three instalments. The advance is normally non-returnable unless you fail to complete the manuscript.

The amount of the advance varies considerably and in the educational and academic field it sometimes will not even make the four figure mark *in total*, so we are not talking the blockbuster five figure sums of money that you hear about in the fiction market. However, seeing your name printed on the front cover of a book published by a reputable publishing house can, for some people, far exceed the finances involved.

Once your book is published you will receive royalties on the book sales. These vary but as a general guide they are likely to be in the region of 7.5% on paperback home sales and 10% on hardback editions.

▶ Journals and magazines

The length of articles that magazines or journals will consider varies enormously, and before rewriting your research with the intention of publication in a professional journal or magazine a little research is necessary. Often journals will give quite detailed instructions of what they require and you should find these out in advance and follow them implicitly if you want to be considered for publication. It is down to you to please editors at this stage, and if you don't bother to find out what they want, why should they even bother to glance at your manuscript.

Start by consulting writers' handbooks for the names of relevant journals or magazines that will be interested in your topic area. You may already know of several publications that you have read frequently in your subject area and with these publications you are at an advantage because you will already have a feel for the type of articles that they commission. When you have identified possible publications, approach each of them individually and find out their requirements. 'Commissioning' a piece of work does not necessarily imply that there will be a payment involved; if you are interested in the financial implications rather than the ability to share your research ideas, you may be disappointed.

Journal requirements

Editors are usually looking for academic-type articles with a well-defined theme and the evidence set out in a concise and significant manner. They will expect it to present argument and counter-arguments of its debate and all appropriate sources cited and set in the appropriate context. Almost all editors require that your feature should be well researched and written in a style that is immediately accessible to the intelligent lay reader.

Some publications require a synopsis (see above) before requesting you to send them the complete manuscript, others will ask you to submit, say, 5,000 words on your topic immediately – the requirements vary enormously.

Journal submission

Unlike book submissions, it is normal to submit an article to only one journal or magazine at a time. When you receive details of the requirements from individual journals you will see that this is often a requisite of your submission. Submission generally implies a warranty on the part of the author that the work is original.

Journals do not normally take as long as book publishers to reply to your request, but if you do want your manuscript returned they normally require a stamped addressed envelope.

Freelance rates of pay

Freelance rates vary enormously from one publication to another. The National Union of Journalists has negotiated minimum rates of pay and you can write to them for up-to-date pay rates. However, publishing in academic journals is not going to make you rich so don't approach publication with the idea of making a fortune.

Journal rejection

One of the biggest differences between book and journal rejection is that the editor of a journal will sometimes give you brief reasons why they have rejected your manuscript. They are not usually open to subsequent dialogue on the matter, but even a short paragraph telling you that the article is one sided, or bogged down in theory, or overlooks some important point in current thinking is a starting point. Don't be offended and when your bruised pride has overcome the initial rejection pay careful attention to what they say, even if you do not agree with them. You then have the choice of rewriting and resubmitting or approaching another journal with a rewritten draft.

▶ Publish it yourself?

Vanity publishing, where the author pays sometimes quite considerable amounts of money to see his name in print, operates on the principle that any book is worth publishing providing someone is prepared to meet the cost (and that someone is not the publisher).

Anyone is entitled to hand over their money to have their publication printed, but the ethics of persuading naive writers to pay for publishing by cajoling them with gratifying compliments and less than truthful assessments of their work is morally unacceptable.

Be wary of advertisements appealing for new authors or requesting immediate manuscript submissions, it is likely to be the contents of your wallet they are aiming at.

If you feel you must take this plunge for fame and fortune, be sure you can afford it, as you may never see your initial outlay returned. Try to visit the publisher's offices if you can (some of them are set up in the corner of a garage!); ask to see reviews of their current books printed in any well-known national newspapers. Ask them how they distribute printed volumes and then check out whether they really do have a contract with any well-known book chains mentioned.

There is always online self-publishing, but this is dealt with in more detail later in this chapter.

▶ Competitions, bursaries, fellowships and grants

Everyone has heard of the Booker Prize for Fiction or the British Book Awards and, while not advocating that you should put yourself forward for these prestigious awards which are normally nominated by publishers, there are other prizes that might be available to you. However, you will almost certainly have to rewrite your manuscript to fit the requirements of the competition or award.

In the competition field there are many awards that you could aim towards, all of which would require you to rejig or completely rewrite your work. So you need to consider whether you have the time to devote to rewriting and the enthusiasm to study or work in an area in which you have been engaged for several months. If you are feeling overkill, perhaps you need a break from this topic before becoming involved in more work around it.

Promethus Award (British Museum Press)

This is awarded annually for the most *outstanding synopsis* for a first book in the field of archaeology, ethnography or ancient history. The aim of the award is to counter the tendency to specialisation among writers and encourage them to think across disciplinary boundaries or a wide historical timescale. One of the past winners was Richard Rudgley for his synopsis 'The Alchemy of Culture: intoxicants in society' which studied the intoxicant use in society drawing on ethnographic data.

The prize is a bursary towards completing the book and a publishing contract. Contact the British Museum Press in London if you are interested and think that your research could fit into that category.

BBC Wildlife Magazine Awards for Nature Writing

If you are interested and your research has centred on human relationships with nature in some way, perhaps this might interest you. It is an annual competition for amateur and professional writers. They require a single essay and there are several monetary prizes in both the professional and amateur categories. Contact the BBC at Broadcasting House, Whiteladies Road, Bristol, BS8 2LR for further information.

Isaac and Tamara Deutscher Memorial Prize

This is an award in recognition of, and as encouragement to, research in the Marxist tradition of Isaac Deutscher. This annual monetary award is made to an author of an essay or a full-scale work published or in manuscript. Contact Gerhard Wilkie, 75 St Gabriels Road, London, NW2 4DU for more details.

Fawcett Society Book Prize

Alternatively, if your research was involved with the concerns, attitudes or roles of women, the Fawcett Society make an annual award to the author of a work of non-fiction. Write to the Fawcett Society Book Prize, New Light on Women's Lives, 46 Harleyford Road, London, SE11 5AY for more information.

Local or specific awards

Awards are made in an array of competitions, some with strict rules of eligibility, which has the advantage of cutting down the opposition. For example, some competitions favour the local author who must have been born in Yorkshire, or Wales and so on, or they must be under 35, or over 50, or have never been published before. To find details of the various competitions or awards available consult a writer's handbook, or take out a subscription to a specialist writing magazine.

▶ Sharing your research without more writing

If you have no wish to become involved in any substantial rewriting of your research work but feel that your findings are important and could be relevant and useful to others, then you owe it to yourself, the subject/s of your research and perhaps your organisation to let others know about it.

There are other ways in which you might think about sharing your work, perhaps as a lecture (or a series of mini lectures), as a workshop when you could invite interested bodies, or by hosting a discussion group. Even simply calling a meeting within your organisation or educational faculty in order to let others know what you've been doing helps the communication process, after all it might be helpful and relevant for them.

If you feel that you do have something important to say and that public speaking is something you might like to pursue, then think about presenting your work to a wide range of people and not just your own section or faculty. The following list is just to get you started on ideas of whom to contact to offer your services, although, depending on the area of your research, some of them may not be relevant.

1. Trade Union branches
2. National/international conferences
3. Professional bodies
4. Adult education classes
5. Evening classes based within your topic
6. Head office meetings (not just your department)
7. Youth clubs
8. Women's groups
9. Mother and toddler groups
10. Groups connected with your research area, for example RSPCC (Royal Society for the Prevention of Cruelty to Children), RSPCA (Royal Society for the Prevention of Cruelty to Animals), RNID (Royal National Institute for Deaf People), RNIB (Royal National Institute for the Blind) and so on.

▶ Further research?

If only you knew at the beginning of your research what you know at the end of it, what a strong position you would have been in. You would have known exactly what to target, what information was or wasn't needed, what were to prove to be false trails and how best to have gone about things.

Some people enjoy research and get satisfaction and a sense of achievement from it. Researching one topic nearly always gives rise to unanswered questions or areas that you did not have time to explore and no doubt you already know of something that you'd like to investigate. Perhaps your workplace would like it investigated too. Maybe you'd like to add an extra qualification to your name or find out more about developing research skills, if this is the case telephone your local university for information. If you are tempted to do more research and you have the time and enthusiasm, then go for it.

PART B

▶ Making your research findings and data available online

Before you embark on placing your information online, make sure that you have read the section on plagiarism (pp. 66–7). How will you feel if someone copies your work and passes it off as their own? Many Web sites contain a copyright notice detailing how the material they contain may be used; you could try doing this, and hope that people would send you an email asking your permission to copy specific areas.

Fair dealing in the digital environment is yet to be defined by the courts, and it would be unwise for anyone to consider that it is fair to copy material from Web sites, however that does not mean that some individuals will not copy your work. Fair dealing for research or private study, criticism, review or reporting current events does not infringe copyright in the normal sense, but is limited by strict conditions.

Although reported cases of online copyright abuse are small or accidental – busy people who don't seek permission, others who are unaware of copyright laws – there are now vast numbers of people using the Internet, and there is a general lack of understanding about what constitutes legal use of material placed on the WWW. So, if you are thinking of putting your research online, be prepared for it to be copied.

▶ Proving it's your work

In the UK copyright of any original work by the author exists if the work is marked in some way, such as with the word 'copyright' followed by the name of the copyright owner and year of production. The international symbol for copyright is © but it is not a requirement in the UK that you use it, however in other countries it is a necessity. If you do use the copyright symbol it might help should you need to turn to legal proceedings against infringement.

Proving that you produced a piece of work before someone else thought of the same idea or did similar research is not always easy. The Copyright Licensing Agency's Web site http://www.cla.co.uk gives sound advice on a number of procedures that you could take to help you to establish when you created a copyright work.

1. Send a securely sealed copy of the work (marked with the copyright details outlined in the first paragraph above) to yourself by registered post and do not open the package when it arrives. Keep the certificate of posting and the package in a safe place.
2. Deposit a securely sealed copy of the work (again marked with the details outlined in the first paragraph above) with a bank or a solicitor.

Their suggestions will help you to prove that you had the work at the date of posting or depositing with a solicitor. In the case of dispute, the sealed package should be opened on the advice of and in the presence of your solicitor.

You could also send a copy of the work to the Registry of Copyright at Stationers' Hall. For more details visit the Copyright Licensing Agency's Web site.

All of the above will help you to prove that the work was in existence at a given time, but it still doesn't prove that the work is actually yours.

Protection outside the UK
There are International Copyright Conventions established to protect copyright works around the world and the UK is a member of these Conventions. Works created by UK nationals or residents are protected by the national laws of all countries who are members of these Conventions and the majority of countries in the world belong to at least one Convention.

Someone's used your work without permission
The worst has happened. You see, word for word, your work that you have placed on the Internet (and marked with your name and copyright details) produced in a journal or magazine. What do you do?

Unfortunately it is up to you to enforce the copyright law and if you feel that you have been cheated out of money you will need to consult a suitably qualified lawyer to take up your case. Alternatively an informal approach to the infringing party may be the more cost-effective method. This carries more authority if you have already joined an association such as the Society of

Authors and you request that they approach the infringing party on your behalf.

Sharing information

It may be that you simply want to share the findings of your research with other interested people because what you have discovered could in some way help someone else. Perhaps you really don't mind whether people copy your work because you feel that the message or lessons learned are far more important than the ownership of the material. If that is the case, go ahead and place your work online.

You can make your own Web site to publish your work, and although you can learn to do this with do-it-yourself books, it might be easier if you attend a short course at a local college or university (see HTML and XML – what are they?, pp. 143-4).

Conclusion

▶ Research is always incomplete

> In research the horizon recedes as we advance, and is no nearer at
> sixty than it was at twenty. As the power of endurance weakens with
> age, the urgency of the pursuit grows more intense . . . And research is
> always incomplete. (Casaubon 1875, quoted by Pattison 1980)

The process of doing the research itself always throws up more questions
than answers. There are always too many leads to follow, and not enough
time to do justice to even the chosen paths. We are human and grow weary
of our subject at times, wishing that the whole business were finished and
done with. And yet, when it is done and a little time has passed, our mind
reflects back to the lessons that we learned and we realise how our horizons
have widened because of the experience.

Glossary of terms

Byte   Storage space in memory. To give you some idea of memory size, think of one byte as being one character on the keyboard.

CD-ROM disc   A disc that is used to store information. When a CD-ROM is placed in the CD drive of the computer it enables the machine to perform the functions it contains, for example play music, a game or a program.

CPU   (the central processing unit) The 'brain' of the computer'. Think of it as akin to the human brain.

DVD   Digital versatile discs and drives are similar to their CD-ROM relative but hold far more information and could, for example, play a full-length movie on your PC. With DVDs the video and the audio are digital, which makes for better quality.

Database   A computer program or a collection of data that can be searched easily to find specific information. For example, a travel agent can access a database of holiday accommodation available for a certain resort on a specific date.

Email   This is a way of sending messages between computers. An email can be just a simple piece of text, or could contain sound, pictures or even moving images.

Floppy disk   A disk on which you save your work. It can be transferred easily from one computer to another so that the information saved can be accessed from any computer providing they have the same software. Always beware of the possibility of transferring viruses when moving disks between different computers. See virus checkers.

Floppy disk drive   Insert a floppy disk in this drive if you want to save your work and then take it away from your computer to use the information on another PC.

Hard disk   Where data is stored within the computer. The size of this is an indication of how much information can be stored by the computer.

Hardware   The physical equipment used in a computer system.

Icon   Small image on screen.

Internet   A network of millions and millions of computers linked by cables over telephone lines. Using the Internet you can shop, get information, talk with friends or make new ones.

KB   Kilobyte. A measurement that is just over a thousand bytes (1024 bytes). See Byte.

MB   Megabyte. A measurement that is just over a million bytes (1,048,5776 bytes). See Byte.

MHz   The symbol for Megahertz, meaning one million cycles per second. This is the CPU speed.

Modem   A piece of hardware inside the computer. It enables you to send and receive information over a normal telephone line. Needed for emails, faxes and the Internet.

Monitor   (or VDU) The screen on which information is viewed – looks like a television.

Mouse   Hand-held manoeuvring device. Moving the mouse on a tabletop makes the pointer move on the screen. Just press the button on the mouse when you're ready to make a choice.

Multimedia   All new machines come with multimedia nowadays, that is, they will come with at least external speakers and a CD-ROM drive, plus a sound card inside the machine. Multimedia allows the user to do a multitude of things, for example, play music, CD-ROMs, interactive responses and so on.

PC Personal computer. Thought of as the home computer but often similar computers are used in offices.

Printer A printer reproduces what you see on the screen to paper so you can print out what you have created. Some printers print in colour as well as black and white.

RAM A form of memory that is essential to a computer. RAM means 'random-access memory'. Data stored in this area can be changed by the computer operator.

ROM A form of memory that is essential to a computer. ROM stands for 'read-only memory'. Data that you can only look at and not alter.

Scanner A scanner copies pictures, photos, images – almost anything you want. It is rather like a photocopier to use but the finished image can be saved on your PC, edited, faxed or used in any document and printed.

Software Programming information that is used by the computer. It is stored within the computer or on CD-ROM. When installed it enables the computer to follow a set of instructions telling it what to do; this could be anything from a game to a word-processing program.

SPSS The Statistical Package for Social Scientists, one of the most common software packages used to analyse and present survey data. Versions of the software available for PC-compatible machines.

Spreadsheet A computer program (or data) that enables the user to manipulate figures, equations and text. Useful for budgeting and financial planning.

Video camera A digital camera lets you take photographs that are instantly available on your PC. You can then add special effects, save to documents or send via email.

Video card A video card predetermines the image resolution on screen and how many colours the computer will display.

Virus checking software A software that gives you an opportunity to check whether or not you have picked up certain viruses on your disks or computer.

Word processing A computer program that enables the user to organise, manipulate and store written text by electronic means.

Bibliography

Ackroyd, S and Hughes, J (1983) *Data Collection in Context*. London. Longman

Allan, G and Skinner, C (1991) *Handbook for Research Students in the Social Sciences*. London. Falmer

Anderson, S and Gansneder, B (1995) Using electronic mail surveys and computer-monitored data for studying computer-mediated communication systems. *Social Science Computer Review*, (13): 33–46

Babbie, E. (1990) *Survey Research Methods*. California. Wadsworth

Bailey, V and Goddard, G (1996) *Essential Research Skills*. London. Collins Educational

Bakeman, R and Gottman, J M (1986) *Observing Interaction: An Introduction to Sequential Analysis*. Cambridge. Cambridge University Press

Bales, R F (1950) *Interaction Process Analysis. A Method for the Study of Small Groups*. New York. Addison-Wesley

Bartlett, P (1999) *Definitive Guide to the Internet*. Christchurch. FKB Publishing

Bell, C and Newby, H (1977) *Doing Sociological Research*. London. Allen & Unwin

Bell, G (1987) *Speaking and Business Presentations*. London. Butterworth

Bell, J (1999) *Doing Your Research Project. A Guide for First-time Researchers in Education and Social Science*. Milton Keynes. Open University Press

Blaxter, L, Hughes, C and Tight, M (1996) *How to Research*. Buckingham. Open University Press

Bodgan, R and Biklen, S (1992) *Qualitative Research in Education*, 2nd edn. Boston. Allyn & Bacon

Bouma, G D and Atkinson, G B J (1995) *A Handbook of Social Science Research*. Buckingham. Oxford University Press

Brause, R and Mayher, J (1991) *Search and Re-search*. London. Falmer Press

Bryman, A and Cramer, D (1999) *Quantitative Data Analysis with SPSS Release 8 for Windows for Social Scientists*. London. Falmer Press

Burgess, R (ed.) (1982) *Field Research: A Sourcebook and Field Manual*. London. Allen & Unwin

Cockton, P (ed.) (1988) *Subject Catalogue of the House of Commons Parliamentary Papers, 1801–1900*, 5 vols. Cambridge. Chadwyck-Healey

Cohen, L, Manion, L and Morrison, K (2000) *Research Methods in Education*. London. Routledge

Convey, J (1992) *Online Information Retrieval – An Introductory Manual to Principles and Practice*. London. Library Association Publishing

Coombes, H (1997) *Text/Word Processing with Word*. London. Thomson Learning

Creswell, J W (1994) *Research Design (Qualitative & Quantitative Approaches)*. London. Sage

Denzin, N K (1970) *The Research Act in Sociology*. London. Butterworth

Desmond, M (2000) *Windows 2000 Professional Bible*. Foster City, CA. IDG Books Worldwide

Dillman, D (1990) *Starting Statistics in Psychology and Education*. London. Weidenfeld & Nicolson

Dunsmuir, A and Williams, L (1991) *How to do Social Research*. London. Collins Educational

Eichler, M (1988) *Non-sexist Research Methods*. London. Allen & Unwin

Feyerabend, P (1981) *Philosophical Papers*. New York. Cambridge University Press

Fielding, N and Lee, R (eds) (1991) *Using Computers in Qualitative Research*. London. Sage

Fisher, D and Hanstock, T (1998) *Citing References*. Oxford. Blackwell

Ford, P and Ford, G (1951) *A Breviate of Parliamentary Papers, 1917–1939*, Oxford, Blackwell. Reprinted by Irish University Press, 1970

Ford, P and Ford, G (1953) *A Select List of British Parliamentary Papers, 1833–1899*, Oxford, Blackwell. Reprinted by the Irish University Press, 1970

Frankfort-Nachmais, C and Nachmais, D (1996) *Research Methods in the Social Sciences*, 5th edn. London. Arnold

Fulcher, J and Scott, J (1999) *Sociology*. Oxford. Oxford University Press

Gilbert, N (ed.) (1993) *Researching Social Life*. London. Sage

Glastonbury, B and MacKean, J (1993) In G Allan and C Skinner (eds) *Handbook for Research Students in the Social Sciences*. London. Falmer

Green, S (2000) *Research Methods in Health, Social and Early Years Care*. Cheltenham. Stanley Thornes

Hantrais, L and Steen, M (1996) *Cross-national Research Methods in the Social Sciences*. London. Pinter

Heyes, M, Hardy, S, Humphrey, P and Rookes, P (1993) *Starting Statistics in Psychology and Education*. Oxford. Oxford University Press

Hitchcock, G and Hughes, D (1992) *Research and the Teacher*. London. Routledge

Hoyle, K and White, H (1988) *Business Calculations*. Oxford. Butterworth

James, A and Christensen, P (1999) *Research with Children*. London. Routledge

Jary, D and Jary, J (1995) *Dictionary of Sociology*. Glasgow. HarperCollins

Langley, P (1987) *Doing Social Research*. Lancashire. Causeway Press

Lavan, A (1985) In E Kane *Doing Your Own Research*. London. Marian Boyars

Lonkila, M (1995) Grounded theory as an emerging paradigm for computer-assisted qualitative data analysis. In U Kelle (ed.) *Computer-aided Qualitative Data Analysis: Theory, Methods and Practice*. London. Sage

Martin, J and Matheson, J (1992) 'Further developments in Computer Assisted Personal Interviewing for household income surveys' in OPCS, *Survey Methodology Bulletin*, (3): 33–6

Mason, J (1996) *Qualitative Researching*. London. Sage

Mathias, H (1991) Presentation and Communication Skills. In G Allan and C Skinner (eds) *Handbook for Research Students in the Social Sciences*. London. Falmer

McKenzie, G, Usher, R and Powell, J (1997) *Understanding Social Research*. London. Falmer

McNeill, P (1985) *Research Methods*. London. Tavistock

McNiff, J, Whitehead, J and Lomax, P (1996) *You and Your Action Research Project*. London. Routledge

Mehta, P and Sivadas, E (1995) Comparing response rates and response content in mail versus electronic mail surveys. *Journal of the Market Research Society*, **37**(4): 429–39

Miles, M and Huberman, M (1994a) *Qualitative Data Analysis*. London. Sage

Miles, M and Huberman, M (1994b) Data management and analysis methods. In N K Denzin and Y S Lincoln (eds) *Handbook of Qualitative Research*. London. Sage

Moore, R (1997) Inner City Immigrants. In Bell, C and Newby, H *Doing Sociological Research*. London. Allen & Unwin

Morison, M (1986) *Methods in Sociology*. Harlow. Longman

Moser, C and Kalton, G (1971) *Survey Methods in Social Investigation*, 2nd edn. London. Heinemann

Nelson-Jones, R (1986) *Human Relationship Skills*. London. Cassell

O'Hara, S, Vega, D and Kelly, J (1997) *Discover Office 97*. Foster City CA. IDG Books Worldwide

Pattison, M *The Oxford Dictionary of Quotations*, 3rd edn, 1980 Oxford. Oxford University Press

Pitter, K, Amato, S, Callahan, J, Kerr, N and Tilton, E (1996) *Every Student's Guide to the Internet: Windows Version*. San Francisco, CA. McGraw-Hill

Roberts, H (ed.) (1981) *Doing Feminist Research*. London. Routledge

Robson, C (1999) *Real World Research – A Resource for Social Scientists and Practitioner-Researchers*. Oxford. Blackwell

Rose, D and Sullivan, O (1996) *Introducing Data Analysis for Social Scientists*. Buckingham. Open University Press

Shipman, M D (1988) *The Limitations of Social Research*. London. Longman

Slattery, M (1986) *Official Statistics*. London. Tavistock

Smith, J (1993) *After the Demise of Empiricism: The Problem of Judging Social and Educational Inquiry*. New York. Ablex

Sprent, P (1988) *Understanding Data*. London. Penguin

Stein, S D (1999) *Learning, Teaching and Researching on the Internet*. Harlow. Wesley Longman

Strauss, A and Corbin, J (eds) (1997) *Grounded Theory in Practice: A Collection of Readings*. London. Sage

Stuart, C (1988) *Effective Speaking*. London. Pan Books

Tapson, F (1999) *The Oxford Mathematics Study Dictionary*. Oxford. Oxford University Press

Taylor, P, Richardson, J, Yeo, A, Marsh, I, Trobe, K and Pilkington, A (1999) *Sociology in Focus*. Ormskirk. Causeway Press

Tesch, R (1990) *Qualitative Research*. London. Routledge

Tittel, E and Pitts, N (1999) *HTML 4 for Dummies*. Foster City, CA. IDG Books Worldwide

Turner, B (ed.) (1994) *The Writer's Handbook 1995*. London. Macmillan

Verma, G K and Beard, R M (1981) *What is Educational Research? Perspectives on Techniques of Research*. Aldershot. Gower

Vorderman, C and Young, R (2000) *Guide to the Internet*. London. Pearson Education

Walsh, J P, Kiesler, S, Sproul, L S and Hesses, B W (1992) Self-selected and randomly selected respondents in a computer network survey. *Public Opinion Quarterly*, (56): 141–4

Warren, M (1980) *Business Calculations*. Amersham. Hulton Educational

Weber, M (1964) *The Theory of Social and Economic Organisation*. New York. Free Press

Whyte, W F (1955) *Street Corner Society*, 2nd edn. Chicago. University of Chicago Press

Woods, P (1999) *Successful Writing for Qualitative Researchers*. London Routledge

▶ **Electronic sources**

Barry, C (1998) Choosing qualitative data analysis software: Atlas/ti and Nudist compared. *Sociological Research Online*, 3(3). http://www.socresonline.org.uk/socresonline/3/3/4.html June 2001

Bell, B (1997) Qualitative Analysis: Web & Software Resources. http://ihs2.unn.ac.
uk:8080/bbqual1.htm June 2001

Coffey, A, Holbrook, B and Atkinson, P (1996) Qualitative data analysis: Technologies
and representations. *Sociological Research Online*, 1(1). Available: http://www.
socresonline.org.uk/socresonline/1/1/4.html June 2001

Collins, P (1998) Negotiating selves: Reflections on 'unstructured' interviewing.
Sociological Research Online, 3(3). http://www.socresonline.org.uk/
socresonline/3/3/2.html June 2001

Copyright Licensing Agency. http://www.cla.co.uk June 2001

Kuczynski, L (1998). Reflections of a Closet Qualitative Researcher. The Genetic
Epistemologist: *The Journal of the Jean Piaget Society*, 26(2). http://www.piaget.
org/GE/1998/GE-26-2.html June 2001

Mehta, R and Sivadas, E (1995) 'Using e-mail as a research tool' ESRC (Economic and
Social Research Council) and JISC (Joint Information Systems Committee). The
Data Archive http://www.data-archive.ac.uk June 2001

Mulder, J (1994) The mechanics of qualitative analysis. *Issues in Educational Research*,
4(2), pp. 103–8. http://cleo.murdoch.edu.au/gen/iier/iier4/942p103.htm June
2001

Palgrave Publications. http://www.palgrave.com. June 2001

Sainsbury, R, Ditch, J and Hutton, S (1993) Computer-assisted personal interviewing.
Social Research Update. http://www.soc.surrey.ac.uk June 2001

University of Essex. *The Data Archive*. http://www.data-archive.ac.uk June 2001

Wheless, B and Ganzel, R *Presentations* Magazine (February 2000). http://www.
presentations.com/techno/soft June 2001

Index

Index of the Microsoft Office software step-by-step instructions

The following functions are particularly useful when using IT for research